"A wholly new approach to the contentious relation between critical theory and theological application. This engaging piece of theological writing effortlessly transforms one of the most misunderstood forms of critical theory—postcolonial criticism—into a valuable instrument for constructing a cogent theology for ordinary people. The author's candor and inventiveness come through forcefully in these pages."

—R. S. Sugirtharajah, University of Birmingham

"This is no ordinary academic book in post-colonial studies. Where so many other volumes offer theoretical, and often a-contextual, readings of coloniality dominated by jargon, Heaney engages post-colonial thought in clear language grounded in particular contexts and experiences. While many postcolonial writers exclude religions/theologies altogether as only and inevitably problematic vehicles of colonialism, Heaney, amid the recognition of theology's propensities for cooptation by imperial interests, calls for the engagement of intercultural theology as a resource for post-coloniality: 'At the heart of the Christian gospel is the revolutionary idea that God interrupted the power of empire.' The result is a *practical post-colonial theology* that interrogates the work of hate in relationships marked by colonized-colonizer enmity.

This work is situated in four particular lived experiences of coloniality. It brings each one into conversation not only with the conceptual framework of postcolonial theory but also with texts and practices of Christian traditions. Starting with his own location as an Anglo-Protestant Christian growing up in Northern Ireland, Heaney engages Irish poet W.B. Yeats to give voice to the ambiguities and instabilities of colonial identities where the boundaries between colonizer and colonized are 'porous.' Heaney considers three other settings shaped by struggles for emancipation from imperial powers—Kenya, Korea, and U.S. Native American contexts. He explores themes of particularity, agency, coloniality, hybridization, and resistance in relation to these contexts, which anchors the book's post-colonial theoretical discourse in lived experiences of colonial contestation. For readers new to this thought world, the book provides a helpful introduction to post-colonial studies with definitions of key terms and concept-linking. For seasoned readers of post-colonial literature, Heaney's book offers a fresh perspective by situating this post-colonial project as a form of *practical theology* that aims toward transformation. This book is a must-read for theologians who are not content with merely describing and uncovering Christianity's role in cultural domination, but who also seek to participate in the life of God whose transforming Spirit is at work to re-humanize us all."

—JOYCE ANN MERCER, Professor of Practical Theology and Pastoral Care, and Horace Bushnell Professor of Christian Nurture, Yale University Divinity School

"Here is the amazing gift of a teachable introduction to the civilizational variations of colonialism. The theological—indeed theopoetic—answer that Heaney offers will revive spirits demoralized by new hate-waves. It will inspire fierce and honest, loving and creative Christian resistance."

—CATHERINE KELLER, George T. Cobb Professor of Constructive Theology, Drew Theological School, author of *Political Theology of the Earth: Our Planetary Emergency and the Struggle for a New Public*

"Robert Heaney makes post-colonial theology accessible to everyone through his clear writing style and nuanced presentation of the material. Given his own social location as a Brit from Northern Ireland, Heaney exemplifies the intellectual humility and curiosity needed for true postcolonial interaction. He shows that postcolonial theology is not a peripheral activity but rather is central to the very act of doing theology. Highly recommend!"

—KAY HIGUERA SMITH, Professor of Biblical and Religious Studies, Azusa Pacific University

"Writing with a deep passion for justice, Dr. Heaney provides a clear and comprehensive introduction to the issues and concerns of post-colonial theology and situates it in the wider discourses of African theology, Black liberation theology, and progressive white theology. I highly recommend this pluriphonic and yet accessible text."

—KWOK PUI-LAN, author of *Postcolonial Imagination and Feminist Theology*

"Embodiments of colonial realities run deep and continue to affect us all—not least the churches and their theologies. How to do theology that is mindful of these realities is the ongoing challenge and Robert Heaney's proposals call for modes of repentance, resistance, and repair that deserve to be engaged critically and constructively."

—JOERG RIEGER, Distinguished Professor of Theology, Cal Turner Chair in Wesleyan Studies, Vanderbilt University

"In a time of palpable white fragility and vulnerability, Heaney's is a poignant theological testimony to the hopeful resistance needed not only to respond to the legacy of hate left by the colonial enterprise, but to constructively forge a new people of God and body of Christ linked across peoples, cultures, ethnicities, and even nations in the present time."

—Amos Yong, Professor of Theology & Mission, Fuller Seminary

"Being a part of a faith tradition with an incarnate God and Cross at its center ought to mean something. Robert Heaney makes that meaning clear especially for an Anglican/white theological tradition that cannot escape its own colonizing theological history. *Post-Colonial Theology: Finding God and Each Other Amidst the Hate* exposes the subjugating and repressive reality of theological colonization. In so doing, Heaney does more than lament a theological past. Rather, he challenges Christian theologians to repent of that past by taking 'a God that becomes incarnate on colonized soil in order that God's people might know the saving message God.' Heaney's book is a call to white theologians to recognize their theological complicity in fostering imperialism and to engage a 'post-colonial theological imagination.' *Post-Colonial Theology* is must read more than an intellectual exercise. It is a call to repentance for those committed to breaking the cycle of colonizing oppression. It is therefore a must read for those who claim to follow the Jesus who died on the cross."

—Kelly Brown Douglas, Dean, Episcopal Divinity School at Union Theological Seminary, Professor of Theology at Union

"Robert Heaney's *Post-Colonial Theology* takes the reality of dominance, hate, and the irreversible nature of centuries of subjugation as its beginning ground. Given that so much of the world's surface has been impacted by the project of imperialism, it is inevitable that most people are either the offspring of landed peoples, the offspring of dispossessed peoples or—like Heaney—the offspring of a hybrid blend of both landed and dispossessed. Elegantly, using poetry, privilege, and precision, he asks serious questions of power; everything comes under his scrutiny: history, doctrine, ecclesial governance, policy, whiteness, liturgy, and apologies. Not satisfied with a distant essay, this book is a demonstration of what engaged academia looks like—Heaney scrutinizes his own story in light of a story of empire, religion, dispossession, and dominance.

Throughout *Post-Colonial Theology*, Heaney amplifies voices that have re-grounded him. This important book honors the seminal work of Korean, South African, Nigerian, Kenyan, and Native American theologians. Weaving poetry throughout the text, the reader is brought on an educational journey that re-envisions the question of God into an exploration for a practice

of humanity with integrity. It is a work of profound impact, both for the academic and the analyst. The text introduces us to the author in a brilliant demonstration of the value of post-colonial studies to be rooted in the specific. We are brought into Heaney's wrestling with the personal and academic question of how theology can contribute meaningfully to a world seeking to tell the truth about the impact of the colonial enterprise. This is a book for generations to study, to learn, and live by."
—Pádraig Ó Tuama, Leader, The Corrymeela Community

"Books like this are a gem, especially those written from one's own context as Dr. Heaney has done, navigating, exploring, and situating himself as a theologian and pastor into his homeland's colonial and post-colonial events, doing this in a very sensitive manner. Reading this book, one can't help but reflect on one's own country/context, and how we can do theology with a fresh memory of what colonialism is or has been (for both the colonizer and the colonized) and (re)defining what post-colonial theology should look like, especially in this current political climate (worldwide). I highly recommend this book to everyone, especially to students of theology."
—Vicentia Kgabe, Rector, College of Transfiguration, South Africa

"This is an excellent addition to works on post-colonial theologies. Dr. Heaney does an amazing job in creatively knitting together theological voices of decolonization from different cultural contexts to reconstruct theology for responding to the hate caused by imperialism—historical and contemporary."
—Muthuraj Swamy, Director, Cambridge Centre
for Christianity Worldwide

"Robert Heaney's book does an excellent job of making postcolonial theory accessible and uses art in several forms to access the liminal spaces where hope, resistance, and reconciliation reside to creatively address the issues of colonialism and the hate and violence that result from it. It is a truly insightful work."
—Damayanthi M. A. Niles, Professor of Constructive Theology,
Eden Theological Seminary

# Post-Colonial Theology

# Post-Colonial Theology

Finding God and Each Other Amidst the Hate

ROBERT S. HEANEY

▲ CASCADE *Books* • Eugene, Oregon

POST-COLONIAL THEOLOGY
Finding God and Each Other Amidst the Hate

Cascade Books
An Imprint of Wipf and Stock Publishers
199 W. 8th Ave., Suite 3
Eugene, OR 97401

www.wipfandstock.com

PAPERBACK ISBN: 978-1-5326-0220-7
HARDCOVER ISBN: 978-1-5326-0222-1
EBOOK ISBN: 978-1-5326-0221-4

*Cataloguing-in-Publication data:*

Names: Heaney, Robert Stewart, 1972–, author.

Title: Post-colonial theology: finding God and each other amidst the hate / Robert S.
Heaney.

Description: Eugene, OR: Cascade Books, 2019 | Includes bibliographical references
and index.

Identifiers: ISBN 978-1-5326-0220-7 (paperback) | ISBN 978-1-5326-0222-1 (hard-
cover) | ISBN 978-1-5326-0221-4 (ebook)

Subjects: LCSH: Postcolonial theology | Postcolonialism | Christianity and culture |
Practical theology | Theology, doctrinal

Classification: BT83.57 H43 2019 (print) | LCC: BT83.57 (ebook)

Manufactured in the U.S.A.                                          MAY 13, 2019

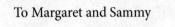

To Margaret and Sammy

We had fed the heart on fantasies,
The heart's grown brutal from the fare;
More substance in our enmities
Than in our love . . .

—W. B. YEATS, "MEDITATIONS IN TIME OF CIVIL WAR"

# Contents

# Preface

I DID NOT SEE W. B. Yeats coming. In retrospect, this might now seem rather odd. For just as Ben Bulben towers over the Church of Ireland graveyard in Drumcliff, so Yeats looms over the deaths and resurrections of empire. Yet, I confess, as I set out upon this road I did not see nor foresee Yeats coming over the brow of the hill. When I began this project I had in view the task of writing an introduction to post-colonial theology. It was my intention to argue that a post-colonial theology is a practical theology and to identify key characteristics of a critical post-colonial theology in conversation with theologians who write from contexts of colonialism or coloniality. This objective has not changed, but in defining the practical and key character-istics, Yeats came into view as both subject and actor.

In preparation for this book I read an essay by Patsy Daniels, who pos-its that post-colonialism begins with Yeats.[1] Whether such an argument can be sustained is not my primary concern. Rather, in identifying the point of departure for the present work this most unorthodox of Irish Anglicans helped me find a place to begin, a place to depart, a place where my own particularity might begin to emerge. Yeats became a conversation partner to help situate myself in relation to the colonialisms and post-colonialisms of Ireland and its provinces. More than once I balked at writing myself into this book. More than once I considered exorcising Yeats from the project. More than once did I fear the prospect of wading into the bloody river that runs through the historical hinterland of Ireland. For if theology still means anything it means giving voice to a vision of the divine or the voice of the divine giving a vision to humanity. Might not talk of Ireland, let alone talk about myself, forestall such a vision? Yet, to talk about practicability and particularity as important to a post-colonial theology would mean that my own voice and context of formation would have to be named. Such a con-

1. Daniels, *The Voice of the Oppressed in the Language of the Oppressor*, 28.

text was shaped by talk about God, it was shaped by segregation, and it was shaped by fear and hate. *Finding God and Each Other Amidst the Hate* became the subtitle of this book, therefore, because it captures something of my own struggle and the struggle of the Irish church. It became the subtitle because it also captured something of the realities at work in colonies and colonialisms and the theologizing that emerges in such circumstances. As a theologian living, teaching, and writing in North America under the 45th president of the United States the title seemed to gain further relevance in a widespread climate of unveiled hate. It is my hope that, amidst such fears, this book can begin to point toward how post-colonial theology might help readers find God and each other anew.

My privilege as a professor of religion afforded me a spring sabbatical in 2017 where much of the writing of this book took place. I am deeply grateful to the board of Virginia Theological Seminary (VTS) and the Very Revd Dr Ian Markham for granting me such sabbatical time. I am also grateful to the Conant foundation for largely funding my sabbatical travel that allowed deeper opportunity to experience and dialogue with leaders throughout the world. Thanks are due to kind and generous hosts, audiences, and conversation partners: The Corrymeela Community, Belfast, Northern Ireland; the Center for Christianity Worldwide, Cambridge, England; the Near East School of Theology, Beirut, Lebanon; the Ming Hua Theological College, Hong Kong; and the College of St. John the Evangelist, Auckland, New Zealand. Each of these contexts have intimate engagements and enmities with different forms of colonialities and colonialisms that made for rich sharing and learning. Others who have been critical and constructive interlocutors as I presented on the topic of this book, and attendant themes, include former mission theologian in the Anglican Communion Bishop Graham Kings and an audience at Westminster Abbey, London; the clergy and leaders of the Diocese of Hawai'i; an audience at a Center for Christianity Worldwide lecture in the faculty of Divinity at the University of Cambridge; Virginia Seminary colleagues at a series of Knowles seminars; and scholars at the inaugural Summer School of Theology, Corrymeela Community, Ballycastle, Northern Ireland. My own students in "GCM classes" and members of the Cross-Cultural Colloquy at VTS continue to inspire inquisitiveness, hope, and the lively possibility of deeper fellowship and justice in the neighborhood and in the nations. Thank you.

Along with particularly gifted VTS students my team in the Center for Anglican Communion Studies, Molly O'Brien and Hartley Wensing continue to ably and gracefully facilitate the growth of our inter-cultural, inter-religious, and international work. Research assistant in the Center, Jean-Pierre Seguin, has been an invaluable help finding sources, proof-reading, and compiling the index for the study. For the duration of my sabbatical, the Revd Dr Melody Knowles generously and gracefully acted as director of the Center. I am in her debt for this kindness and the many other blessings we receive under her leadership as Vice-President of Academic Affairs at VTS. It has, again, been a pleasure to work with Robin Parry and the team at Wipf and Stock. Their guidance throughout the process of writing this book has made the completion of the project always seem within reach—even for me! Lastly and most importantly I am grateful to my family. My wife, Dr Sharon E. Heaney, remains my most important interlocutor. She is my closest ally and, by God's mercy, the source of all that is best in my life. My twelve-year-old son Sam is proving to be an insightful, challenging, mischievous dialog partner. He is quickly becoming a well-read young man with a knack of asking profoundly important questions. Sam, thanks for hanging out and thanks for your grace when I can't hang out. My previous book was dedicated to Sharon and Sam. I humbly dedicate this volume to my parents.

If I could get royalties for my mistakes in life I would have no need for a salary. But, the divine doses us with that which is more important: grace not gratuities. Thus, as with all authors, I must ask forgiveness not only from God, from family, and from colleagues, but also from you the reader. Please note that any misrepresentation or misunderstanding that I have perpetuated here is unintentional and not to be blamed on my sources or on those who have so kindly been part of broader conversations.

In this book I have sought to write a clear and concise introduction to a post-colonial theology. There are many texts available that deal with post-colonial theology. Many of these texts demand a level of familiarity with theory and language that make it difficult for the uninitiated reader to have a clear sense of the intent and practice of the field. It is not my intention in this book to provide a definitive guide to post-colonial theology. I do, however, intend to offer a definition of post-colonial theology. My hope is that you will find this a good place to start. The reader should be aware, however, that I do not seek to present a neutral or dispassionate introduction to the field. This book provides a broad introduction but at the same time offers a deliberate vision for what post-colonial theology could be.

# Introduction

THE CENTRAL PROBLEM FOR the church is the church. The central theological problem of our age is the justification of the church. How is it possible
to call the church "holy?" Theology is the study of witness. It begins with
testimony. It is the testimony of God. It is the testimony of those captivated
by God. It is the testimony of text and context. It is the testimony of the
church through the ages. It is testimony in particularity and it is testimony
in catholicity. However, covenants, conversions, and churches evidence
countertestimony as well as testimony. The claims of God's people, the
witness of opponents, would-be converts, converts, and the ministry of
churches, also deal death. Post-colonial theology is a study of such countertestimony. Post-colonial theologians give voice to such suffering with
a dogged determination that where countertestimony emerges, resistance
might pry open life-giving word and work.

This book will argue that post-colonial theology has five main characteristics. Post-colonial theology begins in *particularity*, is the *agency* of
marginalized voices, considers *coloniality* as the best lens through which
to view imperialist oppression, practices *hybridization*, and seeks to *resist*
dominant forms of theology. Rather than simply theorize on such intent,
the practice of post-colonial theology is considered in the writing of theologians who have experienced particular forms of coloniality. Engaging
with the work of John Mbiti, Wonhee Anne Joh, and Randy Woodley—not
to mention W. B. Yeats—might seem rather eclectic or even arbitrary. I take
some comfort from a leading thinker in the field, Robert J. C. Young. He
depicts postcolonialism as essentially a "montage" made from a variety of
experiences, voices, and relations.[1] Further, I have witnessed how the work
of the scholars engaged with in this study have helped students (and this

---

1. Young, *Postcolonialism: A Very Short Introduction*, 7.

teacher) enter into the complex world of post-colonial studies. The reader is, therefore, invited to read their work and, in this book, consider how each of them illuminate the themes of particularity, agency, coloniality, hybridization, and resistance.

By way of introduction, I will outline the argument of this book and make some initial moves toward defining a post-colonial theology. To begin with, definitions hovering above the particular is at best proleptic and at worst incompatible with what will follow in subsequent chapters. The tension, I hope, is explained by my desire to provide you, the reader, with some initial definitions, direction, and broad themes. This will aid your entry into the book and, it is hoped, serve my desire to write an accessible study of post-colonial theology. As has already been noted, the reader should be aware that I will advance a particular argument for what I think an effective post-colonial theology could be. An effective post-colonial theology will be a practical post-colonial theology. As a practical theology this will mean, at the very least, beginning with (colonial) experience and bringing that experience into conversation with theological questions for the sake of renewed (post-colonial) priorities and practice. It is my hope that many working in and with post-colonial theology would recognize the definitions and themes I provide here. However, the reader should also be aware that the definitions and themes I submit are shaped by the argument of this book and the field itself is rife with contestations. At this early juncture, I will provide some initial definitions for key concepts that will help orientate the reader before defining post-colonialism and outlining the argument of the book. Each of these definitions can be contested, problematized, and nuanced, and I myself would also want to do that. Cognizant of that, I submit them in order to resource initial reflections on post-colonialism and post-colonial theology.

## INTRODUCING KEY TERMS

*Colonization* is the practice of commandeering particular pieces or tracts of land by outsiders motivated by a desire for some kind of increased profit, power, or security. *Colonialism* is the wider movement of such colonization that takes place in a variety of places across history. Colonialism is not only physical action but also philosophical, or theological discourse that may precede or proceed from colonization. The broader term may then include a range of justifications and practices of domination that may include strategies for settling on stolen land for the long term. Colonialism may be dependent on or be accompanied by bloody military conquest, population displacement, or genocide. At other times colonialism may be less directly dependent on military conquest, but rather accompanied by trade expansions and treaties. Indeed, there may be circumstances where colonizers are initially welcomed by a particular section of a population. Given this, a wide variety of colonies and countries come into view, each associated with a foreign power that assumes itself superior to already existing social, political, or cultural arrangements. Both hard and soft power are predicates of colonization and colonialism. If colonization and colonialism are primarily practices, then *imperialism* is, in the first instance, an idea. It is the ambition articulated in, for example, government policy papers, trading priorities, defense strategies, literature, curricula, and sermons for preeminent power and control. Such power can be achieved through colonization, trade agreements, or military threat. Whatever the means, the end is always for a political center to exercise sovereignty over other societies. That ambition can have several real, apparent, contested, and confused motivations emanating from metropolitan centers relating to tropes on overpopulation, unemployment, national security or prestige, global stability, economic growth, and divine providence. Because this book is theological, writings from four contexts will be engaged with not only as illustrative of the nature of post-colonial writing, but also as a means to define what a post-colonial theology is. Thus, authors addressing situations in Ireland, Kenya, Korea, and the United States will illustrate what post-colonial writing is, and at the same time establish the importance of the key post-colonial themes of particularity, agency, coloniality, hybridization, and resistance.

Terms such as "colonization," "colonialism," and "imperialism" can have extended meanings. Consequently, colonization can refer not only to the occupation of *physical* space, but can also mean an unwarranted presence or exploitative presence in *cultural* space, *educational* space, or *theological* space. This study focuses not, therefore, on the so-called "native informant" but on published theology.[2] Imperialism can be an idea for dominance or preeminence that is not dependent on the action of a

---

2. An unintended consequence of a focus on texts is, of course, that it veils the ongoing relational work done with a variety of scholars and practitioners, not least in my work at Virginia Theological Seminary's Center for Anglican Communion Studies. Other publications and forthcoming publications deal more directly with this work. See, for example, Heaney, Sayilgan, and Haymes, *Faithful Neighbors*; Heaney, Kafwanka, and Kabia, *God's Church to God's World*.

nation state, but through other powerful means. For example, economic dominance may be pursued through multinational companies and/or a conglomeration of nations. Unsurprisingly, such colonialist and imperialist thought and practice has met and does meet with resistance in a variety of political, social, economic, cultural, and religious spheres. This resistance can take forms that include armed struggle, political agitation, and religious or cultural revivalism in the cause of *decolonization*. Decolonization, in the first instance, refers to the ending of formal colonial regimes, and is often associated with the 1950s and 1960s and the rise of nationalism after World War II. Given the extended nature of imperialism and colonialism, decolonization can also mean more. It is not only about national independence, but it is also about self-assertion, self-identity, and self-determination in other spheres. In chapter 8, Randy Woodley demonstrates a decolonizing resistance as he submits a renewed theological vision that draws both from Native American and scriptural wisdom. Running alongside the thought and practice of decolonization is the ever-present danger of *neocolonialism*. In simple terms, this is a situation where a former colony has gained flag independence, but an emergent ruling elite continues to maintain many of the injustices of the colonial era. Neocolonialism is often seen in contexts where nationalist leaders continue to govern for the sake of the few over the many. The extended meanings of imperialism and colonialism, along with the reality of neocolonialism and situations of unequal power relations, makes decolonization less than straightforward. Those who seek decolonization have, thus, employed a series of strategies toward post-colonial transformation. This book will illustrate such strategies, especially as they relate to the field of theology.

*Mimicry* is being like, but ultimately unlike, the colonizer.[3] This can refer to an ambivalent surface conversion in the absence of heart conversion where the subject takes on the ways of the imported culture and/or religion, for a range of reasons, without satisfying his or her psychical needs. Mimicry can be more than a process of formation or assimilation that takes on adopted and imported practices and values. It can also be directly subversive. In situations of unequal power relations, it can become a strategy that mocks the authority of the overlords through often exaggerated displays of "loyalty." I have heard the following story in Ireland that, independent of its veracity, illustrates well the subversive power of mimicry. It is a tale set in the era of British rule over the whole island of Ireland and is about an

3. See Bhabha, "Of Mimicry and Man," 125–33.

English dignitary visiting a school. The school was known locally for its republicanism and quiet revolutionary pedagogy. On the guest's arrival at the school assembly, the principal invited all present to stand for the national anthem. The principal shared with the guest of honor that the school had worked hard at not only learning the national anthem, but of translating it "appropriately" into the Irish language. The guest confessed later to some surprise at the children's enthusiasm for the anthem, going so far as to suggest that other schools should adopt this Gaelicized tribute to the monarch. Unbeknownst to the royalist guest, the "appropriate translation" of "God save the King" was closer to "God damn the King." Rather than praying for the divine to "send him victorious," the petition was for God to send him and his servants into the Irish sea. Mimicry is often subversive.

*Hybridization* is a strategy employed toward decolonization that subverts the power of colonial authority and culture by mixing it with, for example, cultural practices, language, philosophy, and texts from the colonized culture. Imperialist practice and texts often assume a binary way of looking at the world, interpreting the world, and teaching the world. There are those who are civilized and there are those who are uncivilized. There are those who are developed and those who are underdeveloped. There are heathens and there are believers. Imperialist mission seeks then to "civilize" subjects by advancing them from their unenlightened state into higher and purer forms of belief and behavior (see chapter 3). Writers such as W. B. Yeats (chapter 1) may well adopt a strategic essentialism that seeks to directly compete with the apparent superiority of imperialist cultures. However, in post-colonial literature there is a rejection of such binaries of opposition, and in Yeats's poetry a strong theme that humans are unable to absolutely choose between opposites is consistently present.[4] Hybridization is not a *direct* move to overthrow a domineering colonialist culture. This may be because of a rejection of binaries of opposition or because power differentials would make it virtually impossible for the "local" to compete with the "imperialist." Thus, the romantic Celtic Ireland of Yeats's early work could never displace the hegemony of Britain. Rather, the strategy of hybridization, in this case bringing a mythic Ireland alive in the English language, aims at interrupting the supposed imperialist superiority. One aspect of the work of theologian John Mbiti that challenges foreign superiority will be considered in chapter 3. His work champions the theological agency of Kenyan believers and the emergence of what might be considered

4. Daniels, *Voice of the Oppressed*, 35.

theological hybridization by challenging the hermeneutical power of foreigners. Taking into account the wisdom of his own Akamba people, Mbiti challenges foreign interpretations of the biblical text. Indeed, he argues that a hybridized New Testament-Akamba eschatology is a more theologically cogent understanding of the end times. Practices of hybridization can have significant impact, not only for cultural production, but even on how human subjectivity is understood. Thus, settled binaries such as heathen/believer challenged by practices of hybridization have implications for a whole series of binary constructions. Not least among these binaries of opposition is that of the colonizer/colonized, which in turn can challenge that most fundamental of all binaries: self/other. Hybridization as a problematizing of "pure" binaries means that one does not simply meet others as *other,* but one recognizes oneself *in* the other and even *as* the other. This will become apparent when we consider the Christology of Wonhee Anne Joh in chapter 6. Joh's hybridized Christology emerges from Korean-American experience in conversation with Korean philosophy and history, "traditional"/white Christology, and feminist philosophy and psychoanalysis.

## INTRODUCING THE BOOK

Post-colonial theology grapples with the complexities, contradictions, and complicities of the church and its mission amidst hate and even as an agent of hate. This book will introduce you to post-colonial theology in five main chapters, defining it in relation to particularity (chapter 1), theological agency (chapter 3), coloniality (chapter 5), hybridization (chapter 6), and resistance (chapter 8). In light of the main characteristics of a post-colonial theology, shorter chapters will draw out broader associations and implications, particularly with discussion groups or classroom settings in view.

Beginning in particularity means that post-colonial theology does not begin with any presumption of universal perspective or cold objectivity. On the contrary, theologians state their location and interrogate their location in relation to imperialism. This will mean, at the very least, some examination of the historical, cultural, and theological narratives that have shaped dominant ways of thought and practice and resistant ways of thought and practice. Given such analysis, the theological agency that emerges is located in a second sense. That is to say, it takes an anti-imperialist stance. Such a position is often marginal in the major assumptions, texts, and processes of theology, especially in the so-called first world. At the very least, this means

I will need to attempt to give voice to my own location. How am I located in and related to the field of post-colonial studies and post-colonial theology? In chapter 1, I will grapple with work of the Irish and Protestant poet W. B. Yeats. He will act as an interlocutor toward locating myself amidst the complexities of Irish histories and identities as they intersect with colonialism and imperialism. As will be seen, locating myself through such means is both promising and problematic. Yeats is considered by some to be a foundational figure in post-colonialism. Certainly, his concern for Irish emancipation seems to cohere with a key task of post-colonial literature. Post-*colonialism* is concerned with emancipation, variously conceived, in response to imperialist and colonialist subjugation. Because it is often argued that the height of imperialism was in the nineteenth century, and that the nature of that imperialism was distinct from earlier ages (at the close of World War I, imperial powers occupied or had some kind of control over nine-tenths of the world), the subjugation commonly in view is that meted out by Europeans. In locating myself in relation to post-colonialism, it will be British imperialism that will be the point of departure in chapter 1. Imperialism in that case is a desire to dominate other peoples and land beyond the island of Britain for some perceived gain for the island of Britain. Of course, this is a dramatic simplification of the histories of Britain that will need to be nuanced in chapter 1. In chapter 2, you will be invited to consider further implications of chapter 1 and the work of Yeats by reflecting on your own particularity and the nature of hate.

The ways imperialists and colonialists articulate their intent is interrogated in post-colonial studies, and the voice and theologizing of those who have been colonized is given priority.

> Postcolonialism . . . begins from its own knowledges, the diversity of its own cultural experiences, and starts from the premise that those in the West, both within and outside the academy, should relinquish their monopoly on knowledge, and take other knowledges, other perspectives, as seriously as those of the West. . . . It's about learning to challenge and think outside the norms of Western assumptions. You can learn it anywhere if you want to. The only qualification you need to start is to make sure that you are looking at the world not from above, but from below, not from the north, but the south, not from the inside, but from the outside, not from the centre, but from the margin's forgotten edge. It's the

world turned upside down. It's the language of the South challenging the dominant perspectives of the North.[5]

Given the globalization of first-world theology and white theology, not least through the expansion of European colonialism, the agency at work in post-colonial theology is "marginal" because of unequal relationships of power. For Christian theologians, emancipation will mean more than nationalist agency but it will not mean less than theological agency. Chapter 3 will consider such agency in the writings of Mbiti, particularly in relation to Christian teaching on the end times (eschatology) in the context of colonialism and foreign mission. Imperialism often, but not necessarily, results in colonization. That is to say, the desire for domination can lead to the theft of land and the settlement of peoples and powers from a metropolitan center to a colonized periphery. Mbiti was born in the white-settler-dominated British colony of Kenya. The Kenyan economy in the post-war era was calibrated for the benefit of these settlers. As is already clear, post-colonialism is not simply interested in a focus on material subjugation. Cultural superiority and its promotion give empire "ideological license."[6] Theological post-colonialism is interested in interrogating thought and texts, produced by Christians, that imply or supply such license and in interrogating thought and texts produced to de-legitimate such license.

*Post*-colonialism indicates a sense of critical beyondness. Post-colonial theology does not simply refer to texts written during a particular colonial rule or after the formal end of that rule. What is in view are texts that adopt a critical stance against colonialism, and a critical stance against theological moves that justify—directly or indirectly—marginalization, subjugation, and colonialism. A reading of Mbiti's work reveals how an imported sense of time disrupted previously held views on temporality. Such cultural importation ultimately forestalled the emergence of an African eschatology that could have avoided a Christian quietism and nourished a deeper sense and practice of agency. Such theologizing, done within historical colonies associated with European powers in the nineteenth and twentieth century, remains key for understanding the nature and intent of post-colonialism. Though currently undervalued, theological voice plays an important role in post-colonialism. Chapter 4 invites readers into a commitment to counter a contextualizing theology. Reflecting not only on the work of Mbiti, this chapter will draw out lessons that theologians from dominant cultures have

5. Young, "What Is the Postcolonial?" 3–4.

6. Said, *Culture and Imperialism*, 222.

learned and that resource a definition and practice of theology that is inherently *inter*cultural. A more critical approach to theology and Christian formation is an intercultural theology. When such theologizing is pursued, the purpose of theology cannot simply be some sort of theoretical coherence. The end of theology is clarified, even in the midst of culturally and theologically licensed domination, as *transformation* (conversion). Entering into intercultural theology is to face such intent for domination or hegemony. However, grappling with such dominance is complex. Chapter 5 will explain what is meant by *coloniality* and why it is theologically important. The cultural subjugation that Yeats and Mbiti wrote about in formal colonial contexts also existed in settings that predated the establishment of colonial conquest and have existed in settings long after formal colonies have been disbanded. Strictly speaking, then, this is not "colonialism." Given that historical reality, coloniality, and not colonialism, is the lens through which post-colonial analysis is done. Chapter 5 argues for the theological significance of coloniality as the ongoing suppression or subjugation of, in this case, theological agency and contextualization. The chapter examines the relationship between culture and power, and the limited notion of critical thought that emerges because of such relationships to cultural power. At the heart of the Christian gospel is the revolutionary idea that God interrupted the power of empire. God becomes incarnate on colonized soil in order that God's people might know the saving message of God. At the heart of the Christian message is an imperial cross. Chapter 6 will, therefore, consider one reading of the cross that emphasizes the key post-colonial characteristic of hybridization. The intercultural theological exchanges across power differences inevitably result in emerging theologies that borrow, adopt, mimic, and subvert a variety of sources. This is done not simply for the sake of some liberal celebration of diversity, pluralism, or relativism. Theological hybridization exists to challenge and dislodge ways of thinking that continue to take no account of imperialism and its continued impact on theology. Chapter 6 will, therefore, explore hybridization as it relates to the central figure of the Christian faith, Jesus Christ. The hybridizing christological work of Wonhee Anne Joh as it relates to the experience, analysis, and vision of Korean and Korean-American thinkers in conversation with fearful division, "traditional" Christology, and psychoanalysis, is considered as a post-colonial reading of the cross. Chapter 7 further draws out the implications of a post-colonial reading of the cross through a rather counterintuitive appeal to recover the language of sacrifice.

Each of these chapters defines post-colonial theology in relation to scholars theologizing within colonialism or coloniality. Each of these writers in their own right and in their own place demonstrates a resistance in the face of powerful forces and the fear, and even hate, such forces evoke. However, because each of these key themes are explored in relation to distinct questions about God and God's mission in *particularity* (given my context, where might I stand before God?), *agency* (how do the Akamba understand the gospel?), *coloniality* (what does it mean to follow God in ongoing situations of subjugation?), and *hybridization* (how is the central symbol of the Christian faith understood amidst empire?)—it is important that a chapter be dedicated to a vision of theological resistance itself. Consequently, chapter 8 considers resistance as a theme in its own right through the work of Randy Woodley, who calls for ongoing Christian resistance in the heart of the world's most powerful nation. Native American theologians point to an experience of coloniality that is internal to the United States of America, deep, and ongoing. Indeed, the experience of Native American peoples can be seen to straddle experiences of proto-colonialism (pre-government policy for expansion), colonialism (deliberate state-sponsored/supported expansion), and coloniality (ongoing subjugation and the impact of historical policies). Woodley demonstrates that resistance is more than simply reactive or deconstructive, but is constructive of a new way. This way he calls *shalom*. Chapter 9 responds to Woodley's call for white people to repent by considering examples of ecclesial repentance and the theological and practical implications of such acts. In a final concluding chapter, I will review and summarize the study pointing beyond the bounds of the present work. Cognizant of my own particularity, a post-colonial theology is not simply theory, but poetic and penitential witness within what I will call a post-colonial imaginary.

# 1

# The Widening Gyre

## The Particularity of the Author

> The heart is devious above all else;
> it is perverse—
> who can understand it?
> —JEREMIAH 17:9

POST-COLONIAL THEOLOGY BEGINS IN *particularity*.[1] The unpronounced hyphen speaks a reality that cannot be elided: colonialism. However, colonialism is plural. It is historically conditioned. It belongs to the history and experience of a variety of peoples and nations in distinct ways.[2] Colonialisms evoke, provoke, and instantiate terror and fear, occupation and resistance, Christ and anti-Christ. To the extent that one can, it is incumbent, therefore, upon the author to name her or his location, to speak what the hyphen might signify (Jer 17:9) before s/he can hear the voice of others and the voice of God amidst the fear and hate. As will become clear, naming my own location consists in at least two tasks. It means heuristically engaging the work of W. B. Yeats toward taking stock of Ireland

---

1. On broader themes and difficulties of defining post-colonialism and post-colonial theology see Heaney, *From Historical to Critical*, 11–30.

2. See Howe, "Historiography," 220–50. Kwok, *Postcolonial Imagination and Feminist Theology*, 38–51.

as my place of formation in light of empire and beyond empire. It means, secondly, an attempt at identifying the ways in which Yeats might have theological significance for the field of post-colonial theology and, more particularly, for this study.

## POST-COLONIALISM BEGINS IN IRELAND

For a young person growing up on the island of Ireland and within Northern Ireland, location meant, at the very least, existential complexity and competing nationalisms. The uncomfortable and unresolvable complexity of my location was forcefully revealed to me while watching a movie in England. In 1996, the Neil Jordan film *Michael Collins* was released. In the title role was Ballymena man Liam Neeson, depicting and interpreting the life of the Irish republican leader of the title who, in 1921, would settle for less than a republic. After its DVD release, I watched it with a group of fellow students in North London. I was taught that Collins was the opposite of who my (Northern) Irish people were and what my people aspired to be. Yet, the people I purportedly belonged to, with all the contradictions and insecurities of a settler people, could "never be English any more than Cambodians or Algerians can be French."[3] I was "a member of the Irish 'other' to England."[4] This became powerfully apparent at the end of the film. As the credits rolled, a fellow student from England scoffed, "Bloody stupid Paddies, they ended up killing each other!" The reaction this evoked in me could not have been predicted, given my religious and political formation. I left the room abruptly and angrily in the wake of a retort that unexpectedly erupted from my throat: "Not so stupid that they couldn't kick the might of the British empire off the island with little more than a few pitchforks!" I did not know in this moment that this admixture of history, myth, confusion, fear, hate, and anger in the face of such jovial jingoism bled into a series of problems and questions relating to a whole set of complex questions

---

3. Said, *Culture and Imperialism*, 228. On the debate around whether Northern Ireland can be considered a colonial settler society, see Cleary, "Postcolonial Ireland," 281–88.

4. This is a phrase Patsy Daniels uses of W. B. Yeats. "Yeats was doubly marginalized: as a member of the Irish 'other' to England and as a member of the Anglo-Irish 'other' to the majority of Irish Catholics in Ireland. . . . [T]hese two forms of 'otherness' were opposite in terms of power: to be Irish in England was to be inferior; in Catholic Ireland, he was Protestant, which was to be superior" (Daniels, *Voice of the Oppressed*, 27).

about hybridized identities, histories, agencies, and theologies that could be described as *post-colonial*.

For Patsy Daniels, post-colonialism begins in Ireland. More specifically, in literature written in English, it begins with the work of W. B. Yeats (1865–1939). In Yeats—and in resistance to the hegemonic intent and cultural dominance of England toward Ireland since at least the twelfth century—themes of otherness, inferiority, liberation, identity, hybridization, resistance, and decolonization are present.[5] Each of these themes continues to remain important in post-colonial literature, including theological literature. This does not mean that the work of post-colonial thinkers and activists is simply reactionary or defined over against dominant political and cultural forces. What Vicki Mahaffrey sees as "icon-elastic" artistry, as opposed to militant and oppositional iconoclasm, is something applicable both to Yeats and post-colonial literature more broadly. Icon-elasticity is a hybridizing strategy that does not simply attempt to overthrow a very powerful rule, but attempts to "evade its power to colonize and predetermine thinking." There is a concentration on "the *elasticity* of thought and language, the reach and capacity for metamorphosis inherent in constructs that have been unnaturally stabilized by the rules governing interpretation."[6] Each of the theologians in this book exhibits such elasticity as they destabilize hegemonic intent in cultural and theological exchange. For Vicki Mahaffrey, Ireland is a place ripe for "conceptual icon-elasticity," not least because of its history of political resistance, which she adjudges to be "curiously reinforced" by a commitment to Christianity.[7] This book will begin to explore why such reinforcement, in a variety of texts and contexts beyond Ireland and Yeats, is not nearly as curious as Mahaffrey imagines.[8]

I grew up in a divided Ireland. I grew up and spent my formative years happily under British rule in Northern Ireland. While division and bloodshed go back centuries in Ireland, it was the high period of the British empire that shaped the context and culture I was born into. Joe Cleary,

---

5. Daniels, *Voice of the Oppressed*, 27–38. I will not spend time here on debates surrounding analyses of Irish history, economics, and politics in relation to colonial categories. For a useful and provocative overview of the debates in relation to broader theorizing in post-colonial studies, see Lloyd, "Ireland after History," 377–95. For a good summary of the postcolonial nature and international influence of Irish literature on anti-colonial struggle elsewhere see Cleary, "Postcolonial Ireland," 257–71.

6. Mahaffrey, *States of Desire*, 9.

7. Mahaffrey, *States of Desire*, 10.

8. See, for example, Bew, *Ireland*, 561–64.

well aware of the complexities of the context, is nonetheless correct to argue that "the development of twentieth-century Irish society has been most deeply conditioned by attempts either to preserve or to surmount Ireland's centuries-old relationship with Britain and the British Empire."[9] It was particularly the First World War era that became generative for both unionism and nationalism. For the Ulster unionism I was formed in, it is difficult to imagine a signifier more potent than July 1, 1916 and the battle of the Somme. Indeed, the "blood sacrifice" of the 36th (Ulster) Division on the Western Front provides the "central foundation myth for the Northern Irish state."[10] On that day, the 36th was tasked with capturing a key German position, the Schwaben Redoubt. Their reckless courage on the day meant they fulfilled the mission, but reinforcements did not reach them. Half of the division was lost in the forced retreat.

> . . . the ghosts of the Somme are never at rest. Their "sacrifice" is constantly recalled, reiterated and, thereby, projected forwards, propelled always and endlessly into the future. . . . [T]he sacrifice of the Ulster Division at the Somme represents an unfulfilled and particularly in the era of peacebuilding, inherently unfulfill*able* promise of salvation.[11]

1916 also has equal and unexorciseable mythical potency for Irish nationalists. That an armed group of revolutionaries should stage an Easter Rising was always meant to deliver a rhetorical and even theological blow above and beyond any military achievement. "Like Christ on Easter, Ireland would rise again out of the blood of its martyrs, and its spiritual kingdom would have no end."[12] As with the Somme, these Irish actors recklessly faced "crucifixion" as a means to bringing about new life for their nation. They succeeded, and the rising became a "source of legitimacy" for the Irish state and for later republican movements that continued to use both force of arms and argument.[13] Stories of soldiers stranded by England and Easter risings against England continue to pump blood into the body politic of Ireland, long after 1916. Since the establishment of both the partition of Ireland and the Irish state, this dancing with ghosts is a rerighting and

---

9. Cleary, "Postcolonial Ireland," 253–54. See also Hempton, *Religion and Political Culture*, 93–116.

10. Grayson and McGarry, *Remembering 1916*, 1.

11. Evershed, "Ghosts of the Somme," 255–57.

12. Mahaffrey, *States of Desire*, 11.

13. Grayson and McGarry, *Remembering 1916*, 1.

rewriting of the past in a bid to recover "a deferred eschatological promise, in the face of deep ontological uncertainty."[14]

> Too long a sacrifice
> Can make a stone of the heart.
> O when may it suffice?
> That is Heaven's part, our part
> To murmur name upon name,
> As a mother names her child
> When sleep at last has come
> On limbs that had run wild.
> What is it but nightfall?
> No, no, not night but death;
> Was it needless death after all?
> —W. B. YEATS, "EASTER 1916"[15]

Yeats's question haunts all communities in Ireland. Was so much death pointless after all? Uncertainty, and thus fear, is alive in the halting steps of loyalist and nationalist dance. Before post-colonial categories were imprinted in learned texts, minds and bodies standing, stumbling, and bleeding on this island turf, knew dislocation, hybridization, porosity, and the struggle for agency. In short, the post-colonial emerges out of such bloody intersections, contestations, contradictions, and doubts.

Post-war Ireland meant partition and ongoing violent competing nationalisms. As is the case in each of the chapters in this book, land boundaries in Kenya, Korea, and the United States of America helped define coloniality. Not for the first time would partition be proffered by the empire in the name of peace. Not for the last time would it fail to deliver peace. The "sacred egoism" of republican politicians in Sinn Féin meant they abstained from politics in Westminster, thus effectively "collaborating" with unionist and British designs for a divided Ireland.[16] Northern Irish nationalists had a right to feel abandoned. Unionist egotism took full

14. Evershed, "Ghosts of the Somme," 244.

15. Yeats, *Collected Poems*, 152–53. Unless otherwise indicated, all the Yeats poems cited in this study will be from *Collected Poems*, published by Macmillan in 2010.

16. Lee, *Ireland*, 44. Indeed, there would continue to be resistance on the side of the Irish state for reunification, even when the British Prime Minister, Harold Wilson (1916–95), sought to work toward British withdrawal. Still today there is some doubt about whether the Irish state has any appetite for reunification. See Bew, *Ireland*, 513–55.

advantage of this. A devolved parliament was set up and opened in Northern Ireland in 1921, keeping six counties within the United Kingdom. A demographic or democratic justification for the contours of the border remain elusive. Southern unionists isolated by this border also had a right to feel abandoned. J. J. Lee's explanation is as fair as it is stark, "The border was chosen explicitly to provide unionists with as much territory as they could safely control."[17] Nationalist leaders assumed that the border would be a temporary inconvenience, but what emerged was little less than a "Unionist and Protestant hegemony in Northern Ireland."[18] The implications of such a skewed settlement continue to play out in British and Irish politics to this day. For the rest of the country, a treaty was eventually negotiated and then ratified in 1922, creating an "Irish Free State" of twenty-six counties under an agreement that gave them, not unlike Canada, "dominion status" within the empire.[19] Inevitably, such a settlement would not be satisfactory. Deep dissatisfaction eventually led to an Irish civil war (1922–23) and ongoing political and violent struggle in Northern Ireland (1968–98).[20]

In the month I was born, the increasing inability of a devolved and partisan Northern Ireland parliament to govern meant that direct rule from London was reinstated. This was just six weeks after British soldiers had opened fire on a civil rights march, killing thirteen innocent people. "Bloody Sunday" was for many the inevitable murderous outcome of hate-filled sectarian politics. That year, declared the "year of victory" by the Provisional Irish Republican Army, saw nearly five hundred people murdered as a result of politically motivated violence in the form of beatings, shootings, and bombings.[21] It is difficult to argue against Paul Bew, who sees the return of direct rule as the "most decisive moment of the crisis" and the *sine qua non* of all that was to follow.[22] Unionists may have had hegemonic intent, but such desire was unable to deliver control, stability, or peace for any citizen. The Ireland of the 1970s continued to dance to the tune of the

---

17. Lee, *Ireland*, 45.

18. Cronin, *History of Ireland*, 207.

19. See Cronin, *History of Ireland*, 199–204; Lee, *Ireland*, 43–55.

20. These dates cover up a more complex picture. The so-called "Troubles" do not neatly fall into such categorization. However, the thirty-year period often cited as the era of "The Troubles" cover the period from Bloody Sunday in 1968 to the signing of the Good Friday Agreement in 1998.

21. Ritchie, "'Descent into terror'"; Bew, *Ireland*, 486–555.

22. Bew, *Ireland*, 509.

1920s. Yeats wrote the poem "Blood and the Moon" in the wake of violence in the 1920s but more than one decade would befit the stanza:

> The purity of the unclouded moon
> Has flung its arrowy shaft upon the floor.
> Seven centuries have passed and it is pure,
> The blood of innocence has left no stain.
> There, on blood-saturated ground, have stood
> Soldier, assassin, executioner,
> Whether for daily pittance or in blind fear
> Or out of abstract hatred, and shed blood,
> But could not cast a single jet thereon.
> Odour of blood on the ancestral stair!
> And we that have shed none must gather there
> And clamour in drunken frenzy for the moon.[23]

Yeats wrote the poem as an exploration of deep-seated and even in-herited enmity in Ireland.[24] As a moderate nationalist, he supported the treaty. However, as in the poem "1916," he was well aware that nationalism, whether British or Irish, had a fecundity that could beget fear, hate, and violence. The relationship between nationalism and post-colonialism is not straightforward. Indeed, post-colonial scholars are critical of nationalism from a number of perspectives. Nationalism can depend upon or draw from a nativism appealing to an essential reality (Irishness) that does not exist. Such nativistic nationalism, while seeking to overthrow the "absolute hierarchical distinction" between ruler and ruled, can actually reinforce it.[25] Further, nationalism may not succeed in overthrowing colonial social arrangements or ways of thinking, but may rather embed them. As has been seen, there is such a thing as neocolonialism. A local ruling elite and agenda can replace, sometimes in cahoots with the departing overlords, a foreign ruling elite and agenda.[26] Nationalism can also smother or flatten out differences and dissonant voices. Feminist, Marxist, and "subaltern" criticism of such nationalism castigates it as the vision of the middle classes

---

23. Yeats, *Collected Poems*, 321.
24. Foster, *W. B. Yeats: A Life: II*, 340–42.
25. Said, *Culture and Imperialism*, 228–29.
26. For a powerful critique of neocolonialism, see wa Thiong'o, *Devil on the Cross*.

writ large in political and social practice.[27] The later Yeats was particularly aware of such problems at work within nationalism:

> Hurrah for revolution and more cannon shot!
> A beggar upon horseback lashes a beggar upon foot.
> Hurrah for revolution and cannon come again!
> The beggars have changed places, but the lash goes on.
> —W. B. YEATS, "THE GREAT DAY" (1937)[28]

The "*déclassé* bohemian" Yeats came not so much to promote or reject, but rather to fret "the proud ideals of nationhood and manhood."[29] While fret means to "restlessly chafe" or to worry, it means more than this. It also means to adorn, "especially with crisscrosses and jewels," and it also refers to the piece of wood in a musical instrument that crosses the strings and thus affects their vibrations. Fretting is "a kind of beauty drawn from the intersection of opposed lines."[30]

> The situation of the Irish writer whose native language is English illustrates how it is possible to be both inside and outside a defining boundary, to be stamped with an identity that is both familiar and foreign, to be fretted (both worried and made musical) by two incompatible states.[31]

My crisscrossing, ever in danger of double-crossing, frets at naïve nationalisms and it frets about Yeats. In the case of Yeats, he was a "hybridized" character with "allegiances both to Ireland and to other nations."[32] Such hybridization in Yeats is unstable and may be both a mark of his post-coloniality and a dilution of his post-coloniality. I feel, though distinctly aware of any hubris that would compare myself to Yeats, a deep empathy with such fretting and double imprinting. While such instability may frustrate the reader, it is part of the post-colonial task to problematize naïve

---

27. Howes, "Yeats and the Postcolonial," 220. For similar reasons, Miroslav Volf explains why Jesus preaches repentance to those oppressed by dominant powers. See *Exclusion and Embrace*, 111–19.

28. Yeats, *Collected Poems*, 267.

29. Mahaffrey, *States of Desire*, 21. Foster, *W. B. Yeats: A Life: I*, xxix.

30. Mahaffrey, *States of Desire*, 21.

31. Mahaffrey, *States of Desire*, 21–22.

32. Mahaffrey, *States of Desire*, 21.

binaries such as "outsider" and "insider," and question the assumption that nationalism straightforwardly aims at or provides decolonization.[33]

Against the backdrop of a 1920s that witnessed a narrow nationalism and a zealous and triumphalist Catholic Church veering toward a confessional state, Yeats feared for the future of Irish Protestants.[34] This desire for a nationalism that is pluralist, in distinction to what emerged in Northern Ireland, points toward a post-colonial sensibility that remains important today. Identities and boundaries and borders are porous, not least because human beings borrow from others and are changed by others. As boundaries are porous, so human identities speak with a fluidity and diversity that does not provide any "pure" foundation for defining nationhood in relation to constructed categories such as race or religion. In a context where such a danger existed, Yeats described his own minority Anglo-Irish tradition in terms that could have graced any northern unionist platform, as "no petty people. We are one of the great stocks of Europe."[35] Such utterances simultaneously point to a constructive impulse and a problematic impulse. While he envisaged a pluralist nationalism, throughout his life Yeats would argue for the leadership of the artistic, imaginative, spiritual, and bold few over the many.[36] Such an oligarchic worldview would result in 1933 with what Edward Said called an "arrogant if charming" flirtation with a nascent Irish Fascism.[37] Authorities on Yeats find no evidence in the particularity of this time and place (before the rise of the Third Reich and the alliance between Hitler and Mussolini)[38] that the "Fascism" Yeats had in view was

33. While the intransigence of Irish unionists may be well known, Bew also points to missed opportunities by Irish nationalists for the decolonization of politics. In the 1990s, the British state explicitly and publicly distanced itself from any strategic or political interest in Northern Ireland. In light of this, nationalist leader John Hume called for a campaign of diplomatic persuasion toward those who doubted the benefits of Irish unity. According to Bew, this path was not taken, nationalists preferring "ethnic grinding" over the "task of gentle persuasion" (Bew, *Ireland*, 574).

34. What Yeats feared largely came to pass. Though intimations toward pluralism begin to emerge in the 1980s, and have accelerated in recent years, Lee depicted the Republic of Ireland right up until the 1980s as a "*de facto* Catholic state" (Lee, *Ireland*, 653).

35. Allison, "Yeats and Politics," 196.

36. Allison, "Yeats and Politics," 185.

37. Said, *Culture and Imperialism*, 230. R. F. Foster prefers the term "para-Fascist" for this movement, commonly referred to as the "Blueshirts," arguing that they were not in fact Fascist but where an organization that had the potential to become "objectively Fascist" (Foster, *W. B. Yeats: A Life: II*, 472).

38. Allison, "Yeats and Politics," 186, 198.

what National Socialists had in view, or indeed what many would-be Irish Fascists had in mind.[39] However, read from a post-war and post-Shoah perspective, such dalliance cannot simply be ignored. In the spring of 1933, Yeats was involved in discussions about forming an "extra-parliamentary opposition" that he described as "a social theory which can be used against Communism in Ireland—what looks like emerging is Fascism modified by religion."[40] The so-called "Blueshirts" developed a vision for a reunified Ireland, opposition to Communism, a national association of farmers, and an ardent Catholicism.[41] Yeats's dalliance was short-lived, and by 1937, he was contributing to a Spanish anti-fascist writer's congress.[42] Despite this, his elitism and oligarchy would persist. His frustration with the results of Irish democracy is apparent: "Our representative system has given Ireland to the incompetent."[43] By the end of the 1930s, he would come to view both Communist and Fascist governments as impediments to the nourishment of a well-bred educated elite:[44]

> I write with two certainties in mind: first that a hundred men, their creative power wrought to the highest pitch, their will trained but not broken, can do more for the welfare of a people, whether in war or peace, than a million of any lesser sort no matter how expensive their education, and that although the Irish masses are vague and excitable because they have not yet been moulded and cast, we have as good blood as there is in Europe. Berkeley, Swift, Burke, Grattan, Parnell, Augusta Gregory, Synge, Kevin O'Higgins, are the true Irish people, and there is nothing too hard for such as these.[45]

For Marjorie Howes, Yeats's work demonstrates the "frustrating, fascinating variations and uncertainties" that post-colonialism itself possesses.[46] Alongside his elitism lie his questioning and subversion of naïve nation-

39. For a fuller treatment of the issue and context, see Foster, *W. B. Yeats: A Life: II*, 466–95.

40. Cited by Foster, *W. B. Yeats: A Life: II*, 472. Also see 627–31.

41. Foster, *W. B. Yeats: A Life: II*, 473. Cronin, "Catholicising Fascism, Fascistising Catholicism?," 401–11.

42. Said, "Yeats and Decolonization," 87. Yeats supports an anti-fascist writers congress in Madrid in 1937 in support of the Republic.

43. Yeats, *On the Boiler*, 11.

44. Yeats, *On the Boiler*, 18–19. Foster, *W. B. Yeats: A Life: II*, 612–13.

45. Yeats, *On the Boiler*, 30.

46. Howes, "Yeats and the Postcolonial," 224.

alisms, his resistance to English hegemonic intent, and his rejection of materialistic reductionist views of the universe. While these latter themes cohere with a critical post-colonialism, his oligarchic tendencies cannot be sustained in a theological post-colonialism that hears God's voice clearest at the margins.

In reading Yeats and reading about him, I had at times the urge to abandon him. Yet, the contestation, hybridization, and even contradiction that are part of Yeats's work are characteristic of any definition of post-colonialism that takes historical particularity seriously. Thus the problems of relating Yeats to the evolving field of post-colonial criticism are, in themselves, characteristic of post-colonialism. That is not to say that he can be cheaply absolved of his sin any more than I can be cheaply absolved of my complicities as a white, heterosexual, Irish Anglican from Northern Ireland. It is the argument of this book that a post-colonial theology should be a practical theology. Whatever else this ascription will mean, it will mean bringing experiences and practices into dialogue with particular texts that have contributed to the embodiment of the Christian traditions and the embodiment of various receptions of these traditions. For this reason, as an initial and interim step, I have begun to bring my own experience into dialogue with an Irish Protestant thinker who, for some, was part of the genesis of post-colonialism.

## BEGINNING TO THEOLOGIZE
## IN A POST-COLONIAL IRELAND

Yeats was a white, privileged, Anglo-Irish Protestant.[47] While he cannot be reduced to such descriptors, they do point to his social and historical location, and they do point to what, in part, formed him, his sensibilities, and his insensibilities. For Said, Yeats was "an indisputably great *national* poet who during a period of anti-imperialist resistance articulates the experiences, the aspirations, and the restorative vision of a people suffering under the domination of an offshore power."[48]

Nonetheless, his work is problematically post-colonial. I have made appeal to Yeats as a means to understand not only the contested nature of post-colonialism as a field of academic study, but also to begin to locate

47. For a more detailed socioeconomic location of Yeats's family, see Foster, *W. B. Yeats: A Life: I*, 6–34.

48. Said, *Culture and Imperialism*, 220.

myself both to the study of post-colonialism and to the ongoing controversies about post-colonialism as experience as well as hermeneutic.
Whatever post-colonial theology is or may become, it proceeds from the
*particular*. If the post-colonial begins in Ireland and begins with Yeats then
already we have seen that to deal with post-colonial theology will be to
deal with a "widening gyre" of controversies, contradictions, and attempts
at emancipation for body, soul, and mind. In short, in seeking to lay bare
the problematic post-coloniality of Yeats I lay bare my own problematic
post-coloniality. Further, it will become apparent that the complexities of
personal identity, the irreducibly religious and theological questions that
emerge in colonialism and coloniality, the centrality of violence and conflict, and a critical approach to nationalisms are not simply definitional for
a post-colonial Ireland. The forms of post-colonial theological literature
studied in this book will also wrestle with these issues. It is clear that Yeats
can frame a consideration of post-colonialism, and given my own cultural
location his thought helps frame my own experiences and formation.

By way of introducing the following chapters of this study, some consideration of the theological significance of Yeats is necessary. For it is one
thing to make Yeats a point of departure or framing presence in a book
on post-colonial literature. It is quite another thing to make him such in a
book on post-colonial *theology*.

> . . . I—though
>
> heart might find relief Did I become a Christian
>
> man and choose for my belief
>
> What seems most welcome in the tomb—play a
>
> predestined part.
>
> Homer is my example and his unchristened heart.[49]

As is seen in this short extract from "Vacillation," Yeats could define
his artistic project *over against* Christianity. Religious authorities were
happy to return the favor by consistently condemning "WBY's theology."[50]
Even after his death and in his "spiritual return" to be buried in Co. Sligo,
the Church of Ireland bishop of Kilmore, Elphin, and Ardagh "felt a little
doubtful as to Yeats's claim to Christian burial."[51] While faith might bring

49. Yeats, "Vacillation" (1932).

50. Foster, *W. B. Yeats: A Life: II*, 628. See Yeats, *Autobiographies*, 115, 173, 205–9,
221, 500, 561.

51. Foster, *W. B. Yeats: A Life: II*, 657. The controversy around the burial of Yeats will
be dealt with in chapter 10.

compelling comfort to the dead, Yeats, like Homer, will accept that the human condition is tragic.[52] To transcend the tragic, a heroic artistic rebirth is required. A rebirth that begins with an epiphany of death, mortality, terror, and the abyss converting the artist to the gay abandon of creative construction, despite the inevitability of creation's destruction:

> Test every work of intellect or faith,
> And everything that your own hands have wrought;
> And call those works extravagance of breath
> That are not suited for such men as come
> Proud, open-eyed and laughing to the tomb.[53]

Few Christian theologians can dispute the call to self-critical reflection that weighs the worth of work and life against the inevitability of death and eternity (Eccl 3:9–15; 1 Cor 15; 2 Cor 7:10). I do not, however, share Yeats's self-confidence. I will not go proud and laughing to the grave, but with *Kyrie eleison* on my lips.

Yeats's art and life-as-art is an apparent rejection of any external offer of salvation in favor of human redemption through self-transformation. He has hope in "Gaiety transfiguring . . . dread"[54] and confidence that "spiritual wisdom" will come from personal history and the "instinctual self":[55]

> The ultimate virtue for Yeats is therefore courage; the artist . . . assumes the mask of heroic gaiety primarily for his own self-realization, but also in order to serve as heroic example to his audience. For Yeats, tragic art redeems life, giving it dignity and power; by providing a means of containing tragic reality, describing it and limiting it, true subjective art provides access to the condition of freedom, calm, and self-fulfillment which Yeats calls "tragic joy" or "gaiety."[56]

It is Brunner's opinion that the later Yeats did test the work of his intellect and faith and found his "self-generated salvation" to have fallen short.[57] Brunner comes close to a post-mortem conversion of Yeats when he writes:

---

52. Brunner, *Tragic Victory*, 4–22. Yeats, *Autobiographies*, 115–16.

53. Yeats, "Vacillation."

54. Yeats, "Lapis Lazuli." See Foster, *W. B. Yeats: A Life: II*, 631–34.

55. Foster, *W. B. Yeats: A Life: II*, 649.

56. Brunner, *Tragic Victory*, 2.

57. Brunner, *Tragic Victory*, 115–50.

His art . . . as the superb, thoughtful craftsmanship that it is . . . deals intimately and directly with the single central concern of humanity—the possibility of salvation from fear and death. . . . What Yeats finally saw is that tragedy *cannot* be a way of life, . . . that heroic gaiety was really inoperative, that it could not deliver the strength and redemption it promised. . . . Yeats finally asserts his search for another system of belief . . . in his turning away from subjectivity as an absolute mode of living we may see something of the drift of his thought toward the end of his life. . . . Yeats's nagging fear that perhaps he might need God or the idea of God for "unity of being" is a large factor in his growing alienation from the subjective doctrine. He wants to hold on to God because he is never fully satisfied that the self without God is complete.

My strong feeling is that, given time, Yeats would increasingly have sought a formulation of experience which would not only include God, but perhaps even center on God.[58]

Yeats's chief biographer, R. F. Foster, is much more circumspect. He cites a letter the poet wrote in the final weeks before his death. In summing up his life's work, he writes, "Man can embody truth but he cannot know it."[59] The words Yeats misquotes come from German theologian and mystic, Jacob Boehme (1575–1624). The source for the quote may well have been a book, dedicated to Yeats, by Arthur Symons:

Jacob Boehme has said, very subtly, "that man does not perceive the truth but God perceives the truth in man"; that is, that whatever we perceive or do is not perceived or done consciously by us, but unconsciously through us. Our business, then, is to tend that "inner light" by which most mystics have symbolized that which at once guides us in time and attaches us to eternity.[60]

In his final weeks, it is true that Yeats had little interest in "psychic promises, occult manifestations, and the prospect of reunion with the dead." Instead, "Faith and instinct outweighed rational philosophic argument."[61] That is not to say, as is Brunner's hope, that Yeats was returning to God

58. Brunner, *Tragic Victory*, 153–55.

59. Yeats to Elizabeth Pelham, 4 January, 1939, cited in Foster, *W. B. Yeats: A Life: II*, 649–50.

60. Symons, *Symbolist Movement in Literature*, 85. See Foster, *W. B. Yeats: A Life: I*, 98–101.

61. Foster, *W. B. Yeats: A Life: I*, 650.

as understood by orthodox Christian theology. Things were, as always, ambiguous between Yeats and God. Poignantly, his final unfinished poem continues, quite literally, to bracket out God:

> Think all a vision of the air
>
> But they will soon be merely this
>
> Not yet my son not yet
>
> For this is no regret
>
> When ghost & dreams walk by
>
> What is out there, those [?]
>
> [cancelled: what men are these that pass in the skies]
>
> A dream [cancelled: by God] of the day to go
>
> That work all done & well
>
> Do I dream this sound in the sky
>
> Do you hear [?] Father
>
> No no not yet not yet
>
> But [?]
>
> Soon soon my son.[62]

Despite this, Yeats knew he could not escape religion and he certainly did not seek to escape the transcendent. He wrote, ". . . Ireland is, I suppose, more religious than any other European country, and perhaps that is the reason why I, who have been born and bred here, can hardly write at all unless I write about religious ideas."[63] His work includes both characters and vision that sit well with Christian radicalism. Indeed, like his "master" William Blake (1757–1827), he could consider his own work prophecy.[64] For "Great art chills us at the first by its coldness or its strangeness, by what seems capricious, and yet it is from these qualities it has authority, as though it had fed on locust and wild honey."[65] As with Blake, Yeats considered clerics and the church to be involved in reducing "divine things" to "a round of duties separate from life."[66] In 1902, he set out to write a play, that

62. Foster, *W. B. Yeats: A Life: II*, 648–49.

63. Foster, *W. B. Yeats: A Life: I*, 269.

64. Yeats and Lady Gregory, *Unicorn from the Stars*, viii. Yeats, *Autobiographies*, 161–64, 253–55.

65. Yeats, *Synge and the Ireland*, 35.

66. Foster, *W. B. Yeats: A Life: I*, 501.

he would not long esteem, about "religious iconoclasm." The central character, Paul Ruttledge, leaves his life of privilege to become a tinker, disrupts the order of a monastery by introducing ecstatic or charismatic spirituality, preaches iconoclastic radicalism, and is eventually martyred. In one scene from "Where There Is Nothing," a group of tinkers put on trial a group of gentlemen to determine if, as they claim, they have lived Christian lives. Paul, who "had never gave in to the preaching of S. Patrick," is the judge. The gentlemen have come to him objecting to his recent decision to spend his money on alcohol for all of the local people. In response Ruttledge says: ". . . I have not done trying the world I have left. You have accused me of upsetting order by my free drinks, and I have showed you that there is a more dreadful fermentation in the Sermon on the Mount than in my beer-barrels."[67]

During the mock trial, Paul warns these respectful men: "You have come into a different kingdom now; the old kingdom of the people of the roads, the houseless people. We call ourselves tinkers, and you are going to put us on trial if you can. You call yourselves Christians and we will put you on your trial first . . . ."[68]

Each of those on trial are found to be living lives that contradict the teaching of Jesus. Colonel Lawley has failed to live up to the teaching of Christ to turn the other cheek (Matt 5:39) because he recruited men for an unjust war. Mr. Dowler is accused of greed and storing up treasures on earth (Matt 6:19). Mr. Green, as magistrate, is singled out for particular censure. For when the poor give the rich opportunity to practice Jesus' command to turn the other cheek, the smiter is punished. When the poor take a coat, fulfilling Jesus' command on his followers to give without expectation of return (Luke 6:30), the taker is condemned. As he examines each, he turns to his fellow tinkers enquiring of them if they think these gentlemen have lived a Christian life. Every time and in unison they cry out, "He has not!"

Beyond the tinkers, and now in the monastery as brother Paul, he continues to judge and to preach:

> The Christian's business is not reformation but revelation, and the only labours he can put his hand to can never be accomplished in Time. He must so live that all things shall pass away. . . . We must

67. Yeats, Where There Is Nothing, 122.
68. Yeats, Where There Is Nothing, 111.

destroy the World; we must destroy everything that has Law and Number, for where there is nothing, there is God.[69]

The tenor of such thinking has a place in Christian theology. Yeats was attracted to thinkers such as Joachim of Fiore (1135–1202).[70] If figures such as Joachim are considered Christian radicals, then space opens up not only for discontinuity between Yeats and Christian theology, but also continuity.

Christopher Rowland and Andrew Bradstock include Joachim and William Blake in the stream of radical Christian thought and action. They identify at least five characteristics of radical Christianity. It makes an appeal to the roots of the faith, especially as found in the teaching and example of Jesus and the early church. It critiques false religion when it props up inhumanity and injustice by protecting the *status quo* institutionally and ritualistically at the expense of the poor. It declares hope for a new order by proclaiming that the reign of God is breaking into the present often *via* a prophetic group or great event. It considers the present as a decisive moment in the purposes of God, thus making immediate action—often under the direction of a charismatic, visionary, or prophetic leader—a requirement. It democratizes the community of faith so that what was assumed to be the preserve of the elite (holiness, knowledge, wealth, and power) is considered to be available to all equally. The interpretation of Scripture is for all through a participatory hermeneutic with an emphasis on the power of the Spirit to open up meaning to the community.[71] Such a definition of radical Christianity echoes in Yeats's religious iconoclasm found in the witness of Ruttledge. This is not, however, an attempt to convert Yeats. It is, rather, an appeal for the possibility that, as well as being significant for post-colonialism more broadly, he may also have theological significance. For, at the very least, there is overlap between the theological literature considered in this book and the themes evident in the Yeats corpus. Both critique false religion that supports the *status quo*, both hope for present change, both see the present as a decisive moment, and both democratize wisdom or faith beyond the circles of the scholars. While Yeats may not straightforwardly make an appeal to the early church of Jesus (though such an appeal is present in Ruttledge) he does nonetheless look to the past, at

69. Yeats, *Where There Is Nothing*, 62–63. See chapter 7 for theological notions of "self-emptying."

70. Foster, *W. B. Yeats: A Life: I*, 177–78.

71. Rowland and Bradstock, *Radical Christian Writings*, xvii–xxvi. See also Rowland, *Radical Prophet*, xiii–xv.

least in his early work, for inspiration toward a better society. This does not make him part of a Christian radical tradition. It does, however, point to particular continuities and inspirations that still provoke post-colonial questions and even post-colonial theological questions. The poet, who never quite abandoned the hope of revelation, faces the tragic, faces the fear, faces the hate, seeks transcendence and, like the radicals, does so ever resisting a religion that speaks one thing and does another.[72]

## LOCATING THE NEXT STEP

Presently, I am a "legal alien" with undoubted privilege as a tenured professor at an American Episcopal seminary. This body speaks of dominance and privilege. It exists as a result of the intertwining and interweaving of my mother's story—a woman with no secondary-level education. It exists as a result of the intertwining and interweaving of my father's story—a man with but one year of high school education. In terms of poetry and progeny I am no Yeats. Yet, my body hides this story and I have often colluded with its innate ability to whiteout the lowly expectations for someone from the time and the place I have left behind. I was often told and it was often implied that I am no one from nowhere. Yet, inscribed privilege serves white people well and I have walked through doors and into spaces no one in my family or community would have ever expected me to walk into. This body has both obvious and tenuous relationships with post-colonial projects. This voice has both tenuous and even oppositional relationship to post-colonial projects. This book, therefore, should not veil my location any more than it can ignore the complexities of considering Ireland a source of post-colonial thought and practice. In turn, existential and historical complexities are joined to other issues at work that make the field of post-colonial studies itself rightly and purposefully difficult to define or delineate. The theorizing and theologizing examined in this book as historically and/or critically post-colonial are inevitably caught in a web of complex strands of history, race, class, gender, sexuality, nationalism, and globalization.

To begin with the particular is already to make an argument about what a post-colonial theology could or should be. It is an invitation to a practical post-colonial theology. If there can be success in the endeavor it will mean, therefore, that both the author and the reader will demonstrate how taking up the invitation has an impact on theology and practice. That

72. Foster, *W. B. Yeats: A Life: II*, 658.

is to say, a practical post-colonial approach should nourish how we act and interact with God and with each other. To consider Ireland a site for post-colonial thought is also to take a position on what post-colonial criticism is and is not. It is to reject the assumption that post-colonialism is temporally, geographically, or racially bound. Time, place, or race are not the cardinal factors in post-colonial analysis and voice.[73] As will be seen in subsequent chapters, the determinative factor in defining a context and response as post-colonial relates to analyses and strategies around exercises of power. That does not mean that race, history, and geography are unimportant in the approach to post-colonial theology being developed in this book. On the contrary, in understanding structures of power and resistance, they remain vital. What is being rejected is any sense that particular races, particular histories, and particular places alone constitute the borders of what is post-colonial. It may well be that those from beyond Europe who have suffered at the hands of Europe, especially in the era of high imperialism, are at the heart of post-colonialism. However, the heart of the movement does not constitute the complete corpus. Rather, a renewed post-colonialism will avoid essentialized nativism, naïve nationalism, and easy binaries of difference in favor of a more expansive intercultural post-colonialism. The particularities of place, race, class, and time are not boundaries to be policed. They are boundaries that make us present to one another. Such particularities can open up avenues for intercultural conversation, analysis, and practice. They can become liminalities toward conversion. They invite us to find God and each other amidst the hate.

Yeats wrote "The Second Coming" in 1919. It is a poem that comes from a particular place and particular time. Amidst his notes he references the upheavals associated with the execution of Marie Antoinette (1793) and the Russian revolution (1917) as backdrop. The ongoing destabilizing impact of World War I and ongoing unrest in Ireland was also still being felt. The poem is apocalyptic. As the old order of things seemed to be passing away with the fall of empires, Yeats envisioned a new era about to break in that would be as uncertain as it would be bloody:[74]

> Turning and turning in the widening gyre
> The falcon cannot hear the falconer;
> Things fall apart; the centre cannot hold;

73. Duncan, "Flexible Foundation," 320–33.

74. Holdeman, *Cambridge Introduction to W. B. Yeats*, 77. See also Foster, *W. B. Yeats: A Life II*, 150–51, 161.

Mere anarchy is loosed upon the world,
The blood-dimmed tide is loosed, and everywhere
The ceremony of innocence is drowned;
The best lack all conviction, while the worst
Are full of passionate intensity.

Surely some revelation is at hand;
Surely the Second Coming is at hand.
The Second Coming! Hardly are those words out
When a vast image out of *Spiritus Mundi*
Troubles my sight: somewhere in sands of the desert
A shape with lion body and the head of a man,
A gaze blank and pitiless as the sun,
Is moving its slow thighs, while all about it
Reel shadows of the indignant desert birds.

The darkness drops again; but now I know
That twenty centuries of stony sleep
Were vexed to nightmare by a rocking cradle,
And what rough beast, its hour come round at last,
Slouches toward Bethlehem to be born? [75]

The colonial, apocalyptic, and even theological, are deeply entrenched in this fearful portrayal of the twentieth century. Yet, it is a poem that has endured beyond the British empire, the era of decolonization, and the proliferations of colonialities. It is a poem that resonates with a work like this on post-colonial theology. For that reason, it will provide a framework for the subsequent main chapters of this book as a post-colonial theology is defined, interculturally, in relation to particularism, agency, coloniality, hybridization, and resistance.

75. Yeats, *Collected Poems*, 260.

# 2

# Implications
## Beginning Post-Colonial Theology

Following each major chapter in the book you will be invited into further reflection and conversation on the implications of the emerging definition of post-colonial theology. Reflecting the title of this volume, each of these chapters will ask you to consider where the hate is found, where we might find each other, and where we might discern the presence of God.

### FINDING THE HATE

> We know in Ireland, and probably they in Poland, in Slovakia and in Russia, and a score of other countries where revolution has succeeded, what is the cost of victorious hate.
>
> —Stephen Gwynn[1]

> We pray this night that thou wouldst deal with the Prime Minister of our country. O God, in wrath take vengeance upon this wicked, treacherous, lying woman: take vengeance upon her, O Lord, and grant that we shall see a demonstration of thy power.
>
> —The Reverend Ian Paisley[2]

1. Quoted in Bew, *Ireland*, 578.
2. Public prayer in Martyrs' Memorial Church, Belfast, 1985 (Bew, *Ireland*, 532).

Sin is back in theological fashion. Any liberal dream that the West had progressed toward some ill-defined democratic enlightenment rings hollow in the face of colonialisms and their aftermath, and the more recent attention to the part that theology played in such colonialism and coloniality. Human beings are sinners and they build structures that oppress. However, such an appeal to sin should not be used to justify any ahistorical move that, intentionally or unintentionally, eschews a hard look at the particularity of bigotry, prejudice, and hate. Yeats knew this reality well and would surely not quarrel with Paul Bew's summation of the modern story of Ireland as the "politics of enmity." Bew is correct to identify the relationship between nationalists and unionists as "mutual contempt."[3] My hope and prayer are that in some way such enmity might be replaced by deeper understanding across differences and imaginative practices that would resource a shared future for Northern Ireland.[4] Bew strikes a tone shaped more by history than hope, seeing the future of Ireland as dependent upon the "management of enmity."[5] Both imagined futures depend on some sort of change in relationships of hate. But, what is hate?

Whatever else the book of Genesis teaches us, it teaches us that sin is local, located, and embodied. Both in my experience, and in the scholarly literature, hate is something that young people in Northern Ireland were socialized into, and the churches took part in such processes of socialization. Inherent to identity in this process is the necessity that one's identity is defined *over against* the identity of others. Enmity is part and parcel of identity. While an appeal to sin may help describe such enmity, it does not explain it. But this is not simply a theological problem; similar problems exist for other fields. Social psychological science does not have answers for why people hate.[6] Defining enmity, Christopher Jones and Chris Loersch write, "Enmity is a social relationship in which one dislikes one's enemy, perceives one's enemy as malevolent, and desires some sort of physical, psychological, or social harm to befall this person."[7] Such enmity has been particularly evident in Ireland since the twelfth century.[8] Hate continued

---

3. Bew, *Ireland*, viii

4. A document called *A Shared Future* was published in 2005 by the Office of the First Minister and Deputy First Minister.

5. Bew, *Ireland*, viii.

6. Jones and Loersch, "Toward a Psychological Construct," 36, 54.

7. Jones and Loersch, "Toward a Psychological Construct," 54.

8. Cronin, *History of Ireland*, 9–38.

(and continues) to be essential for any sense of self and community because that sense of self and community was formed, or apparently formed, in contradistinction to those named as enemies. There is a vicious and violent cycle of hate leading to identity and identity leading to hate here. Decades of intercommunal rhetoric demeaning others, decades of segregation (in, for example, religion, schooling, and sporting activities), and decades of bloody conflict leaves physical, psychological, and social scars. The Belfast (or Good Friday) Agreement of 1998 recognizes the impact of trauma, referring to it as a "deep and profoundly regrettable legacy of suffering."[9] Tragically, and at the time of writing, this peace agreement has come under intense scrutiny and the political institutions set up to implement it are largely dysfunctional.

While the genesis of hate may be impossible to locate, its attendant attitudes and strategies are easy enough to observe in Ireland:

> Identifying a minority . . . as "the other" is the prerequisite to knowing your own identity. You have to know who they are not (they are not, or are different from, you), in order to know who you are. Why does identity seem so important to some people? . . . [I]t is based on the fear of losing something—jobs, neighborhood, prestige, values, tradition, power. The "other" becomes the source of this fear, and is hated. Hatred, then, is ultimately rooted in fear, although of course the hater does not understand this, and would vehemently deny that he, or she, is afraid of anything. Bluster and bullying, and, all too frequently, physical attack, are the cover for fear.[10]

For Jody Roy, hatred is enabled by a series of attitudes that generate a binary view of society where an "us" is always defined over against a "them." Such "polarizing thought lies at the very core of hatred" and is characterized by absolutism, stereotyping, scapegoating, and dehumanization.[11] Absolutism, in Ireland, can take on an almost ontological depth. Identities are constructed and opposing sides in a debate are polarized so that any connection or compromise can seem like an erosion of being. In an Irish context, a range of issues and identities, both historical and contemporary, illustrate such thinking, from the question of political sovereignty to what it means to have the right to live in Northern Ireland. Stereotyping

9. United Kingdom Government, *Agreement*.

10. Oppenheimer, *Hate Handbook*, 14.

11. Roy, *Love to Hate*, 6.

is rife where hate divides people and communities. The myths around the distinctiveness of Anglo-Saxon and Celtic peoples resourced sectarian stereotyping. In colonial tropes, one group had purported propensities toward, for example, industry and critical thought, while the other group had propensities toward indolence and blind obedience to a foreign (Roman) church. Scapegoating blames a group for the ills of society and there are conspicuous examples of such activity with tragic outcomes in history. The Irish context too has witnessed such strategy, not least with some blaming Irish republican politics and naïvely nationalist cultural revivalism as the root of all the ills in twentieth-century Ireland.[12] Such tropes create much fear and an "underlying . . . culture of intolerance" that is the conflict and feeds the conflict.[13]

1. What and who are people afraid of in your community?

2. To what extent is enmity something you can understand and/or how have absolutism, stereotyping, scapegoating, and dehumanization shaped your home community?

3. During your formative years, how have you and your teachers related to imperialism or colonialism and how was that story told?

4. What cultural artifact (for example, a song, poem, film, quotation, parable, or painting) or Scripture illustrates your relationship with colonialism?

## FINDING EACH OTHER

Binaries of opposition—us-versus-them thinking—is one pattern of thought and practice that post-colonial theology wants to overturn. If such thinking can be problematized then there is a greater chance that we can find one another even amidst the hate. But this will not be easy and it will involve critical approaches to history and culture.

First, historical awareness is needed that resources the church to problematize binaries of opposition that are assumed as historically immutable, or necessary in the construction of community identities. The seventeenth-century plantation of Ulster quite literally laid the groundwork for the later

12. Cleary, "Postcolonial Ireland," 258.

13. Office of the First Minister and Deputy First Minister, *Shared Future*, 8.

state of Northern Ireland. Consequently, it is important that theologians interested in post-colonial possibilities in Ireland and beyond have some sense of its significance. As with much colonization, the plantation of the Northeast of Ireland (Ulster) begins with disparaging the people to be displaced and overestimating the acreage of land unpopulated or depopulated. Thus, a 1608 study concluded that the Irish were "fickle," "disloyal," "unskilled," "barbarous," and "irreligious." While the author did not claim direct divine sanction for colonization in Ireland, he did not fail to remind his readers that God had given such sanction in the past. The Old Testament people of God "were commanded by the oracle of God" to "root . . . out" the natives. He was also clear on the benefits to England, pointing to the planting of "true religion" and gain in terms of wealth and national security.[14] In 1610 a final plan, sometimes called the "Articles of Plantation," was published. The Articles were a scheme for Protestant colonization.[15] The plan began to be put into action in 1611. Eventually English and Scottish settlers would drive native Irish people off their lands and into a 20 percent portion of land claimed by the crown. The churches in Ulster were largely reduced to ruins, both by Irish resisters refusing to give them up to an invading force, but more often they were destroyed by English troops. The Anglican Church took over all parishes, Catholics were ruthlessly oppressed, rebellion was put down, and key religious figures were martyred. Despite this, the Catholic Church would not bow to death but, especially due to the work of the Franciscans, would flourish again. Despite such oppression, the settlers did not find plantation easy and had to depend on the Irish in ways that the Articles forbade. Ulster was transformed. By 1622, up to 35,000 Scots and English had settled there. By 1700, the number could have been as high as 250,000.[16]

Jonathan Bardon seeks to draw lessons from this history and the subsequent history of rebellions, financial prosperity, famine, cross-Atlantic colonization, and the rise of an enduring eighteenth-century sectarianism. Against such a backdrop, the dominant narrative of my childhood implied that distinction and separation—ethnic, political, linguistic, cultural, and religious—was rational. That is to say, distinct identities were justifiable and should be maintained, given the clear boundaries of race, religion, culture,

14. Bardon, *Plantation of Ulster*, 129–33.

15. "Loyal" Catholics were also involved in the plantation. See Bardon, *Plantation of Ulster*, 214–34.

16. Bardon, *Plantation of Ulster*, 130–254, 317.

and allegiance. To deny such distinctiveness was to deny the presence of others. To deny such distinctiveness would not be the way to peace, but to deeper conflict. However, an overemphasis on the boundedness of cultural and racial identities does not bear up to historical scrutiny:

> It is not unreasonable to assume that in Ulster the great majority of Catholics are descended from the native Gaelic Irish and that the great majority of Protestants are descended from seventeenth-century British colonialists. However, there is much evidence that planters and their descendants did not separate themselves from the native Irish population as much as was formerly assumed.[17]

Examining the historical evidence, Bardon concludes, "the descendants of natives and newcomers in Ulster became almost inextricably intermingled."[18] Finding one another amidst this hate will demand the ongoing problematization of bounded identities. This is not to deny distinct identities, but it is to recognize a porosity that is too often ignored in this conflict and, arguably, in most conflicts around the world. Post-colonial critics will be suspicious of a tension at the heart of Bardon's work. On the one hand, he details fairly the brutality and oppression of Irish Catholics during the seventeenth-century "plantations" (colonization). On the other hand, when drawing lessons from the plantations, he tends to underestimate the deleterious impact of seventeenth-century colonialism on Catholic leadership and landholding, laying undue stress rather on Catholics who cooperated or willingly extended plantation. Nonetheless, from a post-colonial perspective, his work on problematizing Irish identities and histories remains important. His work demands that I recognize that my own particularity is inherently unstable and pluralist. Inevitably, whatever the dominant culture taught me, I am both planter and native, both colonizer and colonized.

Second, in Ireland, foundational myths pitted one culture against another so that one group's flourishing often depended on the other group's diminishment. I was formed in a Christian community. It was a Christian culture that exhibited both deep fellowship and pathology. If walking into my parents' living room to the evening news covering another murder, I would immediately ask, "One of theirs or one of ours?" I was not alone in such thinking. Given such a mindset, processes of reconciliation or peace-making were often, if not always, suspect. Peace, always requiring

17. Bardon, *Plantation of Ulster*, 342.
18. Bardon, *Plantation of Ulster*, 343.

compromise, meant comprising one's culture and identity. In this light, Ashis Nandy is correct to argue that the sites of colonialism include not only physical spaces, but also psychological spaces.[19] He argues, "colonialism is first of all a matter of consciousness and needs ultimately to be defeated in the minds of men."[20] Minds as well as lands are colonized and this is true of both colonizers and colonized. Finding each other amidst hate means, therefore, the recognition that colonialism dehumanizes *all* people. The process of colonialism in Ireland, and particularly the Ulster plantation, dealt disparagement, displacement, and death. Nandy, keenly aware of the damage done to the colonized, also studies the psychological and cultural damage done to British people as a result of its colonial projects. While imperialism might have been the "final fulfilment" of the dominant middle-class culture of Britain, he proposes, controversially, that the deeper and most negative impact of colonialism is ultimately in the colonizer and not the colonized.[21] Given his own particularly, he has in view the history of India, but because his argument is about the internal and long-term damage done to British culture, his work is apposite for present purposes. The "cultural pathologies" he identifies will be adapted here and described as an exaggerated martial spirit, false homogeneity, isolationism, and exaggerated agency.

The community in which I grew up in Northern Ireland exhibited each of these pathologies.[22] A martial spirit was regularly on parade. A ritual calendar and ceremonial commemorations existed that centered on battles that purportedly brought Protestant gains. For example, the seventeenth-century Battle of the Boyne, or victories seen to be inspired by Protestant values and British honor, such as the Battle of the Somme, were celebrated annually. The false homogeneity that Nandy deals with refers to the opportunity that overseas colonialism presented for those that might otherwise have challenged a societal homogeneity seen particularly clearly in class structures. Being involved in a colony gave opportunities for those that would otherwise not have had opportunities for social mobility. Undoubtedly, this was part of the rationale for some planters coming to Ulster. This, in turn, fed an ongoing appeal to bounded, but actually unstable and porous, racial identities assuming a self-evident and superior Anglo-Saxon

19. Nandy, *Intimate Enemy*.

20. Nandy, *Intimate Enemy*, 63.

21. Nandy, *Intimate Enemy*, 42.

22. Nandy, *Intimate Enemy*, 30–35.

race. Colonialism fed an elevated sense of worth and agency where an almost "magical" belief in "omnipotence and permanence" infected "British selfhood."[23] A bounded sense of identity that presupposes and promotes a separateness from colonized people has, in the end, the psychological effect of colonizers being isolated from each other. No matter how Unionist or British one might have felt growing up in Northern Ireland, there was always a sense of isolation from Britain. Both Irish nationalists and Ulster unionists doubted the trustworthiness of the British state and British politicians.

As has already been seen, common in colonizer narratives was the idea that they were involved in civilizing backward peoples. We have already encountered such narratives in the run up to the plantation of Ulster. Such tropes also had self-reflexive impact, argues Nandy. Depicting the Irish as superstitious, uncivilized, backward, and technologically underdeveloped reinforced a belief that Britain was a beacon and agent of progress. Beliefs in the transformative power of human reason, the inexorable move toward progress, and the conviction that technology and science would liberate were, thus, not only *drivers* of colonialism, but *effects* of colonialism.[24] In sum, the work of Nandy points to a pathology at work in dominant cultures. Already, we have witnessed a martial spirit at work in the settler culture of Ulster, along with a promoted false homogeneity. These themes, along with isolationism and exaggerated agency, will also be met in subsequent chapters. The focus in this chapter is how a stress on particularity might call people beyond hate. In short, how might God be found amidst the hate?

5. How do you tell your family history and the history of your community? In what way does such history-telling depend on competing histories and competing identities?

6. Who is absent in your telling of history? Why do you think this is the case and/or how would you discover these silenced voices in history?

7. Find a voice in literature (poetry, fiction, nonfiction) that represents a different reading of the history of your context. How does the writing challenge or contradict your own assumptions? Select some quotations or excerpts to illustrate your answer.

23. Nandy, *Intimate Enemy*, 35.
24. Nandy, *Intimate Enemy*, 29–35.

## FINDING GOD

If I am to face my own particularity it will mean facing the colonialism at work in Ireland. It will mean facing the historical, formational, cultural, psychological, and spiritual realities of the colonization of Ulster, from which I benefited. It will mean facing the pathologies of a dominant culture. Nandy not only identifies such pathology at the heart of a dominant culture, he also points to reactions those in such cultures exhibit. He sees four responses to the cultural pathologies at work in a dominant British culture. These can be defined as self-hatred, critical morality, apolitical dissent, and interculturality.[25]

In an attempt to develop a critical view of a dominant culture like that of Unionism in Northern Ireland, created and resourced by several iterations of colonialism, *self-hatred* is an ever-present specter. I cannot say that self-loathing has not been part of my own journey and my own struggle within the field of post-colonialism. Even if dressed liturgically as confession and repentance, the dehumanizing spirit of empire is seemingly always locked in battle with the Holy Spirit. Self-hatred in the face of the sin of colonialism is, however, the victory of colonialism. It is the colonization of the mind. Thus, it must be resisted. Self-hatred is not de-colonization. It is the surrender to colonization. *Critical morality* seeks to avoid self-hatred through an attempt to "reassert some of the values which colonialism forced one to disown."[26] Nandy identifies George Orwell as one thinker within the dominant culture who exhibited such critical morality, becoming an ardent critic of the middle-classes as the chief beneficiaries of colonialism. Resistance included a rejection of a patriarchal hypermasculinity (see chapters 6 and 7), an awareness that ideologies of egalitarianism and progress could be the source of oppression, and a conviction that those marginalized by colonialism needed to subvert the *status quo*. Such subversion was at work in *apolitical dissent*. Nandy considers such resistance apolitical because those who embodied it did not consider themselves or their struggles as political. However, such persons became "living protests" against the "worldview" of colonialism. Included in such protest was the Irish writer, Oscar Wilde. The embodied protest of a figure like Wilde challenged the hypermasculinity and martial spirit promoted within a colonialist Britain. At the same time, a particularly restrictive vision of passive

25. Nandy, *Intimate Enemy*, 35–37.
26. Nandy, *Intimate Enemy*, 39.

femininity was promoted, devalued, and associated with so-called lower races and lower classes. Said remains the classic text on how the Orient was depicted in such apparently feminine guise, over against the active and masculine West. But such binaries of opposition were resisted not only in the colonies beyond Britain, but also within Britain by people like Wilde. He rejected such binaries, and in the particularity of Victorian Britain, such resistance, embodied in his homosexuality, threatened categories that were basic to the justification of imperialism and colonialism.[27] The final response to the pathologies at work in a dominant culture is *interculturality*. That is to say, healing for such pathology comes from beyond its site in the metropolitan center. The "most creative response to the perversion of Western culture" comes from its victims.[28] Nandy particularly points to the intercultural work of Mahatma Gandhi and the English missionary priest C. F. Andrews. In Gandhi's resistance to British rule and its concomitant cultural dominance, he too sought a retrieval of, so to speak, a precolonial Britain. Salvation for India included a search for the "other" culture of Britain and a "softer" Christianity. It was in intercultural and interreligious friendship that decolonization for both India and Britain could be envisaged. Of this relationship and its impact, Nandy writes: "It is a comment on modern theories of dissent that the Westerner who perhaps came closest to the Indian cause in two hundred years of British colonial history operated on the basis of religious traditions, not on that of a secular ideology."[29]

For a theologian interested in post-colonialism there is no surprise here. Despite this, post-colonialism, broadly speaking, has largely failed to take account of the decolonizing potency of religion and theology. This current book seeks to define a post-colonial Christian *theology*. Implied in this theological priority is a broader desire to see post-colonialism take theologizing more seriously in its definitions and in its criticisms. Certainly, as this book will unveil, theologizing has served colonialism and imperialism. However, such an assessment must not overstate or oversimplify the complex histories of Christian mission and colonialism. Not every missionary was a colonialist and not every importation of Christianity was imperialist. The history, and thus the theology, is and will need to be complex and nuanced. Finding a vision of God amidst much mission malpractice, and any hope of redeeming the category of mission, is not guaranteed.

27. Nandy, *Intimate Enemy*, 43. See Kiberd, *Inventing Ireland*, 33–50.
28. Nandy, *Intimate Enemy*, 48.
29. Nandy, *Intimate Enemy*, 47.

Nandy, however, gives us some direction in where to begin when he writes, "freedom is indivisible" and "liberation ultimately had to begin from the colonized and end with the colonizers" because both the colonized and the oppressor are "caught in the culture of oppression."[30] In sum, decolonizing theology will need to be intercultural theology. Not only will the church need to tell a history of Ireland that problematizes binaries of opposition, recognizes the need for justice for all, and seeks healing from the pathologies of dominance, all of this will need to be done by creating a new context. That is to say, to find God amidst the particularity of hate means an intercultural theologizing that brings together sources and people from a plurality of particularities. The particularity of hate is only healed within a plurality of particularities. God is only found in intercultural theology. The rest of this book is an attempt at a post-colonial intercultural theology.

8. Define, in your own words, what you understand post-colonialism to be and to what extent it is helpful in thinking about faith and ministry today.

9. To what extent are self-hatred, critical morality, and apolitical dissent part of the dominant culture in your context?

10. If interculturality is so important for a vision of God (theology), where would you look or what can you do to deepen such intercultural theologizing?

11. What questions are you left with? How might you resource these questions?

30. Nandy, *Intimate Enemy*, 63.

# 3

# Things Fall Apart
## Theological Agency and Colonial Christianity

> None of his converts was a man whose word was heeded in the
> assembly of the people. None of them was a man of title. They
> were mostly the kind of people that were called *efulefu*, worthless,
> empty men.... Chielo, the priestess of Agbala, called the converts
> the excrement of the clan, and the new faith was a mad dog that
> had come to eat it up.
>
> But stories were already gaining ground that the white man
> had not only brought a religion but also a government.

—Chinua Achebe[1]

> In the figure of the witness of a postcolonial modernity we have
> another wisdom: it comes from those who have seen the night-
> mare of racism and oppression in the banal daylight of the every-
> day. They represent an idea of action and agency more complex
> than either the nihilism of despair or the Utopia of progress. They
> speak of the reality of survival and negotiation that constitutes the
> moment of resistance, its sorrow and its salvation, but is rarely
> spoken in the heroisms or the horrors of history.

—Homi K. Bhabha[2]

1. Achebe, *Things Fall Apart*, 135, 146.
2. Bhabha, *Location of Culture*, 365.

## POST-COLONIALISM BEGINS IN COLONIALISM

A practical theology begins in particularity. The first step for a theologian is to seek a sense of their location. A practical post-colonial theology needs to work at making explicit a theologian's relation to colonialism and imperialism. The complexity of Yeats and the Irish situation, as a means for locating the present author and for beginning to define post-colonialism, highlights that such work is complex and it is ongoing. Yet, if a post-colonial theology is to be an exercise in critical and practical theology, then the point of departure will have to take into account the particularity of colonialism and wrestle with the "hard questions of history."[3] As was seen in the previous chapter, the histories of Ireland and its relationships to colonialism create intimate enmity.[4] Such intimacy is replicated at other times in other places, and such comparative recognition opens up the need for a theology that is intercultural or intercontextual. What such intercontextual theologizing might mean for understanding post-colonial theology will be the main focus of this chapter.

Famously, Chinua Achebe took up Yeats's lament in "The Second Coming," entitling his first novel *Things Fall Apart*. For Achebe, Yeats knew "intuitively" the "cosmological fear of anarchy" felt both in Ireland and in Nigeria in the face of empire.[5] The novel invites the reader into the richness of Ibo (Igbo) culture and the challenges that the coming of Christianity and the British empire posed for the people of Nigeria. While the novel takes as its title a line from a Yeats poem and both novel and poem tell the story of political, social, and cultural trauma, Achebe's work may have more similarities to Yeats's play "Purgatory." The protagonists in both Achebe's novel and Yeats's play feel deep shame about a parent. That shame drives them to protect their understanding of honor and cultural strength by killing, in both cases, a sixteen-year-old boy:

> Dear mother, the window is dark again
> But you are in the light because
> I finished all that consequence.
> I killed that lad because he had grown up,
> He would have struck a woman's fancy,
> Begot, and passed pollution on.[6]

3. Fitzpatrick, "Instant History," 65.

4. Nandy, *Intimate Enemy*.

5. Achebe, *Home and Exile*, 18–19.

6. Yeats, "Purgatory," 435.

> He heard the blow. The pot fell and broke in the sand. He heard
> Ikemefuna cry, "My father, they have killed me!" as he ran toward
> him. Dazed with fear, Okonkwo drew his matchete and cut him
> down. He was afraid of being thought weak.[7]

Both Yeats and Achebe adjudge that the upheaval of their times had precipitated a loss of cultural, spiritual, and social cohesion. The loss is death and the loss causes death. In Yeats's patriarchal Europe and in Achebe's patriarchal Africa, a terrible beauty was born, and in both cases Christianity was central to the death and birth of that new era. This book is particularly interested in a Christian theological reflection on colonialism. The task is not simply to hear each other speak, but to hear God speak. For that reason, this chapter turns to the work of a key theological voice emerging from a context of British colonialism.

As Chinua Achebe is Africa's best-known novelist and a founder of published African fiction, John S. Mbiti is Africa's best-known theologian and a founder of published African theology.[8] As with Achebe, Mbiti was brought up as a Christian and educated in a Christian school system within a British colonial context. Mbiti's context was Kenya and, as with Achebe, he presents a critical view of the Christianity imported to his home. As a theologian, Mbiti resources a second step. If the first step in a post-colonial theology is to ask, "Where am I in relation to empire/colonialism?" the second step is to ask "Where is God in relation to empire/colonialism?" That question cannot be asked ahistorically or acontextually. Mbiti needs to be read in his context, both because he produced his first major piece of research in the particularism of East Africa, and because of the nature of post-colonial theology being argued for in this book. Mbiti's work provides one answer to the "Where is God?" question in relation to foreign-mission Christianity and the prospect of a contextualized African faith.

In 1895, the year that the British East African Protectorate was declared, the Africa Inland Mission (AIM) founded a mission station in East Central Kenya among the Akamba. In 1931, Mbiti was born in Ukambani and into what was, by then, the British colony of Kenya. His early Christian formation took place within the confines of the AIM's brand of conservative evangelicalism. For his PhD, Mbiti studied the Akambas' reception of Christianity at the hands of foreign missionaries. In a series of moves, he convincingly argues that the traditional understandings that the Akamba

---

7. Achebe, *Things Fall Apart*, 57.

8. Innes, "Chinua Achebe." See also Heaney, *From Historical to Critical*, 3–5.

people had of temporality led to a more coherent reading of the New Testament compared to the reading foreign missionaries brought. Mbiti does not see his work as an exercise in political theology, is suspicious of liberation theology, and would question whether his writings are post-colonial theology. Yet, if nationalism means "not only modernization but also the recovery of tradition and a search for continuity with the pre-colonial past,"[9] then Mbiti's work can be seen in a broadly nationalistic and post-colonial frame. However, to reduce Mbiti's work to nationalism or even a naïve or essentialized nativism would be to read against the grain and would be to go against his own self-understanding. He does not succumb to a nativism that prioritizes the ruled over the rulers, thereby ending up embedding the distinction.[10] Rather, because he is a theologian, the ultimate aim of his work is not simply to win cultural agency for a particular oppressed people, but to evoke a deeper vision of God for all people. On the way to such a vision, Mbiti attempts nothing less than an act of theological decolonization. For in reading New Testament eschatology, it is an African temporality that he favors in the face of an imported temporality from the West. As will be seen presently, Mbiti resources this attempted decolonization by providing a critique of foreign mission and by promoting a more thoroughly contextualized Christian faith.

## MISSION CHRISTIANITY IN THE COLONY

Mbiti provides a critical assessment of foreign missionary thought and practice that emerges from his own experience as a scholar formed in a context dominated by British imperialism. For Mbiti, although missionaries at times opposed colonial policies, they were intertwined in colonialism, and they justified it. Those relationships with colonialism were related to and resulted in practices of cultural acculturation that included subjugation, the disparagement of traditional practice, and the importation of denominational competitiveness.

First, Mbiti's assessment of foreign missionaries is not universally negative. They could persevere through difficulties with "obedience to the commandment of our Lord to evangelize all the peoples of the world."[11] He

9. Peel, *Religious Encounter and the Making*, 3. See also p'Bitek, *African Religions in Western Scholarship*, 41.

10. See Said, *Culture and Imperialism*, 228.

11. Mbiti, "Future of Christianity in Africa," 389.

recognizes that foreign missionaries at times opposed colonial policy and colonial administrators. In Kenya, a clear example of this was the mobilization of Christian opinion against colonial policy on forced labor. In the wake of the First World War, the British government would reward white settlers by granting colony status to Kenya. This meant a degree of self-rule and the real possibility of settlers pushing their agenda forward. Chief among their priorities after the war was the expansion of the plantation economy and that meant a desire for more land and labor. A 1919 Labor Circular from the governor directed colonial administrators, chiefs, and elders to "exercise every possible lawful influence to induce able-bodied male natives to go into the labour field."[12] Such settler pressure on the colonial government created a situation where Africans were effectively forced to work on plantations for two months a year.[13] Some missionaries, including Bishop J. J. Willis of Uganda, Bishop Richard Heywood of Mombasa, and the leader of the Church of Scotland Mission, J. W. Arthur, were concerned that the circular would result in abuses that would undermine any loyalty Africans had for the crown. Other missionaries and mission leaders, including Bishop Frank Weston of Zanzibar, CMS missionary Handley Hooper, and the London-based mission leader, J. H. Oldham, took a more straightforwardly ethical view, contending that forced labor was always morally untenable. Under their influence and activism, the circular was withdrawn in 1921, and in 1923 they secured the "Devonshire Declaration" from the government.[14]

> Primarily Kenya is an African territory, and His Majesty's Government think it necessary definitely to record their considered opinion that the interests of the African natives must be paramount, and that if, and when, those interests and the interests of the immigrant races should conflict, the former should prevail.[15]

Along with such political agitation against settler ambition and colonial policies some missionaries also possessed a more open view on African cultures that resulted in theological agitation for a different kind of missiology against racialist and racist assumptions. In this regard, Mbiti singles out John V. Taylor (1914–2001). As Mbiti was completing his PhD, Taylor published *The Primal Vision*. In that work, he saw himself engaged in a

12. Oliver, *Missionary Factor in East Africa*, 248.

13. Stanley, *Bible and the Flag*, 146–48.

14. Stanley, *Bible and the Flag*, 148.

15. Stanley, *Bible and the Flag*, 149.

"reverent and attentive" intercultural relationship where "presence" and not "assertion" or "action" was paramount:[16]

> The core of Africa's wisdom is that she knows the difference be-
> tween existence and presence. . . . Africans believe that presence
> is the debt they owe one another. . . . A humble reverence that
> never desires to manipulate or possess or use the other is always a
> feature of the face-to-face encounter of true presence, and there-
> fore it flourishes in silence. . . . In contrast to the silence of God
> how much of the mission of his Church seems to be contrived in
> "routines and possessiveness"![17]

Taylor avoided an oversentimentalized view of Africa, while at the same time recognizing the poignancy of the African observation that Europeans are "not all there."[18] Taylor is the exception to the rule. He is an exception demonstrating that a different kind of foreign missionary and mission was possible. This is important to Mbiti's argument, not least because it inoculates him against charges of anachronism. It is indeed possible to criticize missionaries during the British colonial era because thinkers like Taylor, operating in the same colonial context, were able to think theologically in ways that were in continuity with emerging African Christian theology. However, despite such missionary agitation that mitigated against the excesses of white settler appetite for land and labor, and some missionary readings of African culture that mitigated against disparaging and racist views, Mbiti is largely critical of missionary thought and practice. The criticism he has toward foreign missionaries highlights that while some missionaries would stand against the white settlers and colonial administrators of Kenya, they did so as a means to humanize the colony, not to bring it to an end. Of post-First World War missionary opinion in East Africa, Robert Strayer writes, "no one regarded colonial rule as illegitimate and probably very few saw the settler presence as necessarily evil."[19]

While missionaries at times opposed colonialist and settler ambition, they were also intertwined with a foreign colonial vision of Kenya. Missionaries in colonial Kenya generally taught converts to obey the colonial powers and took a dim view of what the general secretary of the Anglican Church Missionary Society (CMS), Max Warren (1904–77), called "feverish

16. Taylor, *Primal Vision*, 135.

17. Taylor, *Primal Vision*, 135–37.

18. Taylor, *Primal Vision*, 136.

19. Strayer, *Making of Mission Communities*, 107–8.

nationalism."[20] As an antidote to such fever, Warren prescribed a theological and imperialist antidote. Preceding Taylor as the general secretary from 1942 to 1963, he published the book *Caesar the Beloved Enemy* in 1955. In it he argued that the "intimate relationship" between Christianity and imperialism had been "an embarrassment and a scandal but also a testimony and an adventure of faith."[21] What was needed for Christians to understand history and for the church to prepare itself for the ramifications of this febrile nationalism in Asia and Africa was "a theology of imperialism."[22] Missionaries and mission leaders needed such a theology to "distinguish the place of imperialism in the providence of God and at the same time recognize its ambiguous character as affording material both for theology and demonology."[23] If imperialism was best understood as one group of people exercising or attempting to exercise power over another group of people, Warren asks, is this always wrong? In response he argues, on the basis of Christian tradition and Scripture, that it is justifiable "in certain circumstances" to subordinate one group to another. Thus, imperialism can have a "place" in the "purpose and providence" of the almighty:[24]

> To be the citizen of a world empire is, for most people, an important step on the road from being a citizen of a tribe to being a citizen of the world. To share in a common culture and so be made an heir of the ages is no small compensation for being deprived for a time of the sweets of anarchy which, after all, more often than not preceded the establishment of an alien *imperium*.[25]

Warren could see empire as preparation for the gospel. Over against the supposed restricted view of traditional societies, empire brought a universal view, and thus a much broader sense of vocation. Colonization brought the social improvements of good legislation and community cohesion.[26]

Second, given that foreign mission strategists and missionaries sought to humanize the colony, were intertwined with it, and even provided theological justification for imperialism, it is no surprise that Mbiti can point to

20. Warren, *Caesar the Beloved Enemy*, 1–14, 39.

21. Warren, *Caesar the Beloved Enemy*, 11.

22. Warren, *Caesar the Beloved Enemy*, 1–14, 39.

23. Warren, *Caesar the Beloved Enemy*, 13–14.

24. Warren, *Caesar the Beloved Enemy*, 14–18.

25. Warren, *Caesar the Beloved Enemy*, 27.

26. Heaney, *From Historical to Critical*, 36–37.

practices of acculturation in foreign missionary practice. In part, what this meant was cultural subjugation, disparagement of pre-Christian traditions, and the importation of ways of thought that threatened African sociality. Mbiti states the problem of cultural subjugation with some poignancy when he writes:

> Often, as African Christians, we feel terribly foreign within the doors of the Churches on our own continent. Lutheran missionaries have made us more Lutheran than the Germans; Anglican missionaries have made us more Anglican than the English; Roman Catholic missionaries have made us more Roman than the Italians . . .[27]

Such foreignness emerged from a "bulldozer mentality" on the side of foreign missionaries.[28] Missionaries "scandalized" and "vandalized" African cultural life without theological justification.[29] Africans have had to suffer "cultural imperialism," but "Africa does not require imported Christianity, because too much of it will only castrate us spiritually or turn us into spiritual cripples who can only move on broken and imported crutches."[30] Cultural imperialism meant an attitude, on the part of foreign missionaries, that their non-African cultures were superior and that any cultural or theological advance depended on some degree of assimilation:

> At the heart of European culture during the many decades of imperial expansion lay an undeterred and unrelenting Eurocentrism. This accumulated experiences, territories, peoples, histories; it studied them, it classified them, it verified them, . . . but above all, it subordinated them by banishing their identities, except as a lower order of being, from the culture and indeed the very idea of white Christian Europe. This cultural process has to be seen as a vital, informing, and invigorating counterpoint to the economic and political machinery at the material center of imperialism.[31]

Mbiti recounts a Christianity that taught him to consider African traditions as demonic.[32] Consequently, for converts to become truly

27. Mbiti, "Future of Christianity in Africa," 393.

28. Mbiti, "Confessing Christ," 138.

29. Mbiti, "'When the Right Hand Washes,'" 433–64.

30. Mbiti, "Christianity and African Culture," 30.

31. Said, *Culture and Imperialism*, 221–22.

32. Mbiti, "Christianity and Traditional Religions," 432–33. See Mombo, "Theological Education in Africa," 131; Nwatu, "'Colonial' Christianity in Post-Colonial Africa?"

Christian meant distancing themselves from much of traditional African cultures. This demand, whether made explicitly or implicitly, could mean suppression of particular traditional practices such as rites of passage and/or it could mean the importation of a way of thinking that was not stressed in traditional thinking. For Mbiti, denominationalism, dualism, and futurism were emphasized in the Christianity imported to Ukambani that stood in distinction to priorities in pre-Christian ways of thinking. He complains that the African church is "a confused jigsaw puzzle of divisions and subdivisions. The church is disfigured by these divisions, which constitute a real insult to our Lord Jesus Christ."[33] Such division is the result of mission societies adopting the colonialist strategy of "spheres of influence" where distinct geographical areas were ceded to distinct churches. But foreign-mission Christianity not only divided territory among itself, it also divided people. Mbiti points to such dualism when he writes, "Certain varieties of missionaries from Europe and America have proclaimed a restrictive understanding of salvation from sin and largely for the soul."[34] In contrast, for many African people, "[h]uman life is a unity, . . . physical threats have spiritual consequences and spiritual threats have physical consequences."[35] As will be seen presently, Mbiti sought to demonstrate not only this distinct approach to reality in Kenya, but sought to prove that it had theological significance in the contextualization and future of religion in Africa. Most controversially, Mbiti criticized missionaries for introducing a temporality that was focused on and fixated with the future as a linear extension of the present and as the defining trait of the identity of the faithful. This, Mbiti argued, unnecessarily contradicted an African priority for the past and the idea that time flowed backwards with people journeying back to their ancestors. It was the past that was the foundation for the identity of the faithful.

In sum, the presence and agency of foreign missionaries in Ukambani created a site for theological dispute. Mbiti's work that challenges foreigners in pursuit of a thoroughgoing contextualization evidences such a dispute. Contextualization, therefore, cannot be seen as a one-way process of inculturating an imported gospel. Contextualization is contestation.

---

353–55; Hastings, *African Christianity*, 51–52.

33. Mbiti, "Future of Christianity in Africa," 391.

34. Mbiti, *Bible and Theology*, 156.

35. Mbiti, *Bible and Theology*, 156.

## CONTEXTUALIZATION IS CONTESTATION

> In colonial times one could protest and one had the people on
> one's side. Today one is colonized and one lies to the people in
> telling them that they are free. To many Africans there is a lack
> not only of drinkable water and of a sufficient quantity of animal
> protein but also of a space of liberty where he can speak "without
> tether or censorship." The Church should liberate the African pro-
> test, allowing the African to speak.[36]

Mbiti recognizes that theological conviction is part of the struggle for independence. Referring to those involved in the anti-imperialist struggle,
he writes that they were "exposed to the biblical view of salvation. Most
of these had embraced the Christian faith, and all had been educated in
Christian schools. . . . The Exodus account in the Bible was certainly a great
inspiration to many, and the cry was as God put it through the mouth of
Moses and Aaron to Pharaoh: 'Let my people go!'"[37]

As has been seen, Mbiti would not want his work reduced to nationalism and does not consider his work to be post-colonial theology. However, he is striving for the theological agency of African believers, which
amounts to an attempt at theological decolonization. The apparatus of intelligibility in Mbiti's experience was foreign. He seeks to change that. The
African church saw extensive growth in the twentieth century. In contrast
to the foreign missionaries Mbiti critiques, he sees the key to such growth
being the traditional African religious background. "It is in the two-thirds
of Africa where African Religion has been predominant that Christianity
is expanding most rapidly. Without this kind of religious background, the
preaching of the Gospel would have been less successful and few Africans
would have embraced the Christian Faith . . . ."[38] It is this "traditional religi-
osity" which is the "basis" for African Christianity.[39] Given such a reading
of Christian history and the context he specifies, Mbiti's resistant theology
begins at the end. Mbiti begins with eschatology and with the Akamba understanding of time.[40]

---

36. Leopold Sedar Senghor, cited by Sundkler and Steed, *History of the Church*, 914.

37. Mbiti, *Bible and Theology*, 163.

38. Mbiti, "Future of Christianity in Africa," 390.

39. Mbiti, "Future of Christianity in Africa," 390.

40. For a more detailed reading of Mbiti's eschatology, see Heaney, *From Historical to Critical*, 62–93. Central to the colonial tropes is often the rhetoric of "progress." It is

According to Mbiti, the reoccurrence of activities associated with the land (planting, growing, and harvesting) and activities associated with human growth (birth, puberty, initiation, marriage, procreation, old age, death) gives a sense of an "ontological rhythm." But it is events that take precedence in Akamba temporality. Events do not exist in time. They create time.[41] Thus, time is "two-dimensional" with an extensive past and an intensive present. The future as "in the linear conception of time is virtually non-existent in Akamba thinking."[42] Neither mythology nor grammar supports a sense of the future beyond two years.[43] Rather, a sense of the future is more properly understood as the "present forthcoming."[44] While the future might be understood in such terms, destiny is not orientated toward the unveiling of the unknown future, but to a return to the community of the departed as the foundation for identity.[45] The long past and the now-period take precedent over any sense or expectation for the future. Thus, Mbiti is prepared to say, "Time as a succession or simultaneity of events 'moves' not forwards but backwards."[46]

The AIM missionaries who came to Ukambani had, argues Mbiti, a very different understanding of time that meant they taught an eschatology with little import for the present or past. Indeed, he depicts it as individualistic and "exclusively 'futurist.'"[47] This futurist eschatology, plotted on a linear conception of time, intersected with Akamba temporality, resulting in theological confusion. To illustrate such confusion, Mbiti retranslates several hymns that the foreign missionaries brought to the Akamba:

> Time is coming to an end, the kingdom is near;
> I believe in Jesus so that I may have life later . . .
>
> He is coming, and He says it is very soon,

of little surprise, therefore, that temporality should become a subject ripe for resistance and decolonization. For example, Nandy identifies temporality as a key resistant and decolonizing category for the work of Gandhi in British India. See Nandy, *Intimate Enemy*, 56–63; Said, *Culture and Imperialism*, 232.

41. Mbiti, *New Testament Eschatology*, 29.

42. Mbiti, *New Testament Eschatology*, 24.

43. Mbiti, *African Religions and Philosophy*, 23–28.

44. See Malina, *Social World of Jesus*, 192.

45. Mbiti, *Akamba Stories*, 17–18.

46. Mbiti, *New Testament Eschatology*, 24.

47. Mbiti, *New Testament Eschatology*, 51.

We will see Jesus that day . . .

When we shed tears as we serve Him,
The promised date of rejoicing in the heart is coming;
When we meet Him we will be like Him.
Then we will rejoice for ever and ever.[48]

The consequences of such eschatological imposition caused deep cultural, philosophical, theological, and psychological displacement. To be Christian, according to the AIM, meant converts had to abandon the notion of a postmortem journey toward the ancestors. An emphasis on a "hereafter" had psychological implications. For some the promise of a future return of Christ, in a context with a concept of the future as the present-forthcoming, could mean deep and unnecessary disillusionment when Christ did not return. For more, however, a futurist eschatology intensified the expectation of the return of Christ and resulted in a "false spirituality" escaping into a "Christian world of the hereafter at the expense of being a Christian in the here and now."[49] Such eschatology creates an escapist and quiescent church. Mbiti's analysis points to a theological colonization of the Akamba that had social, and by implication political, ramifications.

Mbiti contests the imported eschatology at the cultural and theological levels. He castigates the AIM for failing to take part in a serious intercultural exchange toward more robust contextualization. He argues that this acculturation is predicated upon a theological failure. In response, Mbiti seeks a distinct synthesis between Akamba temporality and other readings of New Testament eschatology. He identifies a realized dimension and sacramental mediation for a Christian Akamba eschatology. In such a setting, he will argue that the sacraments are the primary means to convey "eschatological realities." Humanizing rituals in Africa open up the path from childhood to adulthood, and Mbiti proposes a correlation with Christian baptism as the "sacrament of birth." Baptism, practiced as paedobaptism in contrast to the AIM, affirms the Akamba's strong sense of community and corporateness. In a contextualizing move, the sacrament affirms kinship and transforms kinship. A congregational and ecclesial kinship connects the Akamba not only with the departed but, on the basis of the person and

48. Mbiti, *New Testament Eschatology*, 54.
49. Mbiti, *New Testament Eschatology*, 60–63, 86–87.

work of Christ, the kinship extends even to fellowship with the Creator.[50] In light of an imported Christian message that stressed a separation between materiality and spirituality, the potency of the sacraments for the Akamba are further seen in Mbiti's reflections on the Eucharist. "The Sacraments form the nexus between the physical and the spiritual worlds, and through the concrete and material realities, eschatological realities become evident and available in the temporal and physical realm."[51]

While it might not now appear controversial, Mbiti's work on the contextualizing and sacramentalizing of an Akamba eschatology against foreign missionary thought and practice was contentious at the time in which he wrote. Mbiti challenged the authority and orthodoxy of foreign theology and foreign leadership of church and mission. This authority was white and was set within a broader context of colonial authoritarianism and brutality. Given this, to challenge foreign theological agency was dangerous. Indeed, during a 1950s insurgency in Kenya, where up to 11,000 Africans were killed, missionaries did report him as a troublemaker to the colonial authorities.[52] A post-colonial analysis of any theological text cannot fail to acknowledge such locatedness and relationship to social and political implications.

## CONCLUSION

Mbiti's work on an African eschatology has been criticized. Philosophically, he can be accused of essentializing Africans and of caricaturing both Western and African concepts of time. Theologically, he may actually underestimate how the "present-focus" of the Akamba correlates with a New Testament understanding of time. For in a synthetic approach between the Akamba, foreign missionaries, and Western scholarship, Mbiti accepts that the New Testament points to a three-dimensional understanding of time. Consequently, Mbiti, along with the foreign missionaries, may accept too readily modern conceptions of time. Socially, the suggestion that African understandings of time are "backwards looking" seems to legitimize the

---

50. Mbiti, *New Testament Eschatology,* 116–51, 91.

51. Mbiti, *New Testament Eschatology,* 125. Mbiti unnecessarily worries about the "quasi-magical" understanding of the sacraments in his community. It seems he does not consider that such a "problem" does not simply emerge from an African context, but also from a biblical context.

52. Heaney, *From Historical to Critical,* 35; Elkins, *Britain's Gulag,* 366.

notion that Africa is underdeveloped. Consequently, Mbiti lays himself open to the accusation that he gives ideological license to imperialism and the notion that civilization is Westernization. Each of these criticisms might be mitigated. Stressing, as is done in this chapter, the particularity of his work on eschatology to Ukambani weakens philosophical objections. The comparative work he does is not between "Western" and "African" conceptions, but specifically between the AIM and the Akamba. If he were guilty of essentializing, this could be read as "strategic" in his attempts at overcoming foreign theological agency.[53] Integrating more recent work on New Testament eschatology with the recognition of a "present-focus" and the "present-forthcoming" in the biblical text only serves to further substantiate Mbiti's initial work. His use of language, especially relating to the "backward looking" nature of African communities, may actually be in tension with the rest of his argument. For Mbiti identifies the present as the most important dimension of time for the Akamba. If this is indeed correct, then there are grounds to exorcise talk of a "backwards looking" temporality.[54] In short, Mbiti's attempt at theological decolonization is only partially successful. As with Yeats, Mbiti wrote in English and had privileged opportunities. For example, he completed his PhD at Cambridge University. He thus experienced a "double imprinting." He perpetuates and overturns colonial modes of thought. His depiction of "backwards" Akamba time and the further suggestion that this in part explains "underdevelopment"[55] embeds colonial attitudes. However, his argument that Akamba temporality is essential to theological cogency in Africa, and that this takes Christians closer to the meaning of the New Testament, was revolutionary at the time. For this reason, the so-called father of African theology is part of the antecedents of post-colonial theology.

Beginning with eschatology is a powerful way of addressing the "Where is God?" question. It is where Mbiti begins, and in beginning there he seeks to demonstrate that God is knowable and God's ultimate purposes for human beings are knowable within an apparatus of intelligibility that belongs to the Akamba people of central East Africa. For Mbiti, God was present before either colonialists or missionaries set foot in Ukambani. Both, however, deeply affected the material and spiritual worlds. The implication of the AIM teaching on the destiny of humans was that the Akamba

53. Spivak, *In Other Worlds*, 202.

54. Heaney, *From Historical to Critical*, 79–92.

55. Heaney, *From Historical to Critical*, 84–89.

had to adopt a foreign temporality in order to be saved. Mbiti did not accept this. To accept a Christian understanding of redemption did not mean a rejection of Akamba thought. The spiritual world of the Akamba did not need to be colonized in order for them to be followers of Christ. They could be Akamba and Christian. Indeed, because they were Akamba, they could grasp the gospel more fully than the foreigners who brought it to Ukambani. The cultural and theological contestation that Mbiti took part in, especially in his work on eschatology, meant that he could know God and God's purposes at home.

Mbiti completed his PhD in the year that Kenya gained its independence. Alamin Mazrui adjudged Mbiti's work to have had wide influence as one in the "vanguard of intellectual innovation" bringing "aspects of African thought into the global stadium of ideas."[56] Despite this, and writing in 1995, fellow Kenya scholar J. N. K. Mugambi was still asking, "how [can] African Christians . . . be liberated from domination by the missionary legacy on which they have been nurtured, to enable them [to] participate as full members of the international Christian community?"[57] The independence of Kenya in 1963 did not mean the end of cultural superiority, subjugation, or the marginalization of its own theological voices. Given ongoing situations of subjugation, colonialism cannot, in the end, sufficiently define the point of departure for a post-colonial theology. For this reason chapter 5 will explain the analytical and theological significance of coloniality.

56. Mazrui, "Cultural (Re)Construction and Nation Building," 130.
57. Mugambi, *From Liberation to Reconstruction*, 23.

# 4

# Implications
## Voice and Post-Colonial Theology

Mbiti's experience of acculturation and the disparagement of contextualization is not uncommon. However, white theologians do experience interruption and transformation in intercultural encounters. These encounters may point toward a fresh understanding, not only of the theological necessity and inevitability of contextualization, but also of catholicity. In summary, working against hatred, humanity is discovered when the gospel is grasped more fully in intercultural encounter, and God is found when we commit to a vision of the church that is multivocal.

1. Try to sum up the argument of the previous chapter in no more than fifty words.

2. Mbiti takes a critical view of foreign mission that neither romanticizes nor condemns it outright. To what extent do you agree with this position. Why?

3. As a result of the previous chapter, what do you understand by "theological agency" in the context of colonialism? Can you think of other examples of such theological agency?

## FINDING THE HATE

The philosophical and theological richness of the Akamba understanding of themselves and God was disparaged by foreign missionaries. In post-colonialism, such stories are common. In this study we will listen to the work of, for example, African, Korean-American, and Native American voices who testify that the experience of Mbiti has historical precedent and the struggle for contextualization beyond dominant cultures is still an ongoing struggle. In post-colonial theology a common point of departure is the domineering intent of white power and the commonality of that experience. This in part resources the emergence of a field of study that develops common or comparative analysis and visions for change. R. S. Wafula, Esther Mombo, and Joseph Wandera can speak of the continent of Africa as suffering "the harshest effects of colonialism."[1] They point to major figures who have critiqued and stood against oppression in North Africa, West Africa, and East Africa. Albert Memmi experienced, analyzed, and resisted imperial oppression in Tunisia. For Memmi, colonization dehumanized all sides.[2] Frantz Fanon, a psychiatrist writing in the context of the struggle for liberation in Algeria, named race as central to colonial realities and looked to the revolutionary potential of the "peasantry" as the way toward nothing less than a new humanity.[3] Achebe, a Nigerian and son of an Anglican missionary, particularly highlighted the cultural destruction wreaked by colonialism and in colonial tropes. He championed the need for a renewal of identity and voice against and beyond oppression.[4] Ngũgĩ wa Thiong'o, from a Kenyan perspective, presented a "protest discourse" that critiqued British colonialists and foreign missionaries. He subverted key theological ideas such as election, the promised land, the tree of life, and the river of God, displacing the promises associated with Israel—and by colonial logic, Britain—and applying them to the Kikuyu and Mumbi people of Kenya.[5] Each of these figures remains important in the field of post-colonialism and Wafula, Mombo, and Wandera see them as foundational to current African, and particularly Kenyan, work in post-colonialism. They not only analyzed the brutality and oppression of colonialism, but also the ongo-

1. Wafula et al., *Postcolonial Church*, xxvi.

2. Memmi, *Colonizer and the Colonized*.

3. Fanon, *Wretched of the Earth*, 251–55; Fanon, *Dying Colonialism*, 179–81. See Young, *Postcolonialism: An Historical Introduction*, 274–83.

4. Achebe, *Home and Exile*; Achebe, *Things Fall Apart*.

5. Wafula et al., *Postcolonial Church*, xxiii–xxv.

ing dangers of neocolonialism. In a Kenyan context, and from an explicitly theological perspective, Julius Kithinji defines neocolonialism as "impunity" where those with power can act without fear of punishment because of structures of patronage and a compromised judiciary and security force. He calls on Christians to engage the biblical text in such a way that unveils domineering thought, and so in "reordering" the text they learn to reorder the church and the wider society.[6]

Despite major figures like Memmi, Fanon, Achebe, wa Thiong'o, and a growing awareness of the reality of neocolonialism, Wafula, Mombo, and Wandera complain that it is only in recent years that African scholars have come to the place of critical post-colonial analysis in theological scholarship. Unfortunately, they do not recognize the post-colonial significance of earlier African theological voices, not least among them Mbiti. They restrict their view to the work of those who "label" themselves as postcolonial.[7] While they do underestimate the resistance to colonialism and coloniality of earlier theological work, they are, nonetheless, correct to point to the ongoing impact of oppression. This they see particularly identified and engaged with by scholars that include Mosala Itumeleng and his *Biblical Hermeneutics and Black Theology in South Africa*, Musa W. Dube and her *Postcolonial Feminist Interpretation*, and Wafula's own *Biblical Representations of Moab*. Such literature is concerned with challenging an imported, naïve approach to the biblical text, and instead promotes a critical and contextual approach for Bible reading. These scholars seek to identify the social and class bias among biblical authors, while giving voice to contemporary marginalized readers. The translation of the biblical text undertaken or managed by those from dominant cultures is also brought under scrutiny. When such an approach is adopted, the way that Europeans used and use the Bible to justify patriarchy, violence, the demonization of traditional religions, conquest, and globalization is problematized and challenged. At the same time, contemporary and historical evidence emerges that points to a series of "subversive strategies" that empower African Christians to embrace the gospel while rejecting the theologically illegitimate disparagement of African cultures, religions, and contextualizations. Coloniality continues in a range of guises. It continues in "epistemological colonialism,"

6. Kinthinji, "Impunity and Exousia," 43–56.

7. See Wafula et al., *Postcolonial Church*, xxvi fn. 12. For the possible post-colonial significance of Mbiti, see Heaney, *From Historical to Critical*, 182–218, and the previous chapter of the current book.

where authors from former colonies are not valued and where the publishing industry is dominated by the concerns of the global north. There is, therefore, a continued need for contestation.[8]

The recognition of such domineering attitudes and practices is always part of a post-colonial theology. Such theology does not place its trust in naïve nativism or nationalism, but rather recognizes complexities, porosities, and neocolonialisms. That is to say, it seeks to throw off an us-versus-them analysis and vision. Because colonialism and coloniality dehumanizes all people, decolonizing theology will inevitably be a dialectical endeavor. It will involve those deeply or distantly complicit in colonialities, those fighting against colonialities, those with thoroughgoing or nascent historical awareness, those born into settler communities and those born into displaced communities, those whose race has meant privilege and those whose race has meant disenfranchisement. The questions, at this juncture, become clear: Given the evidence that Christian leaders did indeed forestall thoroughgoing contextualization, are there counterexamples? Does this talk of a dialectical and intercultural post-colonial theology have resources even within the modern missionary movement? For if there are no such resources, then we resign ourselves after all to the us-versus-them way of doing Christian theology.

## FINDING EACH OTHER

4. What do you understand by contextualization? Can you succinctly define it and explain it to others?

5. Can you think of an example from Scripture where the message of God's love was announced in a new culture and caused controversy? Explain what the controversy was, how or if it was resolved, and what we can learn for today.

6. Why might contextualization also be contestation? Talk about Mbiti's experience and other experiences that are similar in your context or could be similar if contextualization was taken more seriously.

Mbiti, while critical of foreign missionaries, stops short of total condemnation. Indeed, he points to white theologians who in intercultural work were challenged, interrupted, and transformed by the work of God's Spirit.

8. Wafula et al., *Postcolonial Church*, xxx.

As has been seen, one such figure that Mbiti points to is John V. Taylor. For Mugambi, leaders like Taylor demonstrated an openness and willingness to "recognize that the Spirit of God cannot be contained, controlled or directed by any man or woman."[9] Mugambi, an otherwise ardent critic of foreign missionaries, goes as far as to say that Taylor's intercultural experience, sensitivity, and writing contributed to the genesis of modern African Theology.[10] At least three characteristics were at work in Taylor. He demonstrated a critical awareness of the deleterious impact foreign mission can have culturally. He was aware that he was a guest in another culture, while at the same time being present and open to that culture. As a good guest he committed to being a student of that culture's language, history, and philosophy, adopting an inductive method of theologizing that sought the Spirit's voice in other cultures toward mutual learning and mutual conversion.[11] While Taylor must not be romanticized, he demonstrated a rare willingness to enter into deep intercultural relationship that opened his heart and mind to the richness and complexities of another culture, giving him a fresh perspective on the richness and complexities of his own culture.[12] Taylor's biographers say of this theology that he considered only God to be "catholic" while "we remain sectarian." Taylor thus worked against the small-minded and bounded sectarianism that is at work in every age. He, echoing Mugambi's assessment, was convinced of the "uncontainable, endlessly surprising, endlessly refreshing, endlessly creative" work of the Spirit, who "never read the rubrics."[13] For Taylor, every religion is a response to the self-giving God, but that religion does not represent the truth of God.[14] Each religion represents both obedience and disobedience to God. Thus, all religionists, whether following African Traditional Religions or the religion of the AIM-founded Africa Inland Church, need to experience conversion. That is to say, all are called to a "radical humility" and to a deeper love of God that only comes through a commitment to "presence." Such practice and commitment demands all of our efforts in listening, openness, and hu-

---

9. Mugambi, *Biblical Basis of Evangelization,* 59.

10. Mugambi, *Biblical Basis of Evangelization,* 17. He cites the conclusion to Taylor, *Growth of the Church,* as evidence for this view on the genesis of African theology. See Mugambi, "Introduction," xxii–xxiii, xxvii.

11. Heaney, *From Historical to Critical,* 32–33; Taylor, *Primal Vision,* 146–47.

12. Yates, "Reading John V. Taylor," 153–56.

13. Wood, "Christian Mission with John V. Taylor," 428.

14. Taylor, "Theological Basis for Interfaith Dialogue," 373–84.

mility. Such presence comes under threat when those, particularly in domi-nant cultures, want to quickly flatten out and relativize differences. When that happens, we absent ourselves and disappear the other.[15] Taylor, assess-ing himself, felt he had fallen short of such a call. Particularly in an African context, he concluded that his influence was "in principle regretted by most African theologians."[16] This is not a judgment shared by Mugambi. There is evidence that, in deep intercultural relationships and study, Taylor was changed. We get a glimpse of such change when he writes about the shift in his own theological assumptions and emphases. His mind was "radically" reshaped, particularly as he entered deeper into the study of the Luganda language: "I could no longer discuss theology in abstractions, floating free as air like ownerless balloons—Essence, Union, Conversion, Vocation—but had to ask down-to-earth, concrete questions as 'What experience are we describing?' 'Who is doing what to whom?' Never since have I been able to do theology in any other way but that . . . ."[17] As with Mbiti, he sees such a thought-world as more akin to biblical worlds than what is presented in white theology.

Taylor's articulation of change, however, unhelpfully traded on a set of dualisms (for example, history versus metaphysics, events versus con-cepts, corporate versus individualist, tribal versus national). In doing so, he was in real danger of further embedding an us-versus-them type of approach to culture and theology that—even if he preferred "them" over "us"—someone like Said would rightly critique and reject. A more optimis-tic reading of Taylor is to say that, at least in part, he recognized that these dualisms apparently at work across cultural differences were less stable or static than was widely accepted, and thus he was problematizing them. His intent was to demonstrate the counterproductive dominance of one pole over another, particularly in international Christian mission, theological curricula, worldwide church dialogues, and interreligious partnerships. His intent was to recognize the work of the Spirit in all of God's creation:

> [T]he true nature of God is perceived progressively by prophets
> and poets in the march of history rather than the logic of meta-
> physics. . . . [T]hose narratives of the Old Testament . . . have been
> treasured and retold for each successive generation on account of
> their present, not past, significance. If the word "myth" is properly

15. Wood, "Christian Mission with John V. Taylor," 428–33.

16. Taylor, *Primal Vision*, 146.

17. Taylor, *Primal Vision*, 147.

> applied to them it should not denote truth or untruth, but a uni-
> versal relevance such that all who hear them respond not with
> "That was their story," but with "This is our story." . . . People of
> many different cultures, if not of all, can recognize on both a lit-
> eral and allegorical level such experiences as going up a mountain,
> crossing a river, lake or sea, entering a wilderness. . . . It might
> be called the art of making the world of matter a sacrament or
> incarnation of the world of spirit.[18]

I am not advising readers of this book to go and live in Uganda, as
Taylor did, for ten years. It is unlikely that readers, like Taylor, will learn
Luganda.[19] How might we begin, and here I particularly have in view
people from a dominant culture, to integrate into ongoing processes of formation the lessons that Taylor and Mugambi point to? One place to begin
is with the characteristics of Taylor's approach to "Christian presence" that
can be summed up as critical awareness, cultural humility, and inductive
theologizing.

*Critical awareness* does not mean less than educating oneself about
the history and theology of a particular context as it relates to mission and
the growth of the church. As was have seen in an earlier chapter, that, for
me, means a critical approach to the plantation of Ulster and a problematizing of the historical narratives at work in my context of formation. As an
Anglican, the church I belong to was the settler church. Such an identity,
and the attendant mission strategies at work in Ireland, were replicated in
many communities that eventually became the Anglican Communion. If
the first step of critical awareness is reaching within, then the second step of
*cultural humility* is reaching out. It means learning from the voices of those
marginalized from the dominant narrative. This book is published in the
United States and I belong to a largely white institution and church. However, this church is set within a worldwide fellowship that continues to grow
and flourish in centers far from Washington, DC. To what extent does the
curriculum of Episcopalian and Anglican centers of formation in the global
north reflect the reality that 58 percent of Anglicans are now African?[20] Do
we continue with a kind of cultural arrogance that focuses on "the" tradition founded on Thomas Cranmer, Richard Hooker, and Jeremy Taylor,
largely ignoring colonial histories, settler churches, and the emergence of

18. Taylor, *Primal Vision,* 147–48.
19. Wood, *Poet, Priest and Prophet,* 35–47.
20. Johnson and Zurlo, "Changing Demographics of Global Anglicanism," 38.

post-colonial theology that calls for cultural humility and de-centering? In a globalized communion, it is past time that an international and intercultural group of leaders review the landscape of Anglican formation. How might different contexts within World Anglicanism learn and resource one another in curricula outcomes, resources, and priorities for mission, especially across differences and disagreements? Beyond formal curricula and centers of learning and formation, the same questions need to be raised in local churches. What intercultural training, resources, methods, and partnerships need to be developed for predominately white churches to come to terms with their place in a wider church history where the good news was often, and is often, very bad news? How do we understand settler Christianity and settler churches? What theologians are the people in the pew reading that can resource a cultural humility and a deeper intercultural vision of God and Christian fellowship? The remainder of this book will begin to answer some of these questions, not only on the importance of particularity (chapter 1), but also in terms of other major themes in post-colonial theology that can have clear implications for Christian formation in settler churches.

## FINDING GOD

If critical awareness is a reaching *in* and cultural humility is a reaching *out,* then *inductive theologizing* is reaching *up.* Beginning with experience, inductive theology is a means to a deeper vision of God. At this juncture, to affirm an inductive theologizing is not to pass judgment on deductive theology, thus creating, once more, a binary of opposition. Nonetheless, the example of Taylor suggests an inductive approach to theology. It was because of his experience in Uganda that he had a theological conversion. Luganda had an "intractable concreteness" that took him back afresh to a central Christian claim. By virtue of a theology of incarnation, the idea that the grace of God is translatable into a particular place, time, language, and social location is forever embedded in Christian theology. This translatability of the eternal into the ephemeral points to an infinite translatability at the heart of Christianity. It is the very genius of the gospel.[21] Taylor certainly knew this, but intercultural learning and relationships led him to a deeper theological realization: "every abstract idea, including our idea of God, is derived from experience, and all revelation is given through things

21. Sanneh, *Translating the Message.*

that happen. True theology has to be incarnational."[22] The mission of God is embodied in the life and work of a colonized Palestinian. In ascension (Acts 1:6–11), and through contextual contestation (Acts 15), this Jewish Messiah is recognized as the Lord of the gentiles also. Thus begins a chain reaction of contested interpretation, reinterpretation, contextualization, and recontextualization that continues right up to the present day. However, as Mbiti experienced, white theology subverted the message of divine incarnation. Foreign missionaries in Ukambani too often universalized a localized (Western) expression of the gospel. This apparent inculturation of the gospel into a dominant culture resulted in domineering practices that undermined the genius of the gospel. Further, it stopped the ears of those who most needed to hear the voice of God in intercultural encounter. In Mbiti's experience, the cultural formation and lack of critical awareness of missionaries' own syncretism meant they resisted a deep contextualization of the gospel in an African culture.[23] Of course, the irony was that these same missionaries found the work of scholars like Mbiti to have fallen into syncretism. Given these experiences of intercultural theology in the life and work of Mbiti and Taylor, what lessons can be drawn for experiencing God afresh today? What is to be avoided is clear. A syncretism that emboldens dominance against contextualization and intercontextualization must be resisted. For the incarnate enculturated presence of God in Jesus Christ, and the gift of the Spirit on a multicultural people of God, point toward the necessity of cultural pluralism. Every culture is needed for the fullest possible vision of God. The writer of Revelation captures this in the final vision of God's intent for humanity:

> Then I saw a new heaven and a new earth; for the first heaven and the first earth had passed away, and the sea was no more. And I saw the holy city, the new Jerusalem, coming down out of heaven from God. . . . I saw no temple in the city, for its temple is the Lord God Almighty and the Lamb. And the city has not need of sun or moon to shine on it, for the glory of God is its light, and its lamp is the Lamb. The nations will walk by its light, and the kings of the

22. Cited in Wood, *Poet, Priest and Prophet*, 35.

23. Interestingly, in Mbiti's writing, he uses "syncretism" only once in a positive sense (See Heaney, *From Historical to Critical*, 55). There is much debate about the descriptive and analytic value of the term. For some recent work on the issue, see, for example, Kane, "Ritual Formation of Peaceful Politics," 386–410; Schineller, "Inculturation and Syncretism," 50–53; Boff, *Church*; Starkloff, *Theology of the In-Between*; Leopold and Jenson, *Syncretism in Religion*.

earth will bring their glory into it. Its gates will never be shut by day—and there will be no night there. People will bring into it the glory and honor of the nations. (Rev 21:1–2, 22–27)

Here is an eschatological view of God's intent for creation and re-creation. At the heart of such divine fulfillment, centered on the Lamb, is the particularity of the nations. Indeed, in the new Jerusalem, God will curate the cultural expressions (the glory and honor) of the nations. The universality of the Christian faith does not emerge from any one particular cultural expression of the faith. On the contrary, if the church in history is to be in any way continuous with the church in glory, then its practice of catholicity will need to be actualized in a network of contextualizations. Such catholicity, informed by Christian eschatology, cannot be top-down or center-out, but, as in the vision of Revelation, it will be a *catholicity from below*. God, in renewing Israel, will gather God's re-created universal people into their new home in all their cultural and contextual complexity. The ephemeral particularities of cultural glory will be eternalized in the holy city of God. The seer of Revelation does not detail precisely what such glory consists of, and thus the church militant is left contesting precisely this. However, such contesting catholicity should not be viewed as some sort of inferior fellowship. Rather, as Garrett Green notes, the Christian eschatological hope is "always in tension with our immediate experience of this world."[24] The eschatological fulfillment will be but glimpsed in history, and thus contestation is to be expected and welcomed as part of the pilgrimage toward God's new Jerusalem. Christian theological pluralism and contingency do not constitute a crisis, but characterize the present age. To take Christian eschatology seriously, as Mbiti does in his work (chapter 3), is to commit deeply to a pluralist intercultural sociality. Such an eschatological vision means commitment to theology in and for the church of Christ cradled in a web of contextualizations.

The central and already-emphasized implication of an inductive approach to deepening one's vision of God is to enter into intercultural relationships and theological texts. The rest of this book seeks to demonstrate this further. The next chapter, in the context of a fuller definition of coloniality, will posit that to find God amidst the hate will take nothing less than a conversion experience. Repentance from the status quo, its structures, and theologies that justify it is needed. As will be seen in chapter 6, repentance away from a colonial Christ to a colonized Christ is needed.

24. Green, "Imagining the Future," 78–79.

7. In part, Mbiti answered the question, "Where is God amidst colonialism?" by pointing to God's presence in traditions that colonialists and foreign missionaries distrusted and even sought to displace. From your location, how do you answer the question?

8. John V. Taylor is one example of a Christian who entered deeply into intercultural relationships and theology. In what practical ways might Taylor's example help you to do the same?

9. What questions are you left with? How might you resource these questions?

# 5

# The Rough Beast
## Coloniality and Its Significance

[E]mpire is a recurrent condition, an extraordinary adaptive one that grows rapidly in each new manifestation, voraciously consuming the space it occupies.

—Catherine Keller[1]

The unchained sectarian dragon . . . [is] . . . fear, suspicion, atavistic hatred and memory of ancient wrongs, . . . inaugurating . . . destruction . . . and slaughter.

—Jonathan Bardon[2]

The Akamba were neither helpless nor hapless dupes converted by coercion or trickery to the Christian faith. Even amidst fear and hate, they weighed the Christian gospel in relation to their own traditions. In short, despite actual, apparent, or assumed power differentials, they exercised their own theological agency. Conversion to the Christian faith came as a result of reflection, dialogue, and disputation.[3] Mbiti's argument is that the white missionaries also needed to experience conversion. Had they been more

1. Keller, "Love of Postcolonialism," 222.
2. Bardon, *Plantation of Ulster*, 346.
3. Heaney, *From Historical to Critical*, 94–96.

critical of their own cultures and traditions, in dialogue with Akamba culture and tradition, and in dialogue with the biblical text, they may well have experienced a deeper and intercultural conversion. Such mutual conversion is at the heart of post-colonial theology ranging over various geographical and temporal contexts.

Kenya was a colony established by British law in 1920. As in Ireland, artists, activists, and scholars challenged colonizers and colonial ways of thinking. They wanted to go beyond colonial reality epistemologically, theologically, and politically. They were post-colonial. There was a time in Kenya's history, however, even before it became part of a so-called British Protectorate (1895), when people experienced subjugation and oppression. After it gained independence (1963), many Kenyans continued to experience marginalization and subjugation under nationalist leadership.[4] To distinguish these experiences in a proto-colony, a protectorate, and in a neo-colony, a category beyond colonialism is needed. As will be seen presently, that category is *coloniality,* and is important for at least three reasons. First, it highlights the relationship of theology with exercises of power amidst the ongoing effects of colonialism, innercolonialism, and/ or neocolonialism. Second, its recognition points to the need for deeper critical awareness, especially from those in dominant cultures. Third, the need for changes in analysis, evoked by coloniality, resources a deeper call for change that ultimately means a recognition that the end of theology is conversion.

## COLONIALITY AND POWER

Coloniality is a category that connects experiences of subjugation and resistance across a range of historical settings. On the one hand, the recognition of coloniality distinguishes experiences of colonialism from experiences outside formal colonies. This maintains the importance of historical particularity. On the other hand, the recognition of coloniality provides opportunity to compare experiences of subjugation and resistance across settings affected by colonialism.[5] This provides opportunity for the discovering and development of intercultural and intercontextual (theological)

---

4. See Kithinji, "Impunity and Exousia," 43–58.

5. I have sought to explore the importance of coloniality elsewhere. See "Conversion to Coloniality," 65–77. See also "Coloniality and Theological Method," 55–65.

resources toward more just thought and practice. Writing of the USA context, Lynne St. Clair Darden observes:

> Kwame Touré (né Stokely Carmichael), a founder of the black power movement, and his coauthor Charles Hamilton commented that in an age of decolonization, the situation of Africans in America should be considered as a unique case of internal colonialism: "black people in this country form a colony, and it is not in the interests of the colonial power to liberate them. . . . They stand as colonial subjects in relation to the white society. Thus institutional racism has another name: colonialism."[6]

What is particularly in view in this chapter, in defining coloniality, are situations of subjugation where such circumstances are operative outside a formally established colony, but in a space that has or had experience of formal colonialism. Internal colonialisms are circumstances where people are subjugated—culturally, politically, and/or economically—under, for example, the leaderships of settlers or their progeny. Those suffering and resisting in such circumstances will not have the same rights and opportunities, by law, culture, or convention, as citizens from the dominant culture, and may be segregated to particular land areas. For the purpose of this study, such internal colonialism, along with proto-colonialism and neo-colonialism, will be distinguished by the term "coloniality."

A recognition of coloniality, shaped by historical studies, has the potential to unveil the ongoing relationship between culture and power. There is no "isolated cultural sphere . . . freely and unconditionally available to weightless theoretical speculation and investigation" distinct from a "debased political sphere, where the real struggle between interests is supposed to occur." The two spheres are inextricably linked. They are "ultimately the same" and theology cannot be extracted or abstracted from these spheres.[7] Robert Young captures something of the relationship between the two spheres when he writes:

> To sweep colonialism under the carpet of modernity . . . is too convenient a deflection. To begin with, its history was extraordinary in its global dimension, not only in relation to the comprehensiveness of colonization by the time of the high imperialism period in the late nineteenth century, but also because the effect of the globalization of western imperial power was to fuse many societies

6. Darden, *Scripturalizing Revelation*, 21.

7. Said, *Culture and Imperialism*, 57.

with different historical traditions into a history which, apart from the period of centrally controlled command economies, obliged them to follow the same general economic path. The entire world now operates within the economic system primarily developed and controlled by the west, and it is the continued dominance of the west, in terms of political, economic, military and cultural power, that gives this history a continuing significance.[8]

The history of colonialism and its ongoing impact in coloniality should not be ignored. The wealth of the North Atlantic cannot be understood independent of colonial exploitation. In turn, university endowments, well-established publishing houses, well-paid professional theologians, and disposable income, have decisively resourced the prominence of particular types of theology and theologizing. While such history should not be ignored, it is often ignored. Writing of liberal education, Said argues that there is "massive avoidance" of the "determining, political horizon of modern Western culture, namely imperialism."[9] The same is true for theology that centers itself on issues related to the Reformation, Counter-Reformation, the Enlightenment, modernity, secularization, atheism, and postmodernity, while failing to interrogate the relationship between colonialism, faith, and formation. R. S. Sugirtharajah observes: "Precisely in the 1960s when the process of decolonization was taking place, Western theologians spent their creative energies addressing issues such as secularization and its impact on Christian faith. They were eloquent in their silence when it came to assessing the role of the West in colonial domination . . . ."[10]

When, through colonialisms and colonialities, power is achieved, a conservative movement (marshaling an array of social and cultural products) evolves to maintain that power. That conserving power, as has already been seen, can be theological.[11] James Cone presents the force of such conservatism and coloniality (though he does not use that term) in his book, *The Cross and the Lynching Tree*. Echoing Sugirtharajah's complaint, he writes:

> What I studied in graduate school ignored white supremacy and black resistance against it, as if they had nothing to do with the

8. Young, *Postcolonialism: An Historical Introduction*, 5.

9. Said, *Culture and Imperialism*, 60.

10. Sugirtharajah, *Postcolonial Criticism and Biblical Interpretation*, 26.

11. See Heaney, *From Historical to Critical*, 36–40; Strong, *Anglicanism and the British Empire*.

Christian gospel and the discipline of theology. . . . How could any theologian explain the meaning of Christian identity in America and fail to engage white supremacy, its primary negation?

The Roman Empire that killed Jesus at Calvary was similar to the American Empire that lynched blacks in the United States . . . .[12]

As Said recognizes, there cannot be a bifurcation of the cultural (or theological) realm and the political realm. Cone's work makes this tragically pellucid. Coloniality always has material consequences. In Cone's study, that material consequence is brutalizing murder. In a chapter title that appeals to Yeats, "'The Terrible Beauty of the Cross' and the Tragedy of the Lynching Tree," Cone reminds his readers that between 1880 and 1940, nearly 5,000 black men and women were lynched by white Christians in the USA.[13] In a post-Civil War South, the terror of lynching was deliberately, brutally, and sadistically enacted for the purpose of regaining or further embedding white supremacy. "Although white southerners lost the Civil War, they did not lose the cultural war—the struggle to define America as a white nation and blacks as a subordinate race unfit for governing and therefore incapable of political and social equality."[14]

As coloniality, the purpose of lynching, Cone observes, was to "redeem" the South from purported black domination. The eloquent silence of white theology must be interrupted and is being disrupted by post-colonial theology. It is being disrupted by a counternarrative that says coloniality is close to the heart of a nation whose dominant sanctioned narrative is freedom. Cone's work puts race at the center of coloniality.

During the nineteenth century, part of the justification for subjugation was that the colonized were in some way inferior and thus needed to be governed toward "civilization." Along with African-Americans and Native Americans, the Irish were considered part of the "contagious classes" inclined to biological and social degeneracy.[15] As late as the 1850s, contested racialist tropes on Saxonism were deployed to reassure Protestants in Northern Ireland that they were Anglo-Saxon and not Celts.[16] Further, it was argued by some that Celts were illegitimate occupiers of Ireland be-

12. Cone, *Cross and the Lynching Tree*, xvi–xvii, 164.

13. Cone, *Cross and the Lynching Tree*, 31.

14. Cone, *Cross and the Lynching Tree*, 6.

15. Duncan, "Flexible Foundation," 320–33. Young, *Idea of English Ethnicity*, 94–139.

16. Bardon, *Plantation of Ulster*, 342.

cause they were "racially affiliated" not with Europeans, but with Africans. In order to drive the point home, the Irish were often represented with what were considered "Africanoid features."[17] Such racist hierarchies predicated upon pseudoscience at work throughout the nineteenth century would have, and continue to have, drastic consequences. Distinct ethnic identities assumed to separate, distinguish, and hierarchize settlers from indigenous people cannot be proven. Indeed, even family names often used to signal a particular ethnic identity are much more unstable than nationalist or colonialist narratives would suggest. No less a name than "English" illustrates the point with some verve. The name Gallogley derives from *Gallóglaigh* meaning "foreign warriors." It was mistakenly assumed that *Gall* meant an English foreigner and, thus, the family name was anglicized as "English." As was seen in chapter 2, native and newcomer become intertwined. While the rhetoric of separateness might suppress the truth, it cannot change it.[18] Hate, of course, needs no foundation in fact to build upon: "The unchained sectarian dragon leaped from its cage as fear, suspicion, atavistic hatred and memory of ancient wrongs, gushed to the surface, inaugurating thirty years of destruction, conflict, forced population movement, mutilation and slaughter."[19]

As was seen in chapter 1, those three decades of the twentieth century coincided with my formative years. The irony of that conflict and the tragedy of coloniality is that the cultural and physical subjugation experienced affected *all* sides of the conflict. The dearly held identities, readings of history, and theologies that violently separated communities were indeed legacies of colonialism. Against a backdrop of supremacist ideology in the USA, Cone asks what happened to the hate that led to murder?[20] For any student of post-colonial theology, the answer is clear: the hate remains. And while theology is not the whole answer, and while the actions of the church are not the whole answer, without a deep existential confrontation with theological and cultural malpractice on the part of the church, the hate will remain. An intercultural post-colonial revolution is needed in sanctuaries, liturgies, Sunday schools, seminaries, and on the streets.

The hate remains. The hate is amidst us, even still in Kenya, in Ireland, and in the United States. It is politicized. It is culturalized. It is theologized.

17. Young, *Idea of English Ethnicity*, 104–39.

18. Bardon, *Plantation of Ulster*, 342–43.

19. Bardon, *Plantation of Ulster*, 346.

20. Cone, *Cross and the Lynching Tree*, 164.

It is internalized. It is paraded on the streets. As ever, therefore, culture (including theology) cannot be abstracted from the exercise of power. The power of culture as constructed by supremacists and as constructive of supremacists cannot go unchallenged. Coloniality needs to be named and needs to be identified. To begin with, this means the nourishment of critical awareness.

## COLONIALITY AND CRITICAL AWARENESS

At this juncture, critical awareness that emerges from the recognition of coloniality will mean three things. Critical awareness means the conscious acceptance and integration of post-colonial analysis in one's given field and practice. Critical awareness means an awareness of particularity that not only names the presence of one's context and formation, but also asks: Who is made invisible in this particularity?[21] Further, critical awareness means discerning the presence of God amidst coloniality.

First, academic institutions in the North, dominated by white people, vaunt the critical nature and processes of their education.[22] Indeed, I have been in too many conversations where scholars from or in the USA or Europe question the ability of students from beyond the West or from "non-traditional backgrounds" to exhibit critical capacity and to perform at "an appropriate level" in their studies. These same students often come with deep experience and sensitivities in pluralist and complex contexts where the violence of coloniality, colonial legacies, intercultural identities,

---

21. Young, "Postcolonial Remains," 128–31.

22. Li and Koedel, "Representative and Salary Gaps," 343–54. This study focuses on biology, chemistry, economics, educational leadership and policy, English, and sociology as a window into the makeup of the academy in the USA. Black, Hispanic, and female faculty are underrepresented in relation to their representation in the wider population. White and Asian faculty are overrepresented. Further analysis reveals that a lack of diversity is particularly evident in so-called STEM (science, technology, engineering, and mathematics) fields, whereas non-STEM fields continue to diversify. In theology schools accredited by the Association of Theological Schools (ATS) in 2017–18, there were 175 male and seventy-three female Asian or Pacific Island professors. There were 171 males and 100 female Black Non-Hispanic professors. There were 108 male and thirty-three Hispanic professors. There were four male and one female American Indian, Alaskan Native or Inuit professors. There were fifteen male and seven female visa or nonresident alien professors. There were 2,013 male and 603 female white non-hispanic professors. There were fifteen male and seven female multiracial professors (Association of Theological Schools, "2017–2018 Annual Data Tables").

multilingual communication, and interreligious literacy are daily and lived realities. Those judging them and teaching them may exhibit less capacity in these areas. It seldom occurs to those in the dominant culture that we might also question *our* pedagogies, curricula, or methods of assessment. A recognition of coloniality that identifies the exercise of power through culture (by, for example, defining, excluding, and killing others on the basis of "race" or "civilization") challenges such hubris. The curricula and culture of not a few educational institutions are narrowly conceived. No wonder Robert Beckford is left reflecting that "more books have been written by Western theologians about being nice to animals and the environment than about colonialism or race."[23] Joerg Rieger warns that those who seek to do theology alone or want to be faithful to Christ above the interconnectedness of imperial history and its aftermath "have to face the uncomfortable truth that they might be drawn into the force field of empire unconsciously . . . ."[24] There remains, thus, analysis to be done uncovering how imperialism and colonialism have influenced Western theology.[25] In the absence of such analysis, the ongoing claim that such theology is critical remains unsubstantiated. The challenge to the critical nature of theology is even stronger when it is recognized that theologies emerging in colonial and post-colonial contexts explicitly critique Western theologizing. What critical awareness means, therefore, in the first instance, is an awareness that post-colonial analysis remains important in analysis and practice.

Young notes that for some scholars, especially in the so-called West, there is ongoing disparagement of the field of post-colonial studies. Indeed, for some, post-colonial studies is a blip, a partisan and passing moment that will be superseded by getting back to the core work of scholarship. Young rightly opposes such thought. As an analysis of, a practice, and resistance against colonialism and coloniality, post-colonialism did not need the (Northern) academy for its birth and will not need it for its thriving. The field has never depended on a central method or theory or centralized school to propagate the vision. Rather, post-colonial thinkers and thought emerge from the particularity of colonialisms and colonialities adopting a range of resistant methods including, I argue, theological methods.

> If anti- and postcolonial knowledge formations were generated by such circumstances, peripheral as they may seem to some

23. Cited in Sugirtharajah, "Complacencies and Cul-de-sacs," 22.

24. Rieger, *Christ and Empire*, 313.

25. Rieger, *Christ and Empire*, 313, is a good example of how that might be done.

metropolitan intellectuals, now, as in the past, the only criterion
that could determine whether "postcolonial theory" has ended is
whether, economic booms of the so-called "emerging markets"
notwithstanding, imperialism and colonialism in all their different forms have ceased to exist in the world, whether there is
no longer domination by nondemocratic forces (often exercised
on others by Western democracies, as in the past), or economic
and resource exploitation enforced by military power, or a refusal
to acknowledge the sovereignty of non-Western countries, and
whether peoples or cultures still suffer from the long-lingering
aftereffects of imperial, colonial, and neocolonial rule, albeit in
contemporary forms such as economic globalization. . . . [T]he
issue is . . . to locate the hidden rhizomes of colonialism's historical
reach, of what remains invisible, unseen, silent, or unspoken. In a
sense, postcolonialism has always been about the ongoing life of
residues, living remains, lingering legacies.[26]

As long as hate remains, post-colonial scholarship will be needed. As
long as hegemonic intent in politics, religion, culture, or the assessment
of "non-traditional" students remains, post-colonial theology will remain.
The field of post-colonial studies includes "counterdiscursive practices"
that are aimed at correcting or undoing "Western hegemony."[27] If hegemony means the ideological dominance of a social group or class, then
counterdiscursive practices are the challenges that are made to such power
in cultural, political, economic, and theological work. Yeats, Achebe, Mbiti,
Cone, and other thinkers to be heard in subsequent chapters, contribute to
such counterdiscursive practice. Their aim in disrupting hegemony is not
for the replacement of one type of hegemony with another. This is the very
definition of neocolonialism. Rather, the post-colonial task is conversion to
deeper critical awareness. What is sought is critical work that acknowledges
the reality of coloniality and demonstrates how such intercultural work impacts, in the current case, theology. This is, in large part, the purpose of this
book.

Second, post-colonial critical awareness means identifying and naming those that have been made invisible:

[T]he postcolonial has always been concerned with a politics of invisibility: it makes the invisible visible. This is entirely paradoxical
to the extent that its object was never, in fact, invisible, but rather

26. Young, "Postcolonial Remains," 126.
27. Gugelberger and Brydon, "Postcolonial Cultural Studies," 757.

the "invisible visible": it was not seen by those in power who determine the fault lines between the visible and the invisible. . . .
The task of the postcolonial is to make the invisible, in this sense,
visible.[28]

Young notes that despite this commitment to the visibility of those
made invisible, post-colonial scholars have been slow to make central the
concern of indigenous movements of resistance in, for example, both North
and South America. His explanation for this torpor speaks directly to why
post-colonial theology is important for the broader field of post-colonial
studies. Despite the apparent critical awareness of post-colonial scholars,
they fail indigenous groups because of their bias against religious and/or
theological commitments. As Young notes, "[I]ndigenous activism uses a
whole set of paradigms that do not fit easily with postcolonial presuppo-
sitions and theories—for example, ideas of the sacred and attachment to
ancestral land."[29]

A post-colonialism that emphasizes the politics of invisibility
while making the theological invisible is not sustainable. Post-colonial
theology is concerned with the theology of invisibility. It seeks to make
theologizing bodies visible, including, as will be seen in chapter 9, Native
American bodies. It must be recognized, however, that part of the reason
for exclusionary practices against indigenous work is how post-colonialism
is itself understood. To illustrate and substantiate this insight, Young points
to the now-famous text by Bill Ashcroft, Gareth Griffiths, and Helen Tiffin,
*The Empire Writes Back*. In the book, Young sees a dangerous move toward
equating all revolutionary societies as post-colonial.

It is not an equivalent use of the term to refer to Kenya and the USA
as post-colonial. Taking heed of Native American theology will disallow
any easy assumption that the United States is, in any critical sense, post-
colonial. Woodley's work makes it clear that the *post-* of the USA is as much
about the extension of colonialism as it is about the transcending of colonialism. Young is correct:

*The Empire Writes Back* . . . assimilates all forms of colonial liberation into a single narrative of freedom from the metropolitan
metropolis. What this passes over is the degree to which settler
colonies themselves practiced a form of "deep colonialism," . . .
which underscores the extent to which the achievement of settler

28. Young, "Postcolonial Remains," 128.
29. Young, "Postcolonial Remains," 129.

self-governance enforced the subjection of indigenous peoples and indeed increased the operation of oppressive colonial practices against them. In almost any settler colony one can think of, settler liberation from colonial rule was premised on indigenous dispossession.[30]

As was seen in chapter 1, post-colonialism cannot be in the thrall of any nationalism. Anti-imperialist activism, of course, often leads to national and nationalist emancipation. However, such emancipation and the cultures and societies that emerge from anti-imperialist struggle may include not only the dispossession of colonial rulers, but also the dispossession of a range of people from within the society. If the post-colonial scholars Young criticizes had practiced a deeper sense of critical awareness by opening themselves up to the theological, this would have led them to recognize the importance of indigenous voices to post-colonialism. This, in turn, would have led to a more nuanced reading of history and literature, avoiding the problematic simplification of revolutionary nations all being somehow equally post-colonial. It would have unveiled the "deep colonialism" of that oxymoronic of all peoples, the liberated settler.[31] It is precisely this issue, and its theological implications, that will be examined further in chapter 9.

Third, critical awareness means making the invisible God visible in circumstances of coloniality. This too is entirely paradoxical, for God is not invisible to believers experiencing coloniality. God is made manifest, argues Mbiti, in an Akamba eschatology that prioritizes an African temporality and an African community (chapter 3). God is made manifest, argues Cone, in the black struggle for liberation.[32] In light of coloniality, God is made manifest, argues Joh, in Christ according to Korean concepts of *han* and *jeong* (chapter 7). God is made manifest, argues Woodley, on the stolen land of America in Native American *shalom* (chapter 9). In short, critical awareness names the epiphanic nature of post-colonial theology. God is present even amidst the hate.

The focus of this study is on Christian theology. However, each of the theologians that help define the post-colonial in this study engage in deep interreligious, as well as intercultural, questions. God becomes visible in

---

30. Young, "Postcolonial Remains," 130.

31. Young, "Postcolonial Remains," 130–31. See Veracini, *Settler Colonialism*.

32. Cone, *Black Theology of Liberation*.

Akamba theological agency that engages African Traditional Religion;[33] in Joh's hybridizing, Buddhism and Korean shamanism are always present;[34] and Woodley's resistant theological vision is resourced by Native American religious thought and practice. Critical awareness countering theological invisibility has, therefore, an interreligious dimension. In an academic field that values hybridization, it is ironic that post-colonialism, because of its disappearing of the theological, often effectively excludes or fails to thoroughly address the imbrication and interweaving of colonial, theological, and religious lives. Young rightly chides the field of post-colonial studies for being partial in its reading, or refusal to read, religious and theological resistance to colonialism. This, he sees, has had particularly deleterious consequences for the understanding, presentation, and relationship with religious adherents and scholars. Particularly problematic has been the approach of Western post-colonial scholars to Islam. Young observes, "since its inception in academic form with Said's *Orientalism* in 1978, postcolonial thinking . . . has . . . tended to sideline . . . the question of Islam and the role of religion in anticolonial struggle."[35] This has meant that scholars have become distanced from a broad range of sources for imagining a post-colonial world. To illustrate this, he turns to tenth-century Spain and the Islamic practice of tolerance in Andalucía (*al-Andalus*). Al-Andalus was a place where Muslims, Jews, and Christians lived together with some degree of intercultural and interreligious tolerance. Indeed, such examples resulted in both John Locke and Voltaire citing Islamic precedence for a type of tolerance that European philosophies and societies should follow.[36] Unlike Young, Janina M. Safran recognizes the interwoven nature of theological conviction with Muslim practice on the Iberian peninsula:

> The historical definition of the Muslim self in relation to the non-Muslim other begins with the foundational period of Islam. . . .
> It is true enough to say that from its origins Islam has been defined in relation to Judaism and Christianity. The Qur'an conveys a history of *revelation* to humankind that commemorates God's

---

33. See Heaney, *From Historical to Critical,* 94–125.

34. Joh, *Heart of the Cross,* 27, 99.

35. Young, "Postcolonial Remains," 132.

36. Young, "Postcolonial Remains," 132–38. See also Voltaire, *Philosophical Dictionary,* 387–94. Locke, "Letter Concerning Toleration," 13–14. Locke also appeals to Jewish toleration ("Letter Concerning Toleration," 28–30).

covenant with Abraham and the mission of the prophets who followed, including must prominently, Moses and Jesus.[37]

Safran, herself influenced by post-colonial theory, in analyzing the particular political and social arrangements in *al-Andalus*, notes that, along with jurisprudence and ethics, theology shaped this society. The specific status and welfare for the people of the book (*ahl al-kitāb*), provision as "people of the (pact of) protection" (*ahl al-dhimma*), and an understanding that political opposition was "religious deviance," speak directly to the importance of theology at work among the leaders and people of *al-Andalus*: "Boundary making by Muslim jurists was informed by the fundamental premise that Muslims were distinct from Christians and Jews by their recognition of the Qur'an as God's revelation and Muhammad as God's Messenger."[38]

Any practice of tolerance (and intolerance) was, therefore, ultimately predicated upon a theological conviction. God has revealed God's will to God's people. God wills that provision be made for non-Muslims. Young does not recognize the part Andalusi theologizing plays. I am not expecting him to become a theologian. However, the writing of theology and the theological nature of key writing or key historical events for post-colonial thought can no longer be disappeared by leading post-colonial scholars. This is not to say that *al-Andalus* should be reduced to theological belief. It was much more complex than that and a range of issues relating to, for example, social practices, law, ritual, negotiated culture, and customs, not to mention exercises of power, conquest, and colonialism, need to be considered.[39] Nonetheless, for Young to dismiss the theological in the very act of demonstrating a newfound respect for Islam and religion more broadly is, to say the very least, perplexing. It is to misrepresent this Muslim society and skews any subsequent analysis. To prioritize Muslim social interaction and the idea and practice of "tolerance" independent of the theological is to obscure the very heart of this society. It is to make mute their voices. It is, if it were possible, to make God invisible.

---

37. Safran, *Defining Boundaries in Al-Andalus*, 8. Italics mine.

38. Safran, *Defining Boundaries in Al-Andalus*, 21.

39. Safran, *Defining Boundaries in Al-Andalus*, 9–33.

## COLONIALITY AND CONVERSION

As is seen above, the broad field of post-colonialism needs to undergo a conversion. I invite Young, and post-colonial scholars more generally, to consider that resistance can be inherently theological. This will mean, at the very least, anti-colonialist theological reflection emerging from particular settings of colonialism and coloniality, theological agency toward making visible the so-called invisible, hybridizing theologies, and enacting some kind of resistance against colonialism or coloniality. Such anti-colonial work emerges from a particular, and often contested, vision of God. To be fair to Young, he might well be read as intimating toward the possibility of such theological decolonization. Despite this, he sheds no light on how that might be done.[40] In this final section, we turn then from a call for conversion in the broader field, to a consideration of how, in response to coloniality, conversion is the primary goal of Christian post-colonial theology. The task of theology is to turn people around to a truer vision of God. It is to invite people into a conversional process toward divine life. A post-colonial theologian knows that such a process is undertaken in contexts marred by coloniality. How then, at this juncture, might such conversion be understood from a post-colonial perspective?

First, conversion in light of coloniality is turning away from the *status quo*. In a world where religious adherents and evangelists from dominant cultures have been guilty of displacing, or seeking to displace, the cultures and histories of would-be converts as an explicit or implicit perquisite for entry into faith then they themselves need to be converted (chapter 3). Young defines post-colonialism as the world upturned. It is not simply a field of study or a theoretical construct. Post-colonialism involves the political work to reconstruct "Western knowledge formations, reorient ethical norms, turn the power structures of the world upside down, refashion the world from below."[41] Such a definition echoes to the sound of Jesus' early followers in the Roman Empire accused of "turning the world upside down" and of "acting contrary to the decrees of the emperor, saying there is another king named Jesus" (Acts 17:7).[42] Such a conversion-as-reversal was already announced and envisioned by Mary:

---

40. Young, *Postcolonialism: An Historical Introduction*, 338.

41. Young, "Postcolonial Remains," 126

42. Young, *Postcolonialism: A Very Short Introduction*, 2.

God has shown strength with his arm;

he has scattered the proud in the thoughts of their hearts.

He has brought down the powerful from their thrones,

and lifted up the lowly . . . .

(Luke 1:51–52)

Cone might be seen to exegete the Magnificat when he writes, "the God of Jesus is primarily found where dominant theologians do not look."[43] By implication, therefore, conversion is not the same experience for those in dominant cultures and those beyond such cultures. In Marian logic, God will humble some that they might know divine grace. God will embolden others that they might know divine grace. A potent example of this need for conversion, within the context of coloniality, was seen in twentieth-century South Africa and the now famous *Kairos* document.[44]

The 1980s were a particularly turbulent time in apartheid South Africa. As opposition grew, so too did government suppression of resistance. The white churches in the country rarely exhibited a prophetic ministry amidst violence and death. Against this backdrop, a group of theologians published the "Kairos document":

> We as . . . theologians have been trying to understand the theological significance of this moment in our history. . . . For very many Christians in South Africa this is the KAIROS, the moment of grace and opportunity, the favourable time in which God issues a challenge to decisive action.[45]

The document identified three types of theology. "State Theology" stressed the language of "law and order" resulting in support for the *status quo*. "Church Theology" stressed a form of reconciliation that was predicated upon a justice defined by the oppressors. In calling for nonviolent action, the violence of resistance and repression was collapsed into the same ethical category. Such theologizing was "heretical" and "blasphemous."[46] Any notion of reconciliation in such circumstances was dependent on conversion. Without repentance from those responsible for apartheid, and

---

43. Cone, *God of the Oppressed*, xiv.

44. The document was published in 1985, with a second edition published in 1986 (which give particular attention to an improved section on prophetic theology). Both editions are found in Leonard, *Kairos Documents*.

45. "Kairos Document," in Leonard, *Kairos Documents*, 7.

46. "Kairos Document," in Leonard, *Kairos Documents*, 12–13.

those benefitting from apartheid, reconciliation simply meant acquiescence to the dominant culture. Forgiveness and negotiation required repentance, and before repentance took place, those suffering under apartheid were called to "preach repentance to those who sin against us."[47]

What was needed was not "a theology of reconciliation with sin and the devil" but rather, a "biblical theology of direct confrontation with the forces of evil." Because of an emphasis on the "other-worldly" nature of faith, propagated in "Church Theology," less-than-transformative thought and action dominated. Thus, inadequate "social analysis" and "political strategy" emerged. An inadequate analysis arose from abstracted notions of, for example, reconciliation. Little effort was made to relate such ideas to the realities of South Africa, especially to the "mechanics of injustice and oppression." Once more the importance of particularity in (post-colonial) theology is seen as crucial. As with Young, the theologians of *The Kairos Document* did not shrink from the political nature of change. "Changing the structures of a society is fundamentally a matter of politics."[48] What was needed was a prophetic theology. "The prophets do not have a purely theoretical or academic interest in God and in the signs of the times. They call for repentance, conversion and change. . . . Jesus did the same, 'Repent,' he says 'the KAIROS has come and the Kingdom of God is close at hand.'"[49]

This prophetic theology was a call to action for the church. It meant searching the Scriptures for the liberative word against coloniality, reading the signs of the times, and confronting subjugation while fearlessly declaring hope. How was oppression understood and how were its causes understood? Most importantly, the *Kairos Document* was a call for conversion away from a *status quo* that relied on a god who justified white supremacy. Such a god was an idol.[50] "From a theological point of view the opposite of the God of the Bible is the devil, Satan. The god of the South African State is not merely an idol or false god, it is the devil disguised as Almighty God—the antichrist."[51] For those in dominant cultures there is always this danger that the Christ of our faith is an antichrist. The conversional process

---

47. "Kairos Document," 2nd. ed., in Leonard, *Kairos Documents*, 56.

48. "Kairos Document," 2nd. ed., in Leonard, *Kairos Documents*, 57–61.

49. "Kairos Document," 2nd. ed., in Leonard, *Kairos Documents*, 63.

50. "Kairos Document," 2nd. ed., in Leonard, *Kairos Documents*, 63–77; "Kairos Document," in Leonard, *Kairos Documents*, 12–13.

51. "Kairos Document," in Leonard, *Kairos Documents*, 13.

is always a turning away from an imperial anti-Christ toward the Christ crucified by empire.

Second, conversion in light of coloniality means a turning toward the colonized Christ who makes the invisible visible.[52] Jesus of Nazareth was subject to an empire that was in no way acquired in a fit of absence of mind:[53]

> For them I will not limit time or space.
>
> Their rule will have no end. Even hard Juno,
>
> Who terrorizes land and sea and sky,
>
> Will change her mind and join me as I foster
>
> The Romans in their togas, the world's masters.[54]

Thus, in Virgil's *Aeneid*, Jupiter prophesied the rise of Rome in the place of Troy. As with other imperial visions, ancient and modern, the Romans assured themselves that their superpower status was divinely willed. Roman legions wreaking havoc on the Palestinian countryside were bringing about the will of the gods. Villages and villagers were destroyed, people were enslaved, those who resisted were crucified, and revolts were brutally put down as a means to Rome's expansionist rule. Client rulers, always with the legions at their back, controlled the country and collected tribute. Central to this imperial system and order was the Jerusalem "temple-state" operating, quite literally, under the Roman imperial eagle perching above the gate. It is in such a turbulent context of domination and resistance that the ministry of Jesus should be understood. His ministry was one of renewal for Israel by making the downtrodden both visible and central to the salvific will and actions of Israel's God. Such renewal and visibility was inherently resistant to Roman domination.[55]

The birth narratives announce Jesus as an alternative lord to Caesar, one who immediately and directly threatens Rome's client-king Herod (Matt 2:1–18; Luke 2:1–20). His arrival was, as has already been seen, praised in songs of militancy, not only by Mary, but also by Zechariah and Simeon (Luke 1:46–55, 67–79; 2:29–32). In a country possessed by

---

52. Cone, *Black Theology of Liberation*, 116–36.

53. Horsley, "Jesus and Empire," 77–96; Horsley, *Jesus and Empire*, 59–78.

54. Virgil, *Aeneid*, I.278–80. See Carter, *Roman Empire and the New Testament*, 83–99.

55. Horsley, *Jesus and Empire*, 15–43. Horsley, "Jesus and Empire," 77–84. Perdue et al., *Israel and Empire*, 217–91.

the spirit of imperial supremacy, the exorcisms Jesus performed, ridding individual sufferers of "legion" alien forces, could not be divorced from the broader mission of exorcising the people of demonic conquest and subjugation (Mark 5:1–20). Such healing meant the kingdom of God was breaking in (Luke 11:20) and this signified the dethroning of foreign powers.[56] To replace such subjugation, the followers of Jesus were to pray for the coming of God's kingdom. Richard Horsley reflects that praying the Lord's Prayer for God's reign particularly focused on "the people's economic needs of sufficient food and a (mutual) cancellation of debts . . . the two principal dangers that constantly threaten peasant life because of demands for taxes, tribute, and tithes."[57]

These threats form the background to Jesus' call for community renewal. Imperial domination meant financial hardship and could cause communities and social support to disintegrate. People in desperate situations could be driven to desperate measures. Jesus called his people to renew their relationships by loving those who had become their enemies, and to support one another in such difficult times (Matt 5:38–40; Luke 6:27–36). As Horsley stated:

> This renewal of cooperation and solidarity in local communities would have strengthened the families' and villages' ability to arrest the process of disintegration and to maintain the traditional way of life. That is, it was a resistance to the effects of Roman imperial domination that was driving families into debt, loss of land, and reduction to low-paid wage laborers completely dependent on the wealthy.[58]

When Jesus was directly asked about the payment of tribute, his anticolonial answer was both artful and audacious. The people, he said, should render to God what belonged to God, and to Caesar what belonged to Caesar (Matt 22:21). The sovereignty of God over Israel was clear and thus *all* belonged to God. This displaced any claim to tribute from Rome, implying that what was due to Caesar was the judgment of God. This was a judgment that Jesus acted out at the heart of empire in Judea. The high priests were appointed by the Roman governor and, under their oversight, the

---

56. *Basileia* was commonly associated with the Roman empire. See Carter, *Roman Empire and the New Testament,* 92–98; Horsley, *Jesus and Empire,* 11–14, 98–104; Meeks, *Moral World of the First Christians,* 97–123.

57. Horsley, "Jesus and Empire," 89.

58. Horsley, "Jesus and Empire," 94–95.

aristocratic temple priests collected the tribute. The temple was, therefore, "the primary face of Roman imperial rule in Judea."[59] In this syncretistic space, within the ritual remembrance of Israel's deliverance, Jesus both enacts and predicts God's judgment on the empire (Matt 21:12–13; Mark 11:15–16; 13:1–2; 14:58; 15:29; John 2). At the climax of Jesus' ministry, as he faces death, he shares an exodus meal (Passover) with his chosen representatives of Israel's renewal "in anticipation of eating again in the kingdom of God, no longer subject to the rulers about to kill him."[60] Jesus' ministry was a resistant ministry and the end he met in crucifixion was inevitable:

> He had the audacity to march up to Jerusalem at the highly charged
> time of Passover, carry out a forcible demonstration symbolizing
> God's condemnation of the Temple, and state, however cleverly,
> that it was not lawful to render tribute to Caesar. Those were acts
> of insurrection that the Roman governor and the client-rulers of
> Jerusalem could not tolerate.[61]

Roman governors were little concerned by would-be prophets. However, it was with speed and efficiency that they cut down movements and leaders that even implied threat to the imperial order. From the Roman perspective, his crucifixion implies that they understood him to be "an insurrectionary of some sort." From the perspective of his followers "his mode of execution symbolized his program of opposition to the imperial order." In resurrection, this opposition birthed a renewal movement independent of the "oppressive [imperial] ruling institutions." This was, and is, a temple "not made with human hands" (Mark 14:58).[62]

Tragically, such a movement would not remain immune to the lure of empire and even within the New Testament text there is evidence of a range of positions on how the early church would relate to Rome.[63] For Rieger this makes the reading of biblical texts with an eye on where the "surplus" anti-imperialist meanings emerge to be a crucial interpretative task. The "Christ who never quite fits in" and creates a "theological and christological surplus," pushing beyond "the splendor of the status quo," is his focus.[64]

---

59. Horsley, "Jesus and Empire," 90; Raheb, *Faith in the Face*, 98–99.

60. Horsley, "Jesus and Empire," 84–96. See Cone, *Black Theology of Liberation*, 123–36.

61. Horsley, "Jesus and Empire," 95.

62. Horsley, "Jesus and Empire," 96–97, 131–36.

63. Horsley, *Jesus and Empire*, 135–36. See Meeks, *First Urban Christians*.

64. Rieger, *Christ and Empire*, 9; see also 315–22.

In broader terms, it is the ongoing lure of empire in contemporary times that also makes post-colonial biblical and theological studies an ongoing necessity. Horsley, writing in the context of the USA, is correct to warn against a depoliticized reading of the Galilean Jesus that underestimates the role of empire in the life of the early Jesus movement and in American history and society. From the beginning, he argues, like Rome, the USA strived to be an empire and not just a republic.[65] He adds, "By contrast to the depoliticized Jesus of American imperial culture, among peoples subjected to the American empire Jesus has had direct political relevance and impact."[66] It is precisely this subject that the next chapter will address.

## CONCLUSION

This chapter has argued for the methodological and theological importance of coloniality. Methodologically, coloniality opens up the possibility of comparative and interdisciplinary analysis across distinct places and times, with a focus on the relationship between culture and power. The life of the mind is always also the life (or death) of the body. Scholars, however, in the field of post-colonialism, have been guilty of disappearing and silencing embodied religious experience and voice. Theologically, the place of historical and discursive subjugation is important for understanding the gospel of Jesus. More broadly, the need for constructive theological work that takes coloniality seriously is ongoing. The task in this chapter is described as a conversional process that turns toward the colonized Christ.

Inevitably, to turn toward the colonized Christ is to turn toward the crucified Christ. Post-colonial theology does not speak with one voice on the Christ crucified on an imperial cross. Rightly, there is suspicion of any reading of the cross that divinizes patriarchy by appealing to a passive son and an impassive father. Yet, even for those who have experienced coloniality and colonialism, the cross remains a complicated and complicating symbol not without liberative and transformative and even redemptive power. Cone, alert to the ambiguous and complicated history of interpretation, nonetheless sees in the crucified Christ someone who resisted supremacy:

> When one resists evil, suffering is an inevitable consequence of that resistance. To avoid suffering is to avoid resistance, and that

65. Horsley, *Jesus and Empire*, 137.
66. Horsley, *Jesus and Empire*, 148–49.

leaves evil unchallenged. King challenged the power structures of evil. That was why he was killed. King's suffering, and that of freedom fighters around the world, is redemptive when, like Jesus' cross, it inspires us to resist evil, knowing that suffering is the consequence. To resist evil is to participate in God's redemption of the world.[67]

The next chapter will further consider these issues by engaging with a recent and important work that seeks to develop a post-colonial reading of the cross centered on the characteristic of hybridization.

67. Cone, *God of the Oppressed*, xviii.

# 6

# Blood-Dimmed Tide

## A Hybridized Cross(ing)

... it is always up to us to specify ourselves whereas those who are in the dominant position retain their sense of power through the absence of their specificity.

—Wonhee Anne Joh[1]

... born of the Virgin Mary,
suffered under Pontius Pilate ...
crucified, dead, and buried ...

—Apostles' Creed

For Christians, the cross of Christ is the central site of post-colonialism. Jesus (double) crosses the empire by paying homage to its ordered and ordering power, and by menacing (disordering) its power through love. In exploring such a reading of the cross, this chapter identifies the fourth characteristic of post-colonial theology as hybridization. Wonhee Anne Joh provides a particularly rich reading, but one that is also complex as it faces coloniality while rejecting any reading that divinizes subjugation. As with many post-colonial texts, Joh's work depends on resources, theories, and technical vocabulary that make her work challenging to access.

1. Joh, *Heart of the Cross*, 17.

Nonetheless, it will be the aim of this chapter to provide just such an accessible reading of a post-colonial Christology in light of her book *Heart of the Cross*. The suffering (*han*) of Koreans and Korean Americans is the particular point of departure for her reading of the crucifixion as she seeks to provide a life-giving (*jeong*) understanding of the cross. For Joh, the death of Christ on the cross was deep loss (*han*). But it was more than *han*. It was also disruptive life. It was *jeong*. There was love (*jeong*) in Jesus' life and death.[2]

## SUFFERING *HAN*

Joh warns readers that any translation into English of *han* will remain unsatisfactory. It refers both to historical and psychological suffering. *Han* can be unconscious and conscious, it can be found in individuals and groups, and it can be active and passive. Andrew Sung Park sees its cause in "unjust psychosomatic repression, as well as . . . social, political, economic, and cultural oppression" and is expressed as "sadness, helplessness, hopelessness, resentment, hatred, and the will to revenge." It can be inactive (an acquiescent spirit) and active (an aggressive emotion). *Han* is caused by material, social, and political oppression, and is also the result of psychic experiences. *Han* is "frozen energy" that can implode negatively into revenge, fatalism, mental disorder, and even suicide. It can be converted into "fuel" for community building and social justice.[3] Joh finds Han Wang Sang's definition particularly helpful. "*Han* is a sense of unresolved resentment against injustices suffered, a sense of helplessness because of the overwhelming odds against ones' guts and bowels."[4] For Koreans, *han* is particularly associated with their experiences of empire. Japan occupied Korea from 1910 to 1945, and Joh's own family was involved in anti-imperialist resistance and suffered because of such resistance.[5] Compounding the suffering of Japanese racism and brutality is the racism and crisis in identity experienced by Korean Americans.[6] Thus, *han* is inextricably linked to the coloniality of Koreans in Korea but *han* is not necessarily limited to that experience alone.

2. Joh, *Heart of the Cross*, xxii.
3. Park, *Wounded Heart of God*, 10–34, 137–38.
4. Cited by Joh, *Heart of the Cross*, xxi.
5. Joh, *Heart of the Cross*, xvi.
6. Joh, *Heart of the Cross*, 47.

On the face of it, and unlike some major movements in African Christianity (see chapter 3), Korean Christianity came to be considered anti-imperialist and a galvanizing force against Japanese colonialism.[7] For example, in 1919, when the Korean Declaration of Independence was signed, only 1 percent of the population was Christian, yet thirty-three signatories of the declaration were Christian.[8] Christianity was influential in an emergent Korean nationalism and there is evidence that at least some foreign missionaries gave succor to the cause. However, missionaries also came in for criticism:

> The colonial rulers of Japan . . . tried very hard to suppress . . . [the] . . . growing influence of the Christian churches. . . . [R]egrettably, most of the missionaries who were sent to Korea belonged to denominations in the U.S that were tied to fundamentalism, and they did not want Korean Christians to get involved in political or social issues. Moreover, they went along with the religious policies of the Japanese colonial rulers and tried to transform Christianity into an individualistic, introspective and other-worldly religion.[9]

In the wake of partition in 1945 and the calamitous Korean War of 1950 to 1953, Christianity in (South) Korea would become stridently anti-Communist. Its anti-colonialist worldview was now directed at North Korea's backer, China. South Korea would also turn back to America, who would become its military and economic ally, and the church of the 1950s would give its full support to South Korean's first president, Syngman Rhee.[10] In the post-imperial era, Christianity struggled to maintain a "function of criticism."[11] Only in the 1970s, during a series of military dictatorships, did Christians regain a resistant voice. In the wake of the authoritarian regime of President Park Chung-hee, and an authoritarian change to the constitution, Christians in 1973 went into the streets in protest. The suppression of protest included lengthy prison sentences. In the midst of suppression,

7. Korean Christianity is of course more complex, not least read in light of the later war and considering the ties and influence to the US through, for example, American missionaries. That the US did not come to Korea's aid during the emergence of the nationalist movement also meant that in the 1920s the nationalist movement did exhibit an anti-Western spirit. See Stanley, *Christianity in the Twentieth Century*, 40–48.

8. Kim, "Korean Minjung Theology," 4–5; Park, "Korean Protestant Christianity," 59–64.

9. Kim, "Korean Minjung Theology," 4.

10. Stanley, *Christianity in the Twentieth Century*, 46–48.

11. Kim, "Korean Minjung Theology," 4.

especially against the most vulnerable and marginalized, and in the midst of demands for human rights, *minjung* theology was born. In 1975, Ahn Byung-Mu, a biblical scholar imprisoned for his opposition to the government, associated the *minjung* of Korea with the multitudes in Mark's Gospel: "Jesus did not work for the rich, authorities, the pious and intellectuals. He lived as a friend of the minjung at the side of the minjung, and died for them . . . ."[12] The "Theological Declaration of Korean Christians" (November 18, 1974) stated:

> [T]he poor become poor more and more, and their rights for existence are threatened by unjust intervention of the government and the unjust system of the economy. This (Lk 4:18–20) indicates that those who are poor economically, oppressed politically, blind physically or spiritually, and captivated in real life are liberated personally or collectively from such a bondage and lack, not only from spiritual bondage.[13]

Summarizing the significance of such theologizing, Kim simply states that many Korean Christians opposing the government were, at the same time, proclaiming a gospel that meant a salvation that is "always holistic and structural."[14]

Against the backdrop of various *minjung* movements that were Christian, that involved Christians, and that were non-Christian, theologians made their contribution.[15] Suh Nam-Dong, who also experienced imprisonment, summarized the significance of *minjung* theology. The subjects of history and the subjects of theology are not "kings, but the minjung. The minjung are not to be governed, but to be served. This is the direction of history. So, we have to follow this trend of history."[16] This stress on the *minjung* as the subjects of history is a particular emphasis of the *minjung* movements, and theologians made connections to the biblical exodus, the prophets, and to Jesus:[17]

> Minjung theology was generated through finding out the reality of the minjung. The minjung of Minjung Theology does not indicate one of the many items with which theology is to deal. The

12. Quoted by Kim, "Korean Minjung Theology," 8.

13. Quoted Kim, "Korean Minjung Theology," 7.

14. Kim, "Korean Minjung Theology," 8.

15. Kim, "Korean Minjung Theology in History," 168.

16. Quoted by Kim, "Korean Minjung Theology," 9.

17. Kim, "Korean Minjung Theology in History," 169.

discovery of minjung does not mean that the minjung appeared as the object for theological reflection. The discovery of the minjung means that a new way of doing theology was found. It opens a new perspective for doing theology. This new perspective necessarily brings about a change in the position of those who do theology. This is the Copernican revolution in the work of theology. The discovery of the minjung means the standing at the side of the minjung and choosing the minjung. When we see society and history from the standpoint of minjung and through the eyes of minjung, the upside down structure of historical and social realities is to be set right. . . . Just as the first step in theology is an obedient response to God's call, so the first step to the minjung theology is to hear the voice of minjung and to stand at the side of the minjung. . . . [T]heologians should be converted by the minjung.[18]

Despite this, in more recent times, and during the height of the movements in the 1980s, Christians who did not have a thoroughgoing theological understanding of *minjung* failed to see the ongoing relevance of the movement when social changes were made. However, a theological rationale for *minjung* can be identified that justifies ongoing work:

Theologically speaking . . . minjung includes both the oppressed whom Jesus loved and the followers of the life-giving spirit. It was this minjung-spirit which helped some Korean Christians to see the life-oppressing spirit in the form of totalitarian social structures in the 1970s and to willingly sacrifice themselves for others and join the minjung movements. History is viewed through various perspectives including race, nation and civilization. It is quite possible to interpret history in terms of minjung-spirit, which encourages us to cherish all life and existence as God's precious gift. Everyone, poor or not, educated or not, who joins to promote the expansion of this spirit can be minjung.[19]

This more expansive view of *minjung* theologizing correlates well with an expansive view of *han.* Joh quotes Jan Hoon Lee, who considers *han* a particular Korean concept that ultimately cannot be bound to Korea. Rather, it "speaks" to all humans of "suffering and creativity" at social, structural, and psychological levels.[20] Park further defines *han*, in relation to a capitalist global economy, patriarchy, and cultural and racial discrimination, as

18. Kim, "Korean Minjung Theology," 9.

19. Kim, "Korean Minjung Theology in History," 172.

20. Joh, *Heart of the Cross,* 20; Lee, *Exploration of the Inner Wounds,* 6.

"the critical wound of the heart." He adds, "*Han* reverberates in the souls of survivors of the Holocaust, Palestinians in the occupied territories, victims of racial discrimination, battered wives, victims of child-molestation, the unemployed and exploited workers."[21]

For Joh, *han* is not something simply visited upon the oppressed but is also present in the "deeper psyches of the oppressors."[22] Such insight distinguishes a post-colonial theology from a liberation theology where the latter often "assumes the innocence of *han*-ridden people."[23] Post-colonial theologizing in contrast recognizes that "*han* and *jeong*, oppressor and oppressed, coexist within the individual."[24] "*Han* is not innocent. Innocent suffering is one cause of *han*, but once it becomes *han* it loses its innocence by becoming the source of evil forces that seek revenge on other innocent victims. *Han*, however, can be transformed, just as one personality can be transformed, into a more mature form."[25] This language of transformation raises the possibility of *jeong* and the cross of Christ as a symbol of such transformative grace.

## FINDING *JEONG*

Central to a Korean understanding of deep relationality, *jeong* ensures that *han* does not have the final say.[26] *Jeong* is associated with "compassion, love, vulnerability, and acceptance of heterogeneity as essential to life."[27] As with *han*, Joh makes clear that the concept loses much in translation and cannot be captured by a single English word. Nonetheless, she offers the following: "when the characters that create the word for *jeong* are examined separately, one character means 'heart' another means 'life' when used as a noun but when used as a verb means 'something arising, emerging out of in-betweenness.' It signifies a genesis of becoming that is intimately linked with connectedness and heart."[28] *Jeong* "embodies the invisible traces of

---

21. Quoted by Joh, *Heart of the Cross*, 20–21; See Park, *Wounded Heart of God*, 10, 45–67.

22. Joh, *Heart of the Cross*, 21.

23. Joh, *Heart of the Cross*, 25.

24. Joh, *Heart of the Cross*, 16.

25. Lee, *Exploration of the Inner Wounds*, 151. See also 135–62.

26. Joh, "Transgressive Power of Jeong," 153.

27. Joh, *Heart of the Cross*, xxi, xxiv.

28. Joh, "Transgressive Power of Jeong," 156.

compassion in relationships."[29] It "smooths harsh feelings, such as dislike or even hate." It enriches relationships, not least in the way that it complicates notions of binary and oppositional categories such as oppressor and oppressed. It is "the power embodied in redemptive relationships" and redemption "emerges within relationality that recognizes the power and presence of *jeong* to move us toward life."[30] *Jeong* defines subjectivity/identity of the self as always in relationship with others. It is the power of love. It is the clarity to see complexity. It is openness to others. It is compassionate solidarity in overcoming suffering and alienation and it is more than all of these.[31] In a bid to prevent the concept from being defined simply in abstract terms, Joh turns to the *han*-filled experience of a partitioned Korea and a cultural representation of the deep gloom partition causes. In the 2000 film *Joint Security Area,* Joh sees a "glimpse" of the meaning and significance of *jeong*.[32]

Borders and boundaries and the transgressing of them are themes common in post-colonial texts. The identity crises and hybridizing that borders cause become sites for post-colonial thought. At the drawing of the Irish border in 1922, Yeats, sojourning in England, experienced "deep gloom" reminiscent of the aforementioned definitions of *han*:

> I am in deep gloom about Ireland. . . . I see no escape from bitterness. . . . When men are very bitter, death & ruin draw them on as a rabbit is supposed to be drawn on by the dancing of the fox, . . . all may be blood & misery. If that comes we may abandon Ballylee to the owls & the rats, & England too . . . and live in some far off land. Should England & Ireland be divided beyond all hope of remedy, what else could one do for the children's sake, or one's own work. I could not bring them to Ireland where they would inherit bitterness, nor leave them in an England where being Irish by tradition, & my family & fame they would be in an unnatural condition of mind & grow as many Irish men . . . sour and argumentative.[33]

The boundaries themselves—geographical, cultural, historical, political, and psychological—become sites of generativity referred to in the

29. Joh, *Heart of the Cross,* xxi.

30. Joh, *Heart of the Cross,* xxi.

31. Joh, "Transgressive Power of Jeong," 152–56.

32. Joh, *Heart of the Cross,* 31–41.

33. From a 1921 letter of W. B. Yeats to Olivia Shakespear, quoted in Foster, *W. B. Yeats: A Life II,* 204.

literature as "in-between space," "interstitial space," or "third space."[34] *Joint Security Area* depicts one such space and demonstrates its capacity for transformation (*jeong*). The film centers on an investigation into the death of two North Korean soldiers and the wounding of another at a militarized meeting place between the North and the South. In the wake of the shooting, conflicting accounts emerge. The lead investigator into the deaths of these soldiers who are posted along the demilitarized zone close to the so-called Bridge of No Return[35] is a Swiss-born Korean officer, Sophie Lang. She too will become implicated in the boundaried and transgressive identities and actions at work in Korean history and culture when it is later discovered that her father was a North Korean general. Her own father had crossed the Bridge of No Return in 1953, but refused to continue to align himself with either North or South Korea and eventually found his way to Switzerland. This disclosure allows the South Koreans to press for her dismissal from the case. However, before her early departure she examines the deposition of the surviving North Korean solider named Gyung-Pil and the confession of Soo-Hyuk, the South Korean solider who has confessed to the shooting. Soo-Hyuk claims that he was kidnapped and the death of the soldiers was the result of his escape. This contradicts the deposition of the wounded Gyung-Pil, whose account accuses Soo-Hyuk of storming into their station, killing two of his comrades and wounding him. As the film develops, it becomes apparent that they are covering up what actually happened in order to protect each other. What has happened is *jeong*. The background to the incident was not hate, but love. The soldiers, mimicking the expected posturing of two sides at war, were in actual fact undermining the martial culture and boundaried division of Korea.

Unlike the investigators, viewers of the movie know the back story. Weeks before the shooting, Soo-Hyuk had become separated from his patrol and strayed into the North. Worse, he managed to get snagged on a landmine tripwire. This is when Gyung-Pil and his comrade Woo-Jin discovered him. Instead of abandoning him to his fate, they rescue him and a deep friendship develops that involves letter exchanges and northern visits across the Bridge of No Return. Soo-Hyuk eventually comes to call Gyung-Pil "older brother." The nightly visits that eventually also involve Soo-Hyuk's colleague, Sung-Shik, result in "the sharing of stories, laughter,

34. Joh, *Heart of the Cross*, 62–66.

35. The site where, in 1953, prisoners of war chose to cross into either North or South Korea on the condition that they would never return again. Joh, *Heart of the Cross*, 32.

jokes, and idiosyncrasies regarding each other, as well as through sharing of their personal *han* and mutual collective *han*, they experience *jeong*. The depth of *jeong* that they experience becomes the most important disclosure at the end of the film. . . . *Jeong* is what allows them to see one another's vulnerability."[36]

Despite this *jeong*, and against a backdrop of increased military tension, it becomes apparent to the friends/brothers that their visits must cease. During a farewell visit they are discovered by a superior officer and, in the chaos, the North Korean guards are shot by Soo-Hyuk. Woo-Jin is shot dead. The superior officer is wounded and then, execution-style, killed not by Soo-Hyuk, but by his Northern Korean "older brother," Gyung-Pil. Through a series of flashbacks and interviews conducted by Sophie Lang the truth is delivered. *Jeong* in the film is "vulnerable intimacy forged in the borderlands."[37] For Joh, the film "unfolds the layers of ways that *jeong* expresses itself relationally."[38] Reflecting on the film, she writes:

> [W]hat makes this film interesting is that presences of *jeong* seem not only to counter . . . *han*-filled ideology but also overcome a powerful militaristic ideology. Thus, in the interstices of *Joint Security Area* we find neither clear heroes nor clear villains. The only clear and powerfully redemptive aspect of the film is the experience of *jeong*, which changes the lives of those who come into it relationally through their recognition of mutual vulnerability and humanity. The power of *jeong* allows for a particular kind of audacity, as characters risk the consequences of disobedience by crossing militarized and ideological boundaries and as they risk their hearts by becoming vulnerable relationally.[39]

The border and the fear-filled ideologies that maintain it bear "hardly any significance in relationships filled with *jeong*."[40] The film illustrates that the division and pain of the demilitarized zone (DMZ) is *han*, but that this same site "ironically becomes a site of powerful *jeong*."[41] The location of this *jeong* is important for Joh and will play a role when she seeks to relate it to a reading of the cross:

36. Joh, *Heart of the Cross*, 35.
37. Joh, *Heart of the Cross*, 36.
38. Joh, *Heart of the Cross*, 31.
39. Joh, *Heart of the Cross*, 31.
40. Joh, *Heart of the Cross*, 32.
41. Joh, *Heart of the Cross*, 39.

*Jeong* experienced at the edges often provokes and evokes power of radical change. However, *jeong* rooted within the center of power, advocated within the dominant power structure, works as an accomplice in the oppression of people in the name of *jeong*. I suggest that the experience of *jeong* needs to be distinguished into aspects of *who* is the experiencing agent and *where* it is being experienced.[42]

The particularity of *jeong* in the fretful crossing and recrossing of this Korean site of *han* points poignantly toward what it is Joh wants to say about the cross of Christ. A site of division, militarism, and occupation is also a site of friendship, love, and the subversion of division, militarism, and occupation. This place embodies both *han* and *jeong* just as the cross "works symbolically to embody both *han*/abjection and *jeong*/love."[43] She sees her reading of the cross as emerging from the experience of the Korean people, drawing from Korean understandings of the cross, and rejecting readings that make the cross complicit in coloniality.

## A COLONIAL CROSS

Unveiling "traditional" readings of the cross that promote and perpetuate notions of submission, and even subjection, as being laudable, true signs of devotion to Christ, is to unveil readings complicit in coloniality.[44] Joh gives some detail to the kinds of readings of the cross that she seeks to challenge. These readings she depicts as traditional, Anselmian (after the eleventh-century scholar Anselm of Canterbury),[45] conventional, and inherently violent. The dominance of such readings can be explained, Joh argues, by the dominance of patriarchal understandings of relationships embedded in much Christian theology. These understandings of how relationships work emphasize the dispassionate and distinct power of the father and the need for payment or satisfaction in the face of offense. They sacralize violence, and they glorify the sacrifice of a helpless victim. When the cross is read within such a patriarchal frame it is stripped of its power to subvert such power relations, and instead serves to embed "oppressive

42. Joh, *Heart of the Cross*, 41.
43. Joh, *Heart of the Cross*, 39.
44. Joh, *Heart of the Cross*, 71.
45. Park, *Wounded Heart of God*, 112–14.

power dynamics."[46] In short, the cross can be used to sanction and promote coloniality. Echoing Marx, Joh argues that such a theory means "the cross and its attendant patriarchal misappropriations have drugged many oppressed people."[47] There has been particular danger in such theologizing for women. As Joh notes, "By stressing the traditional concepts of suffering and self-denial, Korean women are often dealt two messages: suffering is justified, and oppression is a natural part of reality and, in its consequent spiritualization of suffering, a 'Christian virtue.'"[48]

For Joh, the churches need to undergo theological rehabilitation. They need to be weaned off readings of the cross that divinize dominating patriarchal power by demanding the "faithful" response of acquiescent submission. To replace the substance of divinized power-abuse, Joh asks if we can "not see the cross as . . . signifying a risk that one encounters as one lives in the fullness of *jeong*?"[49] There is a vital insight here. The liberative potency of the cross is found precisely in the ways it overthrows old patriarchal ways of thinking. Its liberative potency is prevented when the cross is read in ways that further embed patriarchal ways of thinking. The cross is not the "blood dimmed tide" wherein violence and patriarchal power relations are baptized. The cross overflows in *jeong* and washes away such ways of thinking, reading, and acting.

Joh does not condemn in their entirety readings of the cross that stress suffering and self-surrender. Indeed, she finds that they can provide limited potency against ideas and practices of coloniality. One such reading she associates with the work of Jürgen Moltmann. He seeks to go beyond "traditional Christology," but ultimately remains in its thrall. Moltmann sees himself as moving beyond a traditional metaphysical Christology to a historical Christology. He seeks to take seriously human embodiment within the wider natural world. He seeks to read the cross and the sufferings of Christ as sufferings that, because they are apocalyptic, have universal significance. Christ's sufferings are the signs or the birth pains of a new age, and thus have significance for Israel, for the church, and for creation. Moltmann begins by reading the cross in a way that counters a seeming dispassionate and distant Father. The Father was involved in the sufferings

---

46. See Joh, *Heart of the Cross*, 71–82. See too Coakley, "In Defense of Sacrifice," 18.

47. Joh, *Heart of the Cross*, 87.

48. Joh, *Heart of the Cross*, 86.

49. Joh, *Heart of the Cross*, 84.

of the Son.[50] Moltmann seeks to demonstrate the solidarity of the Father with the Son on the cross:

> The Father suffers the death of the Son. He suffers it in the infinite pain of his love for the Son. The death of the Son therefore corresponds to the pain of the Father. . . . What happens on Golgotha reaches into the very depths of the Godhead and therefore puts its impress on the trinitarian life of God in eternity. In Christian faith the cross is always at the center of the Trinity, for the cross reveals the heart of the triune God, which beats for his whole creation.[51]

Nonetheless, Moltmann emphasizes the abandonment of the Son by the Father, and thus can write: "the Father has forsaken 'his own Son' . . . and has given him up to death. . . . The Father forsakes the Son 'for us'—that is, he allows him to die so that he may become the God and Father of the forsaken. That Father 'gives up' the Son that through him he may become the Father of all those who are 'given up.'"[52] Joh sees here an eternalizing of the father's dominance, a sacralization of violence, and faithfulness defined as passivity and surrender. Instead of power relations of mutuality, at the center of the faith stands a cross that signifies an "oppressive patriarchalism" and the "dysfunctional symbolic power of Father-over-Son." Joh is particularly alert to the impact such theologizing has on the human psyche, and especially on the psyche of women.[53] Thus, whatever else a post-colonial reading of the cross will bring, it will bring a reading that seeks to subvert understandings of the cross that perpetuate domineering power relations. In other words, while Moltmann sees himself as providing a reading of the cross that is historical, Joh sees him do just the opposite. She is critical of theologizing about the cross that leaves it "tidy" or "untainted" through elevating it into a metaphysical realm beyond the blood-soaked reality of imperial brutality:

> Moltmann lets the work of redemption be done within the divine Trinitarian relationality. What has happened to the participation of humanity in redemptive work? . . . Does not the work of redemption happen in the process of the historical realm? What happens when the event of the cross becomes divinized?[54]

50. Moltmann, *Way of Jesus Christ*, xvi, 151–52.

51. Moltmann, *Way of Jesus Christ*, 173.

52. Moltmann, *Way of Jesus Christ*, 173. See Joh, *Heart of the Cross*, 82.

53. Joh, *Heart of the Cross*, 81–88.

54. Joh, *Heart of the Cross*, 78.

To interpret the cross in such an "inner-Trinitarian" manner seems, ultimately, to undermine the idea that Jesus experienced abandonment and abjection. Doing so distances Christ from coloniality, while at the same time giving the impression that suffering is somehow essential to the nature of divinity.[55] Indeed, Moltmann states it plainly: "God and suffering are no longer contradictions. . . . God's being is in suffering and the suffering is in God's being itself . . . ."[56] Such a theology of the cross "eternalizes" suffering. But not only is it eternalized, it is also hierarchicalized because the suffering of the Father and the Son remain distinct.[57] Joh writes, "Despite the emphasis on the relationality of the Trinity embodied on the cross, . . . the Father takes the initiative. The Son remains passive . . . ."[58] Such theologizing, given the reality of coloniality and how women particularly suffer under relationships and structures of subjugation, means that Joh looks for more in a post-colonial understanding of the cross. A theology of the cross that further embeds *han* is neither transformative nor redemptive. A Christian understanding of transformation will need to be a pathway away from *han* and toward *jeong* because both are on the cross. To what extent Joh's post-colonial reading can provide this will be the focus of the next section.

## A POST-COLONIAL CROSS

> More and more, theologians are careful as they articulate the power of the cross. This caution is maintained because of our awareness of the potential to reimbue Christology with the remaining shackles of patriarchalism and imperialism. Moreover, this desire to articulate a liberative theology of the cross becomes urgent precisely because we "know" and have "experienced" the power of the cross in liberative ways.[59]

*Joint Security Area* evidences subversive action as the main characters traverse forbidden terrain, both literally and relationally. As characters with relatively little power, they do not undermine the militaristic binary opposition of South/North through a "full frontal assault," which is "usually

55. Joh, *Heart of the Cross*, 78–79.

56. Moltmann, *Crucified God*, 227.

57. Joh, *Heart of the Cross*, 81.

58. Joh, *Heart of the Cross*, 81. Moltmann, *Way of Jesus Christ*, 73.

59. Joh, *Heart of the Cross*, 90.

a luxury afforded to the already powerful."[60] Rather, as marginal actors on this transnational stage of ideology, fear, and hate, their subversive journey toward *jeong* is secretive and guileful. Joh sees here a correlation with the cross as a historical in-between, marginal, colonized space transgressed by Christ. The cross is a site of deep *han* and of deep *jeong*. The temptation for theologians like Moltmann to make the site of the cross an "inner-Trinitarian" space will be resisted by a post-colonial reading. The cross was erected on colonized ground and a colonized Galilean was executed by Roman authority. In short, the cross was political. Jesus was not so much sacrificed by the will of God as executed by a "repressive empire."[61] This then is not the passive sacrifice of a victim, but a revolutionary and resistant act against the power of the empire.[62] Joh particularly draws on Mark Lewis Taylor's work in *The Executed God* to further elucidate this. In Joh's terms, the cross (double) crosses the empire. In Taylor's terms, the cross "steals the show from imperial power."[63]

Taylor is correct to see the ministry and passion of Christ as adversarial and anti-imperialist. As a Galilean, he came from a heavily taxed rural village setting that was a frontier important for Rome to keep under control. It is of no small significance that at a Jerusalem trial Jesus was accused of stirring up trouble "from Galilee where he began" (Luke 23:5).[64] Jesus was formed in a resistant Galilean ethos. A post-colonial reading of the cross seeks to recover the historical and political dynamics of such an interface and the "adversarial politics . . . lodged in the ways of the Galilean Jesus."[65] This Galilean, like the characters in *Joint Security Area*, does not choose a direct assault against the empire that would be easily snuffed out. Rather, his words, actions, and body "theatrically" (icon-elastically) interrupt and subvert the empire with a dramatic confrontation enacting a different ethic:[66]

---

60. Taylor, *Executed God*, 101.

61. Joh, *Heart of the Cross*, 73.

62. Joh, *Heart of the Cross*, 74.

63. Taylor, *Executed God*, 99.

64. Taylor, *Executed God*, 76.

65. Taylor, *Executed God*, 78. Criticism exists that in minjung theology a rather "generalized" christologizing dominates. See Kim, "Korean Minjung Theology in History," 167–82.

66. See Taylor, *Executed God*, 109–19.

The spectacle of crucifixion, which long functioned for *Pax Roma-na* to beat down courage and resistance, now becomes the center of another narrative about power, a story that displaces Rome. In the gospel narratives, the cross is still a spectacle symbol, a great show, but now one that celebrates triumph over the crucifying empire and all that supports it. Rome is rendered by its own cross of torture an interim power. The spectacle of the Roman cross is now wielded against terrorizing Rome. That is to steal the show.[67]

The "theatrics of counterterror" that Jesus plays out disempower and displace the authority and centrality of Caesar. Jesus is an "anti-Caesar." A new gospel is declared that can resource and energize a Jesus movement of resistance that takes an adversarial stance against fear and hate, organizes against fear and hate, and enacts dramatic action.[68]

A post-colonial Christology does not merely provide a reading of Jesus within the *han*-ridden material context of political and social oppression visited upon oppressed peoples by empire; also important in analyzing the "dynamics of oppression" is the concept of abjection.[69] As has already been seen, because *han* is also a psychic experience, the cross will also be read for the related transformative effect on the human heart. The unraveling of this deep *han* can only take place through a healing of relationships within the human heart and between human hearts. "We might be able to wrestle some justice out of the unjust, but we cannot extract the profound trans-formation of the causes of injustice that come only through love/*jeong*."[70] The defeat of the oppressors through cutting them off (*dan*) cannot achieve such deep decolonizing healing. Only the power of *jeong* can heal. This is why Joh seeks after a Christology of *jeong*.[71] In explaining this psychic unraveling, she particularly turns to key concepts from the work of the philosopher and psychoanalyst Julia Kristeva. The depth of *han* in psychic experience goes back to the earliest moments of a human's life. For Kristeva, we journey from the "semiotic" (associated with the mother's womb) to the "symbolic" (associated with the world beyond the womb) by becoming speaking subjects. However, this journey toward subjectivity involves the earliest of all traumas, the separation of the child from its mother's womb.

67. Taylor, *Executed God*, 104.
68. Taylor, *Executed God*, 128–37.
69. Taylor, *Executed God*, 92.
70. Taylor, *Executed God*, 106.
71. Taylor, *Executed God*, 91.

The foundational moment for the self is the "inaugural loss" of the mother's body.[72] This is "original *han*" and the "original wound." As the separated child develops into a speaking subject, she or he jettisons all those things that stand in the way of entering into the symbolic realm and becoming a fully-fledged self. The semiotic is "discharged" into the symbolic. In other words, the preverbal desires and the unconscious drives of the child are articulated in symbols, that is to say, language. The child comes to the realization that there is a distinction between child and mother, between self and subject, between other and object. The child comes, further, to understand that language is not simply the discharge of energy and expression in "coos and babbles" (the semiotic), but can also be referential and point to things beyond itself (the symbolic).[73] This journey is referred to as abjection and should be understood as an object and a process through which individuals and groups move into the symbolic:

> The abject is what one spits out, rejects, almost violently excludes from oneself: sour milk, excrement, even a mother's engulfing embrace. What is abjected is radically excluded but never banished altogether. It hovers at the periphery of one's existence, constantly challenging one's own tenuous borders of selfhood. What makes something abject and not simply repressed is that it does not entirely disappear from consciousness. It remains as both an unconscious and a conscious threat to one's own clean and proper self. The abject is what does not respect boundaries. It beseeches and pulverizes the subject.[74]

The abject defines and threatens the borders of the self just as the loss of the mother's body brings both distinction and danger to a newborn:

> In Kristeva's work the semiotic is explicitly maternal and feminine while the symbolic is paternal, the Law of the Father. The abject then is all that is expelled, repelled, excluded in the process of identification and transition into the unified self and into the symbolic precisely because the abject threatens the stability of this transition from the semiotic into the symbolic. However the subject is never stable in the symbolic because the abject, the repressed or the repelled abject, always haunts at the edges or in the depths of the self in the symbolic.[75]

72. Kristeva, *Powers of Horror*, 5–18. Also see 101–3.

73. McAfee, *Julia Kristeva*, 32–35.

74. McAfee, *Julia Kristeva*, 46.

75. Joh, *Heart of the Cross*, xxii–xxiii.

Abjection is what we "desperately attempt to repress or expel." It is the boundary of the self or the group, "Transgressing borders, abjection is a witness to society's precarious hold over the fluid and disorderly aspects of individual and collective psyches."[76] Haunting the symbolic community of regulated social performance, according to logic and law and despite abjection, the semiotic is never completely absent.[77] It remains even in the world beyond the womb, seen in music, dance, and particular kinds of poetry.[78] Such feminist psychoanalytic theory is critical of Freud. In entering into the symbolic, his concept of ego formation depends on the primacy of the father and the marginalization of the mother and the semiotic. The role of the female is subordinated. This, in feminist critique, means that a less-than-healthy human being develops. A speaking subject whose identity is predicated upon separation and even "matricidal drives" causes a deep sense of loss, abjection, *han*, and individual and collective unconscious violence.[79] "Even prior to any social forms of oppression, the subject has . . . already encountered and experienced 'original *han*' through the abjection of the maternal and the self. The social being is constituted through the force of expulsion."[80] Given such expulsion and the psychic wounds of abjection, how is the cross to be read?

Moltmann's reading of the cross, which Joh does not in the end entirely reject, colonizes the cross by assimilating it into the symbolic dimension of meaning. The cross, in his reading, becomes an "internal divine affair."[81] The depth of *han* and abjection is tidied up and domesticated. It is explainable within the borders and boundaries of a (symbolic) Trinitarian theology. In contrast, the key to understanding Joh's reading of the cross, in light of feminist psychoanalyst understanding of abjection, is that the cross signifies not only *jeong*/love, but the return of what humans have been repressing in their journey to and in the symbolic. The cross is the site of the return of the repressed (the abject) as "the refused refuse" and "refugee of our psyche." It is as if Jesus on the cross is the "crucified people," among whom are included the hybrid Korean-Americans who continue

76. Joh, *Heart of the Cross*, 92.

77. Kristeva, *Powers of Horror*, 91.

78. Interestingly, Kristeva points to Irish literature and James Joyce as one writer that "breaks out" the abject. See Kristeva, *Powers of Horror*, 22–23.

79. Joh, *Heart of the Cross*, 106–7. See Kristeva, *Powers of Horror*, 71–79, 90–112.

80. Joh, *Heart of the Cross*, 110.

81. Joh, *Heart of the Cross*, 105.

to suffer racism, sexism, and classism. Jesus is the "excommunicated, the exterminated abjects of self, memory and history."[82] Joh says, "The event on the cross is a 'God event,' but it is also an abject event. It is not Someone Else on the cross; the cross is full of the abjected other. The cross does not symbolize the death and suffering of one historical figure but rather signifies and points to the abjection of the other as the return of the repressed."[83]

In such a reading, Jesus is not the lone individualized hero. Rather, the cross returns that maternal generativity that problematizes an easy distinction between self and other. The Christ of *jeong* is both Jesus and the community of Jesus.[84] To make this point, Joh quotes Rita Nakashima Brock: "Jesus is like a white cap on a wave . . . it rests on the enormous pushing power of the sea."[85] The solidarity of the cross in view here is not, as is foundational to Moltmann, that between father and son. The solidarity being stressed here is between the subjected Jesus as a colonized Galilean and colonized others as the subjected Jesus. But this cruciform abjection and *jeong* goes even further than destabilizing the identity of the colonized and the Christ. Jesus, in the midst of colonization, exists in the "in-between" demonstrating *jeong* to foreigners, compatriots, collaborators, and the voiceless. The way of the cross does not only destabilize the binaries of Christ and colonized, it transgresses and destabilizes the simple dualisms of colonized/colonizer, friend/enemy, liberator/oppressor associated with many revolutionaries. This is indeed a vulnerable intimacy forged in the borderlands that displaces the way of limited liberation that depends on building up one's identity over against the identity of the other.[86] Jesus opted for "transformation through the power of *jeong* in connectedness."[87] Joh quotes Elizabeth Johnson as illustrative of this: "We seek an understanding that does not divide power and compassionate love in a dualistic framework that identifies love with a resignation of power and the exercise of power with a denial of love. Rather, we seek to integrate these two seeing love as the shape in which divine power appears."[88]

82. Joh, *Heart of the Cross*, 100, 119. For a powerful reading with similar resonances, see Cone, *Cross and the Lynching*.

83. Joh, *Heart of the Cross*, 77.

84. Joh, *Heart of the Cross*, 98.

85. Joh, *Heart of the Cross*, 98; Brock, *Journeys by Heart*, 67.

86. Joh, "Transgressive Power of Jeong," 156.

87. Joh, "Transgressive Power of Jeong," 157.

88. Joh, "Transgressive Power of Jeong," 162.

Further, this reading disrupts the tidiness of "doctrinal theology" and challenges atonement theories that reduce the *han*/abjection and *jeong*/love of the cross to legalistic transactions of debt and payment.[89] *Jeong* is "the power embodied in redemptive relationships."[90] This return of the abject opens up the "possibility of our redemption."[91] For abjection/*han* and *jeong*/love are seen as simultaneously present on the cross. Thus, an understanding and experience of redemption as relationality and not sacrifice emerges. While Joh rejects Moltmann's framing of the cross in inner-Trinitarian terms, she does see his reading of the cross as "revealing an irreducibly and divinely felt depth of suffering" that is close to her understanding of "what Jesus would have experienced as he embodied the power of *jeong*."[92] Jesus' suffering signifies embodied *jeong* in solidarity with the abject and, at the same time, challenges the powers that repress *jeong*.[93] In this, Joh sees herself as presenting a new way of understanding the cross *via* this powerful concept of *jeong*. Salvation ultimately concerns the "'intensity of divine presence' in relationship."[94] For if *han*, in part, is disintegrating selves and relationships (seen clearly in *Joint Security Area*), then self-giving *jeong* for the other, with the other, and as the other, is the power to heal such disintegration.

## CONCLUSION

As with many texts in the post-colonial field, an obvious criticism of Joh's work is its dependence on specialized argot. The dense material of the *Heart of the Cross* deserves further elucidation, and had that happened, a much larger book or even two books would have resulted. However, it is equally correct to say that the complexity of the language often reflects the complexity of the situation. Coloniality impacts a range of interconnected phenomena across a range of cultures and histories and this is evident in Joh's narration of Korean-American experiences. Given this, a range of analyses across a number of fields, and the borrowing, adaptation, and hybridization of diverse methods from a variety of disciplines, is inevitable. Those

89. Joh, *Heart of the Cross*, 111.

90. Joh, *Heart of the Cross*, xxi.

91. Joh, *Heart of the Cross*, 95, 103, 118.

92. Joh, *Heart of the Cross*, 100.

93. Joh, *Heart of the Cross*, 101.

94. Joh, *Heart of the Cross*, 102–3.

especially from dominant cultures would do well to spend time reading and slowly becoming accustomed to the language, concepts, analyses, and proposals of thinkers such as Wonhee Anne Joh. In the following chapter, further reflection on Joh's work and feminist readings of the cross will be submitted. I will particularly revisit the contention that love and the deep relationality at work in the world require the abandonment of the language of sacrifice.

# 7

# Implications
## Hybridizing Sacrifice

> There can be no doubt, that a tribe including many members who, from possessing in a high degree the spirit of patriotism, fidelity, obedience, courage, and sympathy, were always ready to aid one another, and to sacrifice themselves for the common good would be victorious over most other tribes; and this would be natural selection.

—Charles Darwin[1]

Joh hybridizes a reading of the cross with historical, cultural, psychological, and theological resources borne out of the experience of Koreans and Korean-Americans. She appeals to *Joint Security Area* as one means to unveil a deep relationality that illustrates what *jeong* means. This reading of *Joint Security Area* is contested. Indeed, the movie may be suggestive of violent sacrifice. Instead of eschewing the language of sacrifice entirely, this chapter will submit, in light of Joh's depiction of *jeong* in Jesus' ministry, that the language of sacrifice is consonant with a post-colonial reading of the cross.

---

1. Quoted by Coakley in *Sacrifice Regained*, 21; Darwin, *Descent of Man*.

## FINDING THE HATE

1. If possible, watch *Joint Security Area*. Write a short synopsis of the plot. What major theme did you detect in the movie?

2. If you do not speak Korean, what expression, image, or term in your first language captures something similar to Joh's definition of *han*? In your context, where is *han* found?

3. How does Joh's definition of *han* help you understand the circumstances of Jesus' crucifixion?

A strategic essentialism is sometimes adopted by those who are seeking to overcome hate.[2] Yet, this is a dangerous move. In the case of the early Yeats, a strategic Irish essentialism ran the risk of embedding racist constructions of Irish people. In the case of Joh, a strategic feminist essentialism runs the risk of embedding already existing sexist, racist, or imperialist constructs that presume or promote ideals of homogeneous identities.[3] Further, a strategic essentialism may psychically reinforce the dissonance that people in coloniality experience by distancing the reality of their everyday experience from an identity and a home that seems ever out of reach:

> For many people, home is always on many thresholds, such that these people are not quite fully allowed entrance but always live on the borderlands of many realities. Home then is not only contingent on many different dynamics but also always provisional so that we are strangers in our supposed "homeland" as well as in our new places of being. As a result one repeatedly feels out of place within what are familiar but also differing worlds. This unsettling feeling causes us to scrutinize questions of settlement so "as to make it easier for the diversely unsettled ones to bear the anxieties of unwonted seclusion."[4]

Korean North Americans particularly experience *han* in a hybridized identity, belonging fully neither to Korea nor to the United States of America.[5] As has been seen in each chapter of this book, a sense of what might be termed "unbelonging" is a common trait of those experiencing

2. Joh, *Heart of the Cross*, 7.
3. Joh, *Heart of the Cross*, 8–11.
4. Joh, *Heart of the Cross*, 9. She cites here Minh-ha, *When the Moon Waxes Red*, 194.
5. Joh, *Heart of the Cross*, 118–19.

colonialism or coloniality. In post-colonial literature, this unbelonging is more constructively rendered as "interstitial" or as a "third space." Bhabha explains it in typical Daedalian style:

> The intervention of the Third Space of enunciation, which makes the structure of meaning and reference an ambivalent process, destroys the mirror of representation in which cultural knowledge is customarily revealed as an integrated, open, expanding code. Such an intervention quite properly challenges our sense of the historical identity of culture as a homogenizing, unifying force, authenticated by the originary Past. . . . It is only when we understand that all cultural statements and systems are constructed in this contradictory and ambivalent space of enunciation, that we begin to understand why hierarchical claims to the inherent originality or "purity" of cultures are untenable . . .[6]

Whatever else the theorizing points to, it points to the in-betweenness experienced because of colonialism and coloniality. It points to the fantasy of a pristine foundation for personal, cultural, or ecclesial identity. It points to borrowings and hybridizations at work in human constructions of identities and societies. In such circumstances, *han* is, as has been seen, a deep sense of ongoing resentment against injustice. Living in a perpetual in-betweenness and the hatred that, in this case, Korean-Americans have faced, it is of little surprise that a theologian like Joh seeks the theological significance of hybridization. The fantasy of a pure foundation and sanitized point of departure is ultimately rejected. A post-colonial theology begins amidst the hate. Joh recognizes her own dynamic hybridized identity and this alerts her to the possibility of the hybrid nature of all identities. "Cultural spaces are unfixed, unsettled, porous, and hybrid."[7] Arising, then, from historical migrations and countermigrations, there is also movement and countermovement among key characteristics and categories in post-colonial literature. Joh captures this with some beauty when she writes the "metaphor of 'journey' embodies both the remembering of our past roots

---

6. Bhabha, *Location of Culture*, 54–55.

7. Bhabha, *Location of Culture*, 51. For a criticism of the "valorization" of hybridization as itself predicated upon binarism and as a privileged "identity category," see Hogan, *Empire and Poetic Voice*, 4–20. To avoid Hogan's criticism, this study does not want to theorize about the term abstractly, but simply point to specific cases where, in the face of subjugation, it opens up creative and liberative responses and, more particularly, theological imagination.

and the forging of new routes." Joh calls such a journey "sacred."[8] Amidst the strategic ploys toward decolonization and amidst bloody patriarchy, *jeong* is possible. As we have seen, Joh interprets *Joint Security Area* as an artistic glimpse of what *jeong* might mean in relational migration amidst militarized hate.

Joh's perspective on *Joint Security Area* is contested. The boundaried existence of the characters, their transgressions of those boundaries, and their growing experience of *jeong* in the midst of fear and hate, should not occlude a reading that might point to the victory not of *jeong*, but of *han*. Certainly the film was controversial. The Joint Security Area Veterans Association opposed the film, and the release of a statement saying it was a work of fiction came as a result of their lobbying.[9] Critics too were circumspect about the power of *jeong* in the film. For Xan Brooks, *Joint Security Area* is a "pungent military drama."[10] A. O. Scott sees it as a demonstration of how the "logic of political conflict works itself out in stark, brutal ways that ordinary people, however brave or decent they might be, are often powerless to oppose."[11] Scott notes that the revelation of *jeong* in the film may seem "anticlimactically simple."[12] Further, in a final scene, Soo-Hyuk kills himself. After shooting himself with a stolen pistol he lies cruciform on the ground. The pin taken from the landmine during his rescue has been worn around his neck ever since. In this scene, blood trickles beneath the pin that Gyung Pil gave him after saving his life. While reading such scenes cross-culturally is notoriously difficult, it does, nonetheless, raise questions and evoke deeper reflection. What rules of bloody honor or even patriarchy are at work in the broader storyline of *Joint Security Area*? Even if the popular saying, "You die, I die; you live, I live" expresses a deep sense of *jeong*, we might still ask, did Soo-Hyuk have to kill himself?[13] What themes might be at work in this movie that work against a post-colonial reading of the cross? This is a story, to the say the least, that seems to offer a limited vision of a new beginning and new relationships. *Jeong* may indeed unravel *han*, but *Joint Security Area* depicts much blood soaked into contested ground. Is this bloodshed indicative of *jeong* or is it symbolic of the victory of *han* or is

8. Joh, *Heart of the Cross*, 9.

9. Wheeler, "JSA."

10. Brooks, "Joint Security Area."

11. Scott, "Dear Enemy."

12. Scott, "Dear Enemy."

13. Joh, "Transgressive Power of Jeong," 155.

it suggestive of a return of violent sacrifice? The *jeong* in *Joint Security Area* that interrupted the divisions across "no-man's land," and that erupted into the lives of enemies-become-friends, seems to be short lived. The apparatus, structures, and strictures of war and violence, in the end, seem to snuff it out. In the artistic and historical crossroads of *Joint Security Area*, things remain unstable. Interpretations of *Joint Security Area* can be contested and Joh admits that *jeong* is elusive in human history. The movie may not provide as deep a sense of relationality as Joh requires. Thus, at least read cross-culturally, it may not communicate the potency of *jeong*. That does not, however, mean that *jeong* is not the complex, rich, transformative force that Joh identifies as a source for Korean life and for a post-colonial reading of the cross. Before considering the contention that sacrifice remains important to a post-colonial understanding of the cross, one more step is needed. In the next section, and in preparation for a proposal that sacrifice is consonant with Joh's description of *jeong*, the *jeong* in the ministry of Jesus of Nazareth is considered.

## FINDING EACH OTHER

> *Jeong* emerges within connectedness to foster hope for unraveling *han* and engendering new beginnings. Thus, it is within relationality, within the in-between space of the Self and the Other, that allows for the transformation of *han* into *jeong*.[14]

As was seen in the previous chapter, *jeong* is deep relationality. It is the power of love (*agape, eros*, and filial). It is the clarity to see complexity. It is openness to others. It is compassionate solidarity in overcoming suffering and alienation.[15] *Jeong* has "multiple and shifting dimensions" and "embodies the invisible traces of compassion in relationships." It is "most often recognized when we perceive our very own self, conscious and unconscious, in the mirrored reflection of the other."[16] *Jeong* is a relational ethos prevalent in Korea. It is associated with "compassion, love, vulnerability, and acceptance of heterogeneity as essential to life."[17] It has the power to move beyond contestatory either/or understandings and framings of

---

14. Joh, "Transgressive Power of Jeong," 156.

15. Joh, "Transgressive Power of Jeong," 152–56.

16. Joh, *Heart of the Cross*, xxi; Joh, "Transgressive Power of Jeong," 152.

17. Joh, *Heart of the Cross*, xxi.

suffering. It is the power of redemptive relationships.[18] Its "backbone" is loving relationships with others.[19] Those who hate and oppress depend upon and promote polarizations. In contrast, Joh depicts *jeong* as being like the "power of eros that forges its presence in the interval between the Self and the Other."[20] This deep relationality brings a certain porosity or openness between the self and the other that is not necessarily predicated upon a mutuality between people.[21] It can, thus, have a transgressive quality existing even on the interfaces between hate and love, oppressor and oppressed, and between the intent of Jesus and the intent of his disciples. *Jeong* is present in the relational spaces or potentialities between hate and love, self and other, material and spiritual. *Jeong* creates "indeterminacy" in these "unaccounted-for" spaces. It makes people vulnerable one to another, and makes personal identity open to corporate identity.

It is debatable the extent to which *Joint Security Area* points toward this complex and rich view of *jeong*. In contrast, Jesus of Nazareth radically lived out and embodied *jeong*.[22] Such embodiment is not simply the thoughts, words, and actions of an individual, but it is *jeong* made manifest in the deep relationality of the Jesus movement. The witness of Jesus and his followers is inseparable as the power of *jeong* ensures that *han* does not have the final say.[23] Even when that relationality was threatened by *han* in the corporate body, *jeong* rang forth. Christian *jeong* was manifest in Palestine in love for enemy. It was seen in compassion for those marginalized by the dominant culture and religion and for those complicit with coloniality.[24] Jesus and those he ministered to were struggling with the *han* of an oppressive imperial regime.[25] Jesus, as a colonized person and as a member of a colonized people, experienced *han*. His response to such suffering was to exist in the in-between. He demonstrated *jeong* to foreigners, compatriots, collaborators, and the voiceless. Jesus did not choose the simple dualism

18. Joh, *Heart of the Cross*, xxi.

19. Joh, *Heart of the Cross*, 18.

20. Joh, "Transgressive Power of Jeong," 152–53.

21. Joh makes a distinction between *mi-uwn jeong* that emerges in mutual relationships and *go-eun jeong* that emerges in relationships "full of discontent" (Joh, "Transgressive Power of Jeong," 155).

22. Joh, "Transgressive Power of Jeong," 157.

23. Joh, "Transgressive Power of Jeong," 96, 153.

24. Joh, *Heart of the Cross*, 126.

25. Joh, "Transgressive Power of Jeong," 156.

of colonized/colonizer, friend/enemy, liberator/oppressor associated with many revolutionaries. That path leads to a limited liberation that depends on building up one's identity over against the identity of the other. It demands a cutting off (*dan*) of the other.[26] In contrast, the major tenor of Christ's mission was to opt for "transformation through the power of *jeong* in connectedness."[27] The deep relationality of the Jesus movement did not, however, come without risk.

The cost of Christian *jeong* was famously summarized in Mark's Gospel: "those who want to save their life will lose it, and those who lose their life for my sake, and for the sake of the gospel, will save it" (Mark 8:35). For Joh, such teaching hints at a deeper understanding of *jeong via* a "comparativist hermeneutic . . . suggestive of transreligious hybridities."[28] In other words, Jesus of Nazareth was not a Westerner, and to understand the riches of *jeong* in his life and teaching, one would do well to read them in conjunction with Buddhist ideas and practices. Particularly relevant to a *jeong*-filled understanding of Jesus are the ideas of self-emptying toward self-fullness. Jesus lived out of *jeong*, resulting in self-emptying. In wilderness temptation (Matt 4:1–11), in betrayal by friends (Matt 26:17–25), in the refusal of vengeance (Matt 26:52–56), and in the conscious turning toward death (Matt 26:36–42), Jesus empties himself. Dangerous though this concept is, Joh sees Jesus exercising his agency to empty himself of those things that prevent a fuller life for Jesus and the Jesus movement. Satan seeks to negate the messianic call in Jesus' life (Matt 4) and, in response, Jesus negates himself of this negation. In the face of his friends' disloyalty (Matt 26:31), Jesus faces the depths of self-emptying in the agony of Gethsemane (Matt 26:36–46). There is *han* here and there is *jeong* here.[29] An interreligious hybridizing impulse no doubt runs through Joh's work and her understanding of *jeong* and the holding together of seemingly contradictory notions. Nonetheless, Joh does not take time to explicate a thoroughgoing Buddhist-Christian reading of Christ's self-emptying. It would be folly to assume that that can be achieved here. However, some intimation in the direction of what this might mean as a further example of the implications

26. Joh, "Transgressive Power of Jeong," 156.

27. Joh, "Transgressive Power of Jeong," 157.

28. Joh, "Transgressive Power of Jeong," 157. For some work in this area, see Faden, "No Self, Dōgen," 41–54. For a related artful, narrative-based view of practical hybridization, see Farwell, "On Whether Christians Should Participate," 242–56.

29. Joh, "Transgressive Power of Jeong," 156–59, 162.

of the post-colonial characteristic of hybridization is needed. In this regard, Joh cites the work of John P. Keenan. He writes that emptiness counters the "security of self-centered knowledge by undermining the belief that human ideas and images represent the very essence of things."[30] In reading Mark's Gospel, Keenan sees a constant tug-o'-war between Jesus and his disciples. They consistently clung to their own ideas of who they were, who Jesus should be, and constantly rejected his messianic path toward death. Yet by the end, in a gospel where the resurrected Jesus remains absent, both disciples and readers are left with "simply nothing to hold onto."[31] A Buddhist (Mahāyāna) reading brings to this gospel a concept of emptiness that is not nihilistic, but potentially liberative:

> Without the realization of no-self (anātman), no salvation is possible. This means much more than not being selfish. It means that one must abandon the final validity of all the definitions of self which we construct in our coping with the world. . . . The emptying and abandoning of an imagined inner core to our lives frees one to engage in the true dependently co-arisen beauty and joy of human being.[32]

Through Jesus' jeong for the world, Jesus resolves to empty himself for the world, and in emptying himself he finds a renewed world and renewed life for that world. This self-emptying, understood now by the gospel text and Buddhist insights, is the only way to unravel han.[33] In the emptiness at the end of the Mark's Gospel, disciples and readers are invited into a renewing story. They are invited into the interdependence of a new community:[34]

> Mark's abrupt ending embodies the silence of the risen Lord and issues a call for his followers to awaken to his presence in the everyday. . . . The story of Jesus has no final conclusion, for the resurrected life of Jesus is not a given data, once learned and perhaps

30. Keenan, Gospel of Mark, 25.

31. Keenan, Gospel of Mark, 27.

32. Keenan, Gospel of Mark, 205. The ideas of no-self (anātman) and dependent co-arising (pratītyasamutpāda) are complex, controversial, and depend upon a series of other Buddhist commitments. Roughly, no-self is the rejection of the notion that an individual enduring self (ātman) exists. Given this, dependent co-arising means entities arise and then pass away in a deep relationality or network of causes and conditions. See also Mackenzie, "Enacting the Self," 239–73. See also Keenan's more recent commentary, Emptied Christ of Philippians, 169–83.

33. Joh, "Transgressive Power of Jeong," 161.

34. Keenan, Gospel of Mark, 28–30.

imitated. Rather, it is the life story of each Christian, embodied in particular circumstances and taking specific courses . . .[35]

As already noted, Joh acknowledges that reading the ministry and cross of Jesus by emphasizing self-emptying is dangerous. For such a so-called "Asian" reading of the cross and the power of God in the self-emptying lordship of Christ may be distinguished over against a more so-called Western and triumphalist reading of the lordship of Christ. Sarah Coakley is similarly aware of such dangers. On the one hand, she avers that Christian freedom may occur through a "*special* form of human 'vulnerability'" or self-emptying (*kenōsis*). On the other hand, she is aware that such self-emptying can be construed as passive and the particular charism of women, non-Westerners, or the laity, all the while acting to define and empower legions of men.[36] Nonetheless, both Joh and Coakley want to argue for the importance of the concept and practice of self-emptying. Coakley, however, goes further than Joh. In Coakley's kenotic readings, she makes the further move of arguing for the rehabilitation of a feminist understanding of sacrificial language. In the next section, her insights will be submitted as an extension and enrichment of Joh's *jeong*-filled reading of Jesus' life and cross.

4. In light of the movie, or the previous chapter's description of it, how do you understand *jeong*? Is there another movie or piece of art that you would use to help explain *jeong*?

5. How do you understand Mark 8:35?

6. To what extent is the suggestion useful in your context that a hybridizing of interpretation, with Buddhist help, deepens an understanding of Jesus' call to his disciples?

## FINDING GOD

It is the cross that points in the direction of hope, the confidence that there is a dimension to life beyond the reach of the oppressor.[37]

35. Keenan, *Gospel of Mark*, 396–97.

36. Coakley, *Powers and Submissions*, 31–34. Joh briefly refers to this work in *Heart of the Cross*, 86–87, 95.

37. Cone, *Cross and the Lynching Tree*, 161–62.

In *jeong*, Joh sees a way to "shift our focus from a salvation obtained through sacrificial suffering to a salvation based on the relational power of jeong."[38] Nonetheless, the movie *Joint Security Area* and her depiction and emphasis on the self-emptying involved in *jeong* are suggestive of sacrificial language. Is it possible to maintain her emphasis on the deep relationality of *jeong* and recover a language of sacrifice that does not fall into patriarchal power relations and the divinization of bloodshed? Coakley aims at precisely such a task and it is to her work that we turn in this section. She begins by questioning the move by Christian theologians, particularly since the twentieth century, to set aside the language of sacrifice. While such a move is designed to undermine patriarchy and the necessity of violence, it might, in fact, have the opposite effect. Coakley argues that to reject a life-giving understanding of sacrifice is to concede that the only understanding of sacrifice is patriarchal and violent toward the (purportedly) powerless. This, however, need not be the only understanding of sacrifice.[39] Coakley argues for an understanding of sacrifice that is about the purgation of false desire in favor of desire for God's life-giving will.[40] This she sees in the story of Isaac's binding and, by implication, the cross of Christ.

The rejection of sacrificial language gives in to a dominant strand of thinking, particularly influential in theology through the early work of René Girard, that posits social progress and stability on violence. Girard's well-known, if not pervasive, theory can be succinctly stated. He theorizes that at the very root of culture and religion lies selfish, violent desires that threaten to dismantle human society. Lest this happen, a scapegoat is identified and sacrificed to avert the crisis.[41] When such a theory is accepted, it is assumed that sacrifice is essentially violent, foundational to human nature, and necessary for the emergence and sustainability of human societies.[42] For Coakley, assuming that sacrifice is essentially violent is a "deadly caricature."[43] Thinking that one can avoid the caricature by evacuating Christian language of sacrifice does not work. For when one

38. Joh, "Transgressive Power of Jeong," 162.

39. Jay, *Throughout Your Generations Forever*, 128–50.

40. Coakley, "Pleasure Principles," 20–33.

41. I have oversimplified Girard's work here. See Girard, *Violence and the Sacred*; Jay, *Throughout Your Generations Forever*, 128–33.

42. Coakley, *Sacrifice Regained*, 13.

43. Coakley, *Sacrifice Regained*, 5–6. See Klawans, *Purity, Sacrifice, and the Temple*; McClymond, *Beyond Sacred Violence*.

rejects sacrificial language, one is, at the same time, accepting that sacrifice is essentially violent. What is needed, argues Coakley, is not the rejection of sacrificial language (already prefigured in the language of *jeong* through an emphasis on self-emptying), but an understanding of sacrifice that rejects the primacy of violence. She argues against both the assumption that violence is intrinsic to societal progress, and that violence is intrinsic to a Christian understanding of sacrifice. She resists the false sacrificial logic of patriarchy with its domineering themes of male violence and scapegoating. In its stead, she argues for a "feminist significance of sacrifice."[44] In an attempt to overthrow theoretical commitments to a competitive and violent substructure for creative processes, she appeals to another foundational theory. She makes an appeal to recent work done in evolutionary theory as a way to understand creative processes that eschew the primacy of either competition or violence. Coakley refers particularly to the work of Martin Nowak as one basis for the return of the sacrificial. Nowak studies "evolutionary dynamics" and argues that the natural tendency in the evolutionary process is co-operation (sacrifice).[45] "The cooperation of reproducing entities is essential for evolutionary progress. Genes cooperate to form a genome. Cells cooperate to produce multicellular organisms. Individuals cooperate to form groups and societies. The emergence of human culture is a cooperative enterprise."[46]

Cooperation means that a "donor pays a cost" and a "recipient gets a benefit." Such sacrifice (cooperation) aids "reproductive success" and is "abundant in biology."[47] Indeed, Nowak argues that alongside mutation and selection, cooperation should now be considered the third principle of evolution.[48] Given such developments in evolutionary mathematics, for Christians to abandon the language of sacrifice seems, at best, injudicious. Here is an understanding of deep relationality that opens a door to sacrifice removed from patriarchy, subjugation, and intrinsic violence. It suggests the possibility of sacrifice that is "purgation-into-life" and not "sacrifice-as-death."[49] This idea has interpretative significance not just for science,

44. Coakley, "In Defense of Sacrifice," 25–30.

45. Coakley, *Sacrifice Regained*, 22.

46. Nowak, *Evolutionary Dynamics*, 5.

47. Nowak, *Evolutionary Dynamics*, 90.

48. Coakley, *Sacrifice Regained*, 23. See Nowak, "Five Rules for the Evolution," 1563; Coakley and Nowak, *Evolution, Games, and God*, 1–5.

49. Coakley, "In Defense of Sacrifice," 23.

but for feminist (and post-colonial) interpretations of the biblical text. To demonstrate this, Coakley turns to the story of Isaac's binding in Genesis 22 and the central idea that Isaac is the main actor self-emptying himself of that which is not God.

In Christian theology, Isaac is a type of Christ (Gal 4:28–31; Rom 8:32) and, thus, a feminist reading of the Genesis 22 story has implications for reading the cross. Coakley's rereading of the text is resourced not only by her Christian and feminist commitments, but also by artistic representations of the story, Jewish midrash, and later Christian readings of the text. Her aim is as clear as it is bold. She argues that only in a return to right understanding of sacrifice can a feminist account of human transformation, in relation to God, be constituted.[50] Drawing on rabbinical sources, her reading of Isaac's binding focuses not on Abraham, but on Isaac, who is not a helpless child, but already a mature adult.[51] Thus, the binding of Isaac is a moment of "genuine consent" given to God's call to align one's self with the divine, life-giving will.[52] Isaac aimed at "the fullness of life" through a "voluntarily purgative" act.[53] However, while such a reading retrieves agency for Isaac, the agency remains male. The text absents a feminine presence. To counter this, Coakley sees Isaac as "genderlabile" and, ultimately, a type of "feminist selfhood transformed."[54] She reads Isaac as an "honorary woman" because instead of submitting to patriarchal patterns of sacrifice, a deeper reading of the text subverts such patterns. Isaac sought to demonstrate that his desire was not "bound" to the idolatry of patriarchy, rather his desire was for God. This desire was honored by divine interruption. The site of the binding, in danger of descent into violent sacrifice through an intensifying patriarchal duality of Father/Son, is interrupted and pluralized by a third agent. Considering the second angelic speech in 22:15–18 to be an interpolation, Coakley prioritizes the first interruption of the angel in Genesis 22:11 as the "ambushing" and "transforming" of a negative duality. The first interruption, in stark contrast to the second, "breaks patriarchal attachment" through a confirmed and deeper commitment to the fear of God (Gen 22:12). By the end of the story we discover that the final *telos* of Isaac and Abraham's desire is God, and God meets Isaac in

---

50. Coakley, "In Defense of Sacrifice," 19.

51. Coakley, "In Defense of Sacrifice," 23–25.

52. Coakley, "In Defense of Sacrifice," 25.

53. Coakley, "In Defense of Sacrifice," 26.

54. Coakley, "In Defense of Sacrifice," 19.

this desire.[55] Such a feminist reading, for Coakley, means that genuine freedom is achieved because that which Isaac desires comes to Isaac through heavenly interruption and presence. The gendered and binary construction of the story is broken by an interrupting divine third.[56] Such a reading is the divine call to "purgation" that leads not to "sacrifice-as-death," but to a deeper relationship with God. It is the response to divine grace, consensually voiced, through letting go of destructive desires for the gift of God's life. While such a reading may rehabilitate sacrificial language (as purgation into life) in the bloodless story of Isaac, how might the same reading strategy impact a reading of the cross?

As Coakley reads the binding of Isaac with the end of the story in view, this too is the way that the cross of Jesus is to be interpreted. As Isaac self-empties (purges) himself from that-which-is-not-God, a divine third interrupts. The purgative self-emptying of Jesus as the crucified people[57] (which is in continuity with his self-emptying ministry as described in the previous section) is interrupted in the life-giving resurrecting agency of the Holy Spirit. The violence of the cross and the danger of a regnant patriarchal duality is destabilized and overcome through the interrupting life-giving power of the Spirit. On the cross the abject returns in both *han* and *jeong*, and commonsense logic and order (the semiotic) can neither contain nor explain the depth of the relationality at work. Jesus purges the locus of the cross and the locus of interpretation from that-which-is-not-God. The self-emptying of Jesus leaves us, so to speak, empty. The cross is both icon and iconoclastic. The idol, malleable and manipulatable, is fallen. The imperial idol, with its will to power over resistant witness, is brought down. The idol that puts colonial crucifixion on a metaphysical plane is broken. The idols of neatly defined atonement theories, dependent on patriarchal power relations, is toppled. The idol of ontological containment submitting what we presume to be divine to the philosophical limits of a particular human system is cracked. *This* sacrifice breaks such a sacrificial code. The divine third invites us beyond the idols that depend on and define theologies of divine exchange through manipulation, control, and even

55. Coakley, "In Defense of Sacrifice," 26–27, 36n36. See Coakley, "Pleasure Principles."

56. Coakley, "In Defense of Sacrifice," 19. It appears, unlike the previous Buddhist (*Mahāyāna*) reading of self-emptying, Coakley remains robustly committed to what Keenan calls disenabling "classical ontologies and ontotheologies" (Keenan, *Emptied Christ of Philippians*, 169–74).

57. Joh, *Heart of the Cross*, 100, 119.

Father-Son fidelity.[58] For Coakley, that call is ongoing and opens up a path to our own self-emptying pilgrimage where we seek to align our desires with the desires of God. In short, a key implication of this post-colonial feminist reading of the cross is a call to discipleship and formation. It is a call to prayer.

In the "adventure" of prayer, Coakley speaks of the necessity of spiritual breakthrough where God's Spirit interrupts and destabilizes our self-serving images of divinity. Indeed, she calls this intervention "spiritual terror." To get at what she means, it is worth quoting her counterintuitive, unsettling, and controversial reflections directly:

> The smashing of [the] idol, whether through patient prayer or personal disaster—or both—is a crisis of huge spiritual signifi-cance: I can walk into the dread, in which, seemingly, God has become nightmarish threat, or I can retreat. But at the heart of this nightmare is the same irresolvable conundrum of the "binding of Isaac," or of the cross: for this new God who magnetizes me and allures me and demands of me nothing less that everything, and whom I desire above everything, is the same God who also *seems* to turn on me and slay me, even as he "binds" and hands me over with Christ in the Passion into a new posture of pure, passive love. The contradiction is, in human terms, seemingly unbearable. But the point about this moment, if the great spiritual guides of both Jewish and Christian tradition are right, is that it is also purposive, purgative and transformative. It is, in fact, the very *death* of vio-lent, "patriarchal" religion . . . .[59]

As will be seen further in the next chapter, this understanding of sacrifice as purgation-into-life is not the spirituality of colonizers. The sacrificial spirituality of empire is death to those who would stand in the way of the aggrandizement of the powerful. The spirituality of empire, in Girardian-style, is landed stability through death (Matt 27:24–26; Mark 15:15; John 19:15). It is the justification of the status quo. Thus, a reading of the cross emphasizing notions of self-emptying and sacrifice—hybridized by Buddhist thought and evolutionary science—in post-colonial theology does not mean passivity. It means ongoing resistance to a patriarchal and imperialist expectation that death is necessary for the progress of society and stability.

---

58. See Coakley, *Cross and the Transformation*, 21.

59. Coakley, *Cross and the Transformation*, 22.

7. In your context of formation, how is the cross of Jesus understood?

8. Given the work of Joh and others in these chapters, to what extent has your understanding of the cross changed?

9. Try to articulate your understanding of the cross in light of chapters 6 and 7.

# 8

## The Ceremony of Innocence Is Drowned

### Resisting the Powers

A popular Native American belief is that we, who were here in America, never left our garden of Eden. . . . [I]t doesn't take much imagination to figure out who replaces the snake as the interloper in the Eden story.

—Randy Woodley[1]

The cross has often been misappropriated and misapplied. Famously, and according to Lactantius, it was appropriated by the Roman Emperor himself in 312: "Constantine was directed in a dream to cause the heavenly sign to be delineated on the shields of his soldiers, and so to proceed to battle. He did as he had been commanded, and he marked on their shields the letter X . . . being the cipher of CHRIST. Having this sign, his troops stood to arms."[2] Yeats too reflected on this episode, depicting the apparent Christianization of the empire not as "conversion of the crowds" nor a "general change of opinion" nor "pressure from below," but as "an act of power."[3] For Native Americans, such imperialist misappropriation is ongoing. For Woodley, the "cultural dilemma" they encountered when meeting

1. Woodley, *Shalom and the Community*, xv, 68.
2. Lactantius, *De Mortibus Persecutorum*, chap. XLIV.
3. Yeats, *Vision*, 278.

124

settlers for the first time is the same dilemma they face today. The values and lifestyles of many Native Americans, who claim no allegiance to Jesus, reflect more closely the Christian gospel than those who actually claim to be Christ-followers. It is as if settler baptism is itself submerged in a sea of colonialism and coloniality. The ceremony of innocence is drowned:

> European and American history is replete with ungodly people doing god-awful things, including land theft, rape, murder, enslavement, torture, pollution, depleting the earth's resources, and even attempted genocide, by those who held "correct" theological beliefs. There exists a philosophical disconnect in the Euro-western mind between what one believes and what one does.[4]

Too often in church and in the academy do those who have benefitted from imperialism and those who are descendants of colonial settlers relativize, excuse, and even justify colonialism. At the very least, such impulses would be problematized if the literature produced by the colonized was taken seriously. Woodley's "god-awful things" echoes one of Yeats's most disturbing poems. "Leda and the Swan" is a poem about colonization. In it he reinterprets the Greek myth where Zeus, in the form of a swan, visits a mortal woman. For Yeats this colonizing visitation was rape:

> . . . How can those terrified vague fingers push
> The feathered glory from her loosening thighs?
> And how can body, laid in that white rush,
> But feel the strange heart beating where it lies? . . .
>
> So mastered by the brute blood of the air,
> Did she put on the knowledge with his power
> Before the indifferent beak could let her drop?[5]

The trauma of colonialism continues to have ramifications in a form of coloniality that Woodley associates with the "American dream." The dream of an "immaculate origin" disavows the presence of Native Americans and

---

4. Woodley, *Shalom and the Community*, 151, 106. The population numbers are contested and some have argued for a pre-1492 figure as high as 16 million. That the Native American peoples experienced catastrophic loss of land and life cannot be contested. For the impact of war and disease on Native populations see Carpenter, *"Times are Altered with Us,"* 2–4, 22–28.

5. Yeats, *Collected Poems*, 292. See Daniels, *Voice of the Oppressed*, 38.

"founding violence."[6] The dream stresses freedom, equality, justice, progress, and providence. Even when disavowal is faced by those in dominant cultures, there is often an appeal to a revised American dream. The revision states that, in a post-civil-rights era, the sins of mothers and fathers have been corrected or redeemed.[7] For Woodley, both the dream and the revised dream act as social location and pseudo-place. This "location" then acts as the "site" for the construction of white (acontextual) theology. But it is theology built on no-place. It is theology that ignores the realities of the land and the events that took place on that land—events that for Native Americans do not amount to a dream, but to a nightmare.[8] Woodley embodies resistance against such whitewashing and submits a theological vision for a different future in relation to storytelling, *shalom*, and renewal.

## HISTORY-TELLING AND THE NEED FOR RESISTANCE

There is a dominant way of telling the history of the USA. It is a romance. It is the story of a people from an old world escaping an abusive relationship. It is the story of a people finding freedom through the waters into a new promised world. It is the story of a budding courtship in an expansive land where expansive liberties, equalities, and opportunities flower. It is the romantic retelling of the exodus story.[9] It is the story told by a dominant culture around thanksgiving tables, under fireworked skies, and beneath white flagpoles. However, for many people, such tables, such skies, and such flagpoles stand not for remembering, but for *dis*membering. They signify limbs cut off; voices silenced. Some cannot breathe. For Native Americans dismembering meant dispossession, schemes for assimilation, and genocide.

From the 1820s to the 1840s, "anti-Indian sentiment" was high and fed rhetoric and policy for the removal and relocation of Native Americans. The Reverend Jedidiah Morse, a leading intellectual, civic, and religious figure of the time, explicitly stated that the mission of the church was the

---

6. Veracini, *Settler Colonialism*, 78–80.

7. Veracini, *Settler Colonialism*, 75–116.

8. Woodley, *Shalom and the Community*, 131–35.

9. See the PBS television show, *God in America*. http://www.pbs.org/godinamerica/. Veracini, *Settler Colonialism*, 75–116.

mission of the United States of America.[10] In making recommendations to the government in 1822 he wrote:

> The field of our labor is wide. It is a wilderness, in which successful cultivation has but recently commenced.... "The harvest," already beginning to whiten for the sickle, "is great"; and seeing that there are such numbers of qualified reapers offering themselves for the service of gathering it in, and our means for paying them their wages are so abundant, let us not be constrained to add, "*but the laborers are few!*" ... The arm of the Lord, in whom we trust is strong. His power can do all things. The old adage, full of pith and meaning is, "no cross, no crown." ... It is animating in no common degree, that the rulers and lawgivers of our favored nation lead in this godlike work. ... Surely the hand of God is here; the thing which we desire will be accomplished. None shall hinder it. May every heart and voice respond—SO BE IT.[11]

In 1819, the government passed the Civilization Act to furnish "capable persons of good moral character" with provision to prevent the "further decline and final extinction of the Indian tribes . . . and for introducing to them the habits and arts of civilization."[12] The funds were mostly distributed to churches and mission agencies. Addressing a group of Ottawas at Michillimackina, it might appear that Morse sought to bring good news:

> Your fathers, the christian white people . . . are devising plans for your happiness. The Congress of the United States, the Great Council of our nation, feel for you, also, and have put money into the hands of your Father, the President, to promote the welfare of the Indians. ... Among the means for your civilization . . . we will bring you the best, the only *effectual*, means of making you truly happy—we will bring you the Bible, the best of all Books. ... This book causes the wide difference which exists, as you see, between the white man and the Indian. We will bring you the blessed book.[13]

Morse, who could be critical of government policies, the military, and the morality of other white people, nonetheless accepted that it was the government's objective to "civilize the Indians." Reflecting on the role of

10. Hawk and Twiss, "From Good," 48.

11. Morse, *Report to the Secretary of War*, 93–96.

12. Act of March 3, 1819 ch. 85, *Stat. 2* in Peters, *Public Statutes at Large*, 516–17.

13. Hawk and Twiss, "From Good," 48–49; italics are the author's.

both Canada and the United States as Christian nations, Morse considered Native Americans and First Nations to be under the care of white people by the hand of providence. The mission was to "raise the long neglected native tribes . . . from their present state of ignorance and wretchedness, to the enjoyment, with us, of all the blessings of civilization, and of our holy religion." He found himself arguing against other "shocking" views, which included plans for the extermination of Native Americans.[14] In contrast, he was convinced that:

> Indians are of the same nature and original, (*sic*) and of one blood, with ourselves; of intellectual powers as strong, and capable of cultivation, as ours. They, as well as ourselves, are made to be immortal. To look down upon them, therefore, as an inferior race, as untamable, and to profit by their ignorance and weakness; to take their property from them for a small part of its real value, and in other ways to oppress them; is undoubtedly wrong, and highly displeasing to our common Creator, Lawgiver and final Judge.[15]

He was, nonetheless, not ignorant of the colonial realities. The best land was selected and settled by treaty depriving the Native people of their identity and the means to life. "This is no fancied picture. In a few years it will be sad reality, unless we change our policy toward them. . . . How many tribes, once numerous and respectable, have in succession perished, in the matter described, from the fair and productive territories, now possessed by, and support to TEN MILLIONS OF PEOPLE!"[16] If, argued Morse, the government failed in justice, education, and religion to "civilize" Native Americans, then their land should be given back to them. However, he had confidence in the government and made recommendations that included the removal of Native American tribes that lived "within the settlements of the white people"; provision of chaplains for each military establishment; implementation of an agricultural "revolution" that would move them away from a hunting culture; and commitment to widespread vaccination programs. Guardianship would combine the firm implementation of the rule of law with missionary activity (*via* what Morse calls "Education Families") and be predicated upon recruiting people who were "principled" and of "fair moral character." Such recommendations once implemented, Morse

14. Morse, *Report to the Secretary of War*, 12, 20, 80–81.

15. Morse, *Report to the Secretary of War*, 82.

16. Morse, *Report to the Secretary of War*, 65–66.

opined, would "call forth the thanks of the Indians, and secure for our nation the applauses of the world."[17]

The syncretistic theology of Morse justified dispossession, acculturation, and violence. Yet, he considered Native Americans to have "imperfect" claims to their land and sovereignty. He conceded that, "Each tribe possesses many of the attributes of independence and sovereignty."[18] With the election of Andrew Jackson (1767–1845), child of Irish immigrants, to the presidency, even such begrudging recognition of Native Americans would be swept aside. President Jackson viewed as risible earlier treaties that considered tribes to be independent nations. Though some resisted, the Indian Removal Act of 1830 resulted in dispossession of the eastern tribes "by methods of persuasion or bribery or threats, or some combination of these."[19] While individual missionaries opposed removals, Christian agencies generally supported government policy.

In the late nineteenth century and into the twentieth century, it would be removals to boarding schools that would present a new wickedness. By 1899, $2.5 million was being spent each year on 148 boarding schools and 225 day schools designed to civilize/Christianize 20,000 children. The late nineteenth century would see a preference for "off-reservation" boarding schools. The best known of the schools was Carlisle Indian Industrial School, Pennsylvania, founded in 1879 by Captain Richard H. Pratt. In regard to the so-called civilization of Native Americans, he considered himself a "Baptist" because he believed in "immersing the Indians in our civilization and when we get them under holding them there until they are thoroughly soaked."[20] Such violence in boarding schools continues to have present-day effects. After a national symposium in 2011, the National Native American Boarding School Healing Coalition (NABS) was set up. The coalition works for a "national strategy" that raises awareness and cultivates healing for the trauma caused by boarding schools.[21] Decolonization as healing continues.

17. Morse, *Report to the Secretary of War*, 20, 60–93.

18. Morse, *Report to the Secretary of War*, 67–69.

19. Hagan, *American Indians*, 57–58; Cuéllar and Woodley, "North American Mission and Motive," 67.

20. Hagan, *American Indians*, 105–6.

21. www.boardingschoolhealing.org. See also Dunbar-Ortiz, *Indigenous Peoples' History*, 211–14; Smith, "Forever Changed," 57–82; Brave Heart, "American Indian Holocaust," 60–82.

Ethnocide can lead to genocide. In what would become the United States of America, it is estimated at the time of Columbus (1492) there were more than five million Native Americans. In 1900, there were less than 300,000.[22] Woodley is clear, "Native Americans have experienced genocide as a result of Euro-American ethnocentrism."[23] Daniel Hawk and Richard Twiss reference Mbiti's distinction between the gospel and Christianity as they seek to make sense of the missionary past of the USA. The former could be consonant with Native cultures, the latter could not:

> [T]he ultimate goal of the missionary agenda, was a process of removing native differences and distinctives and assimilating indigenes into the European moral economy and civilization as measured against a single value that claimed to be absolute truth. Over time this process would not efface human differences but would slowly try to absorb them into a kind of homogenized European system, a single scale of social, spiritual and material inequality. . . . [T]he stage was set for "humane imperialism." . . . [These] hegemonic realities of colonialism are deeply embedded in the ethos of American Christianity. . . . The effect . . . is . . . the imposition of a consciousness that negates and denies the lived reality—hence the identity and value—of indigenous people.[24]

From Woodley's perspective, the Euro-Western church has little to be proud of in its understanding and practice of mission to Native Americans.

As has been seen, genocide is physical violence. But, it can also be discursive or administrative violence. Walter Ashby Plecker was Virginia's Chief of the Bureau of Vital Statistics from 1912 to 1946. He was at the forefront of racist and anti-miscegenation attitudes and policies constructed to safeguard white power and authority. For Plecker, no Native American in Virginia was "free of African ancestry" therefore "their Indianness . . . was considered null and void." Given his conviction, he made it his mission to detribalize Virginia and to categorize people as either black or white. This lead to the "near documentary erasure of Virginia's Native peoples." For Virginia's Native peoples this was "paper genocide." Included in this systematic detribalization were all divisions of the Monacan, Chickahominy,

---

22. Woodley, *Living in Color*, 23.
23. Woodley, *Living in Color*, 23.
24. Hawk and Twiss, "From Good," 56–57.

Rappahannock, Mattaponi, Nansemond, and Pamunkey.[25] Gonzales, Kertész, and Tayac quote the words of Felix S. Cohen (1907–53):

> [T]he Indian plays much the same role in our society that the Jews played in Germany. Like the miner's canary, the Indian marks the shift from fresh air to poison gas in our political atmosphere; and our treatment of Indians, even more than our treatment of other minorities, reflects the rise and fall in our democratic faith.[26]

The Racial Integrity Act was repealed in 1967. However, in order to be acknowledged as an "Indian tribe" the federal government demands documentary evidence that a people have been identified as Native American continuously since 1900.[27] Plecker's legacy of disappearing Native Americans continues.

Such history-telling challenges a dominant narrative of discovery, romance, and providence. As a Keetoowah Cherokee, Woodley writes, "We must remove the legacy of colonialism, not just forget it . . . ." He does not avoid criticism of white theology, but in his understanding of resistance he goes beyond criticism to develop a "harmony ethic" for the sake of "indigenous well-being."[28] He seeks an intercultural theologizing that will bring about "redemptive correction" aiming at nothing less than intercultural partnership toward "a new theological system."[29] He proposes a decolonizing resistance that is constructive and life giving. For Euro-Westerners, this means recovering the centrality of *shalom* as a path to walk. For Native Americans it means a recognition that their traditions, including the "Harmony Way," relate closely to the biblical vision of *shalom*.

---

25. Gonzales et al., "Eugenics as Indian Removal," 63–66.

26. Gonzales et al., "Eugenics as Indian Removal," 66.

27. Gonzales et al., "Eugenics as Indian Removal," 65.

28. Woodley, *Shalom and the Community*, 150, xiv–xvi. It should be noted that "indigenous" and "indigene" have particular colonial histories, and for that reason are not innocent categories. They are used in this chapter because Woodley employs them.

29. Woodley, *Shalom and the Community*, xv–xvi. See also 61–66. On other Native American theologies, see, for example, Treat, *Native and Christian*; Kidwell et al., *Native American Theology*; Tinker, *American Indian Liberation*; Twiss, *Rescuing the Gospel*.

## *SHALOM* AS RESISTANCE

For Woodley, a vision and practice of *shalom* is shaped by Native American wisdom, God's closeness to an interconnected creation, the biblical text, and the person and life of Jesus.[30]

### The Harmony Way

As a result of experience and research, Woodley has argued for a "construct" called the "Harmony Way" that expresses common values present in the life and teaching of Native American communities. Among such communities there is a deep commitment to "maintaining harmony or balance in life."[31] This begins with an acknowledgement that "everything that humans do has an effect on the rest of the world around us."[32] This is not simply a philosophy, it is "how life operates" and "it is the only way that life can continue."[33] Appealing to Cherokee concepts, Woodley names *Eloheh* and *Duyukta* as key expressions of this harmony. *Eloheh* may be translated as "balance" or "Harmony Way," and *Duyukta* can be translated as "justice" or "righteousness." Both terms might be interchangeable. When quoting an Eastern Cherokee elder, Woodley notes that while he is describing *Duyukta* he could equally be describing *Eloheh*:

> Duyukta is a moral code that might be roughly translated as "the right way," "the right path," or "the path of being in balance . . . ." It is the traditional Cherokee way of living: placing importance on the good of the whole more than the individual; having freedom but taking responsibility for yourself; staying close to the earth and all our relations. And how does one do this? By taking time to dream; by understanding our nature and our needs and taking care of them; by doing ceremonies that keep us in balance like going to water and using the sweat lodge; by listening and praying; by recognizing our dark and light sides; by having the support of the family, extended family, clan, and tribe. The medicine people

30. Post-colonial theology simply cannot be associated with "liberal" or "progressive" theologies. See, for example, Smith et al., *Evangelical Postcolonial Conversations*.

31. Woodley, *Shalom and the Community*, 18–22, 67.

32. Tinker, *American Indian Liberation*, 68.

33. Woodley, *Shalom and the Community*, 64.

say it requires understanding ourselves and our place in the world around us.[34]

This "harmony concept" is a "foundation for living" among Native Americans. It is a concept that is holistic and integrative. It distinguishes itself from the dualisms of modernity and any theologizing that pits creation against salvation, community against individual, and the land against its inhabitants. The disintegration that such dualisms result in is often represented as a broken circle or hoop. A complete circle or hoop, in contrast, represents the Harmony Way and its holistic and integrative emphasis:

> [T]he spirituality of my people is wholeness. It certainly is related to a view of life which does not separate or compartmentalize. The relationship of health with ourselves, our community and with all creation is spiritual relationship. The need of the universe is the individual need to be in harmony with the Creator. This harmony is expressed by living in the circle of life.[35]

The Harmony Way envisions an interrelatedness between all peoples and all of creation. It is a vision and way of life that values and practices "reciprocity and familial relatedness."[36] However, in today's USA and today's world, such reciprocity and relatedness seem in short supply.

It is particularly a connectedness and balance between identity and the land that Woodley sees as "perhaps the single most glaring difference between a Euro-Western worldview and an indigenous Native American worldview."[37] In Said's propagation of post-colonialism, particularly in reference to Ireland and the early Yeats, a primary mark of resistance was to "reclaim, rename, and reinhabit the land."[38] For Woodley, the traditional wisdom and interconnectedness to land and creation that has the potential to inform political and policy discourse is a theme central to biblical faith. Indeed, he considers the Harmony Way to be "essentially one" with the biblical vision of *shalom* and thus divinely given.[39]

34. Woodley, *Shalom and the Community*, 71–72.

35. McKay, "Aboriginal Christian Perspective," 54.

36. Woodley, *Shalom and the Community*, 20–21, 73–81.

37. Woodley, *Shalom and the Community*, 65.

38. Said, *Culture and Imperialism*, 226.

39. Woodley, *Shalom and the Community*, xiv–xv, 19–20. This interconnectedness to the land is particularly strong in early Yeats as he appeals and interprets ancient myths and legends of the Celts (in, for example, "The Stolen Child" (1886), *The Rose* (1893), and *Countess Cathleen* (1899)). Said, rightly, sees such writing as a search for "a more

## God and Creation

The foundational myth of the Keetoowah illustrates a God-given interconnectedness to the land: "Those who became Keetoowah people went due
south until a sign was given for the seven clan leaders to . . . fast and pray
for seven nights. . . . [A] messenger from the Creator appeared. . . . The
messenger told them . . . that the land they were presently in was the land
the Creator had chosen for them since the world began . . . ."[40] For Native
Americans, land, history, religion, and culture form a "single conceptual
integration." Motherhood, reciprocity, and gratitude are themes emerging from such interconnected thinking. The earth is "our mother, God [is]
our Father, and all the creatures . . . our relatives."[41] *Prima facie*, Woodley
does not go as far as George Tinker, who argues that this divine closeness
and spiritual interconnectedness denies any privileging of human beings.
"There is no sense . . . that God . . . has any different regard for human beings than for the rest of creation . . . ."[42] For Woodley, humans have a unique
role and one that he defines as ministry or service toward maintaining
harmony and restoring harmony.[43] Nonetheless, the category of "creation"
is problematic for Native American theologians if it suggests or promotes
an "objectification" of creation. Humans cannot somehow exist outside or
stand over against creation.[44] Interconnectedness is a fundamental reality:
"All things are designed and created beautifully by their Creator. Each part
of the created whole bears the mark of its Creator. Each element works in
relationship with all the others."[45] Humans must learn from creation the
harmony that emerges in reciprocal relationships. Reciprocity is "fundamental to the human participation in world balancing and harmony."[46] Acts
of reciprocity are consistently ritualized and often practiced when people

---

congenial national origin than that provided by colonial history, for a new pantheon of
heroes and (occasionally) heroines, myths, and religions—these too are made possible by
a sense of the land reappropriated by its people." Herein is, quite literally, grounded resistance toward "decolonized identity" (Said, *Culture and Imperialism*, 226). See Daniels,
*Voice of the Oppressed*, 28–30.

40. Woodley, *Shalom and the Community*, 123–24.

41. Woodley, *Shalom and the Community*, 66.

42. Tinker, *American Indian Liberation*, 62–63, see 57–68.

43. Woodley, *Shalom and the Community*, 64.

44. Kidwell et al., *Native American Theology*, 34–35.

45. Woodley, *Shalom and the Community*, 42.

46. Tinker, *American Indian Liberation*, 68.

put natural materials to use, when they hunt, when they go to war, and when they harvest crops. "Maintaining harmony and balance requires that even necessary acts of violence be done 'in a sacred way.' Thus, nothing is taken from the earth without prayer and offering."[47] Ritual that expresses such interconnectedness and reciprocity is lacking in Euro-Western cultures and Woodley sees this as significant. The salvation of the earth may depend on Euro-Westerners becoming "indigenous once again."[48]

It is not surprising to Woodley that it was under Latin America's first indigenous president, Eva Morales, that the "Law of Mother Earth" was promoted.[49] Morales framed the vision in terms of rights, "Sixty years after adopting the [Universal Declaration of Human Rights], Mother Earth is now, finally, having her rights recognized."[50] The Bolivian legislation passed the law for the defense of Mother Earth in 2010. The law reflects the language that Woodley uses in defining indigenous values toward the interconnectedness of the divine, the land, and its people. The binding principles emphasize *harmony* between human activity and the processes inherent in creation. The *collective good* means attention to the care of all creation. The state must ensure *regeneration,* creating conditions where the ecology of the earth can "absorb damage, adapt to shocks, and regenerate without significantly altering . . . structural and functional characteristics." Mother Earth has rights and this means the state must *respect and defend* these rights. These rights include life, diversity of life, clean water, clean air, equilibrium, restoration, and pollution-free life. Living systems and the processes that support them cannot be *commercialized* or used for anyone's private property. *Multiculturalism* is inherent in living in harmony with the earth; thus, all the cultures of the world and their understandings and practices are to be respected and brought into dialogue with one another toward resourcing harmony with the earth.[51] For Woodley, such indigenous values and practices can be favorably correlated with the biblical image of *shalom.*

---

47. Tinker, *American Indian Liberation,* 70.

48. Woodley, *Shalom and the Community,* 64–66.

49. Woodley, *Shalom and the Community,* 64–66.

50. Global Alliance for the Rights of Nature, "Bolivia's Leadership." Robert Young notes that among post-colonial scholars there has been a slowness in recognizing the important of indigenous struggles (Young, "Postcolonial Remains," 128–29).

51. Neill, "Law of Mother Earth"; Chávez, "Bolivia's Mother Earth Law." See Hill, "Is Bolivia Going to Frack?'"

## Scripture

Rather than adopt a straightforwardly skeptical approach to the Scriptures, Woodley turns to the Bible and biblical scholarship to substantiate the centrality of the restorative and decolonizing effects of *shalom*. He quotes Walter Brueggemann as illustrative of *shalom*'s path:

> Shalom is the end of coercion. Shalom is the end of fragmentation. Shalom is the freedom to rejoice. Shalom is the courage to live an integrated life in a community of coherence. These are not simply neat values to be added on. They are a *massive protest* against the central values by which our world operates. The world depends on coercion. The world depends on fragmented loyalties. The world as presently ordered depends on these very conditions against which the gospel protects and to which it provides alternatives.[52]

The idea that *shalom* is a "massive protest" points to how this biblical category can be understood as holistic resistance. Visions of *shalom* (and their concomitants in Jubilee, Sabbath, and kingdom of God) in Exodus 16, Leviticus 25, Isaiah 2:3–4; 11:6–9; 61, Luke 4:16–27, Colossians 3:12–15, and Ephesians 2 mean it is both a personal and structural imperative. *Shalom* is "communal, holistic, and tangible."[53]

God placed humans in a garden (Gen 1); the Abrahamic covenant centered on the promise of place (Gen 15); the people were "married" to the land (Isa 62:3–5); the Babel project was defeated because of God's desire for diversity (Gen 11). Moses (Exod 1–12), Ruth (Ruth 1:16; 4:10; Matt 1:1, 5), Esther (Esth 2–5), and Paul (Gal 2:3–5; 1 Cor 9:20) are types of inter-cultural hybridized interlocutors whose ethnicity remained foundational to God's purpose in their lives. Peter and Cornelius reveal the cultural expansiveness of God's mission (Acts 10). Pentecost spread good news through diverse languages and cultures (Acts 2). The Council of Jerusalem (Acts 15) ratified the commitment that the gospel must be expressed in gentile cultures. In the heavenly eschatological vision of God's throne room and the new Jerusalem, the diversity of cultures and ethnicities is maintained (Rev 5:9–10; 21:24). Both place and cultural diversity are at the heart of God's creative (and re-creative) intent. The Scriptures testify to a God who works against ethnocentricity and choses diversity to reveal divine grace.

52. Woodley, *Shalom and the Community*, 24. Brueggemann, *Peace*, 51. Italics are mine.

53. Woodley, *Shalom and the Community*, 10–40.

For the God of Trinitarian monotheism cannot be captured in one culture, language, or nation. The distinctions between cultures should, therefore, be respected. Such respect does not serve ethnocentricity and any naïve notion of imperviously boundaried identities. Rather, it is a vital means through which human beings discern the nature and calling of God. Thus, the particularity of place and culture, divinely ordained, leads to cultural conservation, regeneration, and intercultural relationships. Important to Woodley's thought here is the idea that God intends particular people for particular land:[54] "From one ancestor [God] made all nations to inhabit the whole earth, and he allotted the times of their existence and boundaries of the places where they should live, so that they would search for God and perhaps grope for him and find him—though indeed he is not far from each one of us" (Acts 17:26–27).

From such texts Woodley deduces that God has appointed particular (indigenous) peoples as "host peoples on lands all over the world." These people are "keepers," "stewards," "gatekeepers" of that land and are responsible to God for what happens on it. The Bible speaks of spiritual pollution because of bloodshed, immorality, broken treaties, and idolatry (Lev 18:24–30; Job 31:38–40; Isa 24:4–5; Jer 12:4; Ezra 9:11; Rom 8:20–22). That the land is cursed because of colonialism and coloniality means that, in some sense, the fullest blessing of God is absent. Such colonialism and coloniality, in the USA, includes ethnocentrism, white supremacy, ethnocide, genocide, slavery, and structural racism.[55] He states plainly, "the long history of cruelty after slavery . . . has quenched the Spirit of God in America" and "as human beings we have cursed the land, and we are the ones who must pronounce its redemption in Christ."[56] Woodley is aware that settlers and settler theology find such Scripture and the theology it provokes "bizarre." However, that such theologizing exists in the Bible and resonates with Native American history, experience, and communities cannot be denied.

54. Woodley, *Shalom and the Community*, 119.

55. Woodley, *Living in Color*, 92–120, 149–80. Woodley, *Shalom and the Community*, 119–36.

56. Woodley, *Living in Color*, 171, 176.

# Jesus

Given the trauma associated with colonialism and coloniality, on the land and in the people of the land, the idea of "redemption in Christ" is associated with a renewal of interconnectedness to creation and decolonization. Both these themes are present as Woodley presents Jesus as the Creator-Son reconciler, *shalom*, teacher of multicultural peace, and the bringer of the kingdom.

Joh, as is not uncommon in post-colonial theologizing, makes a distinction between the Jesus of Nazareth and the Christ of God. So too do some Native American theologians. Clara Sue Kidwell, Homer Noley, and George Tinker, citing Rudolf Bultmann, see the distinction as important in Native American theologizing. In their reading of John 1 they argue that to assume that the Logos must be limited only to Jesus or that the preexistent Logos means that Jesus was preexistent is a mistake. John is focused on how the Logos (or Christ) is at work in Jesus, but that does not mean that the Christ was not at work in other times and places.[57] For Woodley, continuity between Christ and Jesus is important. It is a means to a christological integration or interconnection between Creator and creation. To open up space between Christ and Jesus is to once again fall into dualistic ways of thinking that Native American theology should be resisting.[58] The importance of christological continuity is seen to reflect the value Native Americans put on a holistic or integrative view of reality. In this case, that stress on holism means that the Creator and the redeemer are the same agent. Sean McDonough, in a major study of Christ's role in creation, sees such an integrative reading as part of the New Testament witness: "If the one true God worked so evidently, and so dramatically, through his Messiah to sustain and re-create the world (both at the physical and 'spiritual' level), there was every reason to believe that the Messiah's mediating role reached back to the very origins of creation."[59] John 1:1–2, Colossians 1:15–17, 1 Corinthians 8:6, and Hebrews 1:1–2 and 2:10 seem to point to the preexistence of Christ and Christ's role in creation. Woodley feels that Western theology underplays the role of Christ in creation and thus perpetuates imbalanced or dualistic thinking. A charge of dualism may well be justified. However, major figures in theology do grapple with the relationship of Jesus to God's

---

57. Kidwell et al., *Native American Theology*, 79.

58. Cone makes a similar argument. See Cone, *God of the Oppressed*, 106–26.

59. McDonough, *Christ as Creator*, 235.

creation and creating.[60] McDonough cites, for example, Justin Martyr, Irenaeus, and Athanasius. In modern theology, he points to Karl Barth, Wolfhart Pannenberg, and Jürgen Moltmann. Irenaeus argues, "The creator of the world is truly the Word of God, and this is our Lord, who in the last times was made man."[61] In the Johannine passage where Jesus heals the man born blind (John 9), Irenaeus offers this exegesis: the "hand of God which formed us at the beginning, and which does form us in the womb, has in the last times sought us out who were lost, winning back His own, and taking up the lost sheep upon His shoulders, and with joy restoring it to the fold of life."[62] Moltmann writes, "If Christ is the foundation for the salvation of the whole creation, then he is also the foundation of creation's very existence."[63] Similarly, Woodley argues that if God is to heal the brokenness in creation, then the divine nature and will need to enter into the frailty of creatureliness.

Woodley does not posit one model of atonement theory nor does he make appeal to foundational narratives of vicarious self-sacrifice in Native American thought.[64] He does, however, understand Jesus as the one who makes *shalom* with all creation through his "redemptive atonement":[65]

> Jesus died for all creation. . . . Redemption (our salvation) is for the whole earth. . . . In the Cherokee language we have a phrase that points to Jesus as the *Creator-Son* [*Oo-nay-thla-nah-hee Yo-way-jee*]. . . . In this simple formula Jesus is acknowledged as both divine Creator and divine Son. The implications of embracing this broader understanding, of Christ as the one who creates all things and as the one who restores all things, has tremendous missional significance.[66]

Such a christological focus, for Woodley, overturns the colonizing attitude of much missionary activity that depicted Native Americans

---

60. Woodley, *Shalom and the Community*, 57–60. See Athanasius the Great of Alexandria, *On the Incarnation*, 50–52; Dionysius the Areopagite, *Mystical Theology and the Divine*, 76–79.

61. McDonough, *Christ as Creator*, 240–41.

62. McDonough, *Christ as Creator*, 242.

63. McDonough, *Christ as Creator*, 253–54.

64. See Kidwell et al., *Native American Theology*, 79–83.

65. Woodley, *Shalom and the Community*, 58.

66. Woodley, *Shalom and the Community*, 60.

as pagans worshipping false gods. Christologizing is, thus, "resistance in search of genuine American Indian liberation . . ."[67]

If Christ is present in God's creation then the implications for the monotheistic worship of Native American communities prior to any intervention by foreign Christian missionaries is clear. Native prayers were directed toward Christ and the blessings they received were through Christ. Further, this intimate relationship between Christ and creation means that a Native American theology will shun what might be termed an Augustinian doctrine of the fall. Many Native Americans do not have a word for sin. Being human is good. Humans make mistakes.[68] What makes actions shameful is the desire to take the place that rightly belongs to the Creator. Such shame arises from forgetting one's humanity. Sin need not be

> inherited or permanent for it to be present in everyone. . . . Among traditional Native Americans, restoring broken harmony is less individualistic, being more about restoring the community—less guilt ridden, not inherent, more tangibly rectifiable, and much more oriented toward restoring harmonious relationships in all of creation, rather than simply obtaining human forgiveness.[69]

Given this understanding of shame, and Christ's entry into creation, a telling of a decolonized Christian gospel that is good news for Native Americans begins to come into view:

> Jesus, as the Creator-Son, brought the good news of the relational aspects of the Trinitarian God to earth by creating a place. Eden was where human beings were placed in order to enjoy the fullest possible sense of place on earth. God's original intention was to allow humans to relate in the parameters of a shalom garden. One could say that the garden culture was the original human culture from which one could come to know God, a God who relates in and through community.[70]

The Christ that birthed the whole world was the very same Christ that was willing to die for the whole world.[71] This self-giving of the Creator-Son

---

67. Kidwell et al., *Native American Theology*, 63.

68. Kidwell et al., *Native American Theology*, 100–112.

69. Woodley, *Shalom and the Community*, 69. See Tinker, *American Indian Liberation*, 90–91.

70. Woodley, *Shalom and the Community of Creation*, 136.

71. Woodley, *Living in Color*, 87. For deeper female imagery in a Native American theology, see Kidwell et al.'s work on the narratives of the First Mother (Corn Mother) in

brings *shalom* by revealing a deep interconnectedness and interrelatedness that flows from the Creator. Within Woodley's thought, the Trinity is *shalom*, Jesus incarnates *shalom*, and God's intent in Jesus is to restore *shalom* to the world. Thus, in Nazareth, Jesus announces that he is the fulfillment of the scriptural promises for Jubilee (Luke 4:21). For Woodley, Jubilee (Lev 25) is one of a number of biblical descriptions for *shalom*. Peace, in light of Jubilee, is God's word to the oppressed, rescue of the poor, healing of broken hearts, and liberation for captives. Standing on the colonized soil of his childhood, Jesus declares that he is this Jubilee. He is *shalom* and he brings *shalom*: the "mission of birthing and restoring shalom to the world is in Christ, by Christ, and for the honor of Christ."[72] The life of Jesus and the teaching of Jesus in the Gospels embody this Jubilee-*shalom* or Harmony Way. In the context of imperialism, his was a call to a *shalom* "kingdom." A kingdom open to the outcast, the marginalized, the stranger, the widowed, and the orphaned. This is a different kind of community even amidst the fear and terror of colonialism and coloniality. For this reason the next chapter will reflect on resistance as renewal.

## CONCLUSION

In broad terms, Woodley's depiction of a holistic Harmony Way that stands over against a "Euro-Western" Cartesian dualism serves his argument well. Yet, if crucial to a post-colonial theology is resistance to binaries of opposition that serve coloniality, there is opportunity for his work to be strengthened further. Nandy is correct when he argues that the so-called West is not simply part of an "imperial view," its traditions include "protest against the modern [colonialist] West."[73] To the extent that Woodley recognizes this, his call for intercultural theology resources post-colonial theology.[74] As has been seen in this chapter, a dualism between Christ and Jesus may be present in theology labeled "Western," but there are other voices, perspectives, and readings of Scripture also present.

If Joh underestimates the subversive and surplus readings of Scripture, Woodley may tend toward a reading of Scripture that does not fully recognize its potency to subvert his intentions. In part, he recognizes this,

---

*Native American Theology*, 79–84.

72. Woodley, *Shalom and the Community*, 25.

73. Nandy, *Intimate Enemy*, xiv.

74. See Woodley, *Shalom and the Community*, 56–57.

calling the text of Joshua, a "narrative of bloodthirsty terrorists killing men, women, and children" that is the result of "Jewish nationalistic redaction."[75] He does not dwell on the significance of such redaction. Rather, he chooses to relativize the place of Israel in the plans of God as one nation among many, while at the same time applying other promises made to Israel to Native American histories and lands. Criticisms of all kinds of naïve nationalisms are important in post-colonial theology.[76] The relativizing of the place of Israel in the biblical text and theology by Christian scholars is, however, problematic. The Christian gospel stands in continuity and not discontinuity with the Hebrew Bible. No doubt Woodley's appeal for renewed intercultural (and interreligious) theologies and communities further opens our eyes and hearts to the consequences and unintended consequences of our readings of Scripture and tradition.

From a Native American perspective, Woodley's resistant theologizing presents not only a deconstructive critique of white theology, but it also presents a practice of resistance that is constructive. He begins from his own experience and research to weave a tragic counternarrative of the USA. Both Native Americans and colonizers lose in this history. Blessings that could have been widely shared become corrupted, and defensive communities and faith commitments emerge. In contrast, Woodley sees at the heart of Native American theology and the gospel a call to the Harmony Way. Fundamentally, and particularly for white Christians, this call is a call to repentance. As will be seen in the next chapter, such a return to God is a return to the land and a renewal of holiness, communion, and mission. However, it is a long and slow turning and will be led by those marginalized by dominant cultures and theologies. Even amidst fear, hate, and brutality, Woodley holds onto the hope that the turn from crisis to *kairos* is possible.

---

75. Woodley, *Shalom and the Community*, 122n19.
76. See Ateek, *Justice, and Only Justice*; Ateek, *Palestinian Theology of Liberation*.

# 9

# Implications
## Toward a Post-Colonial Renewal

> [T]hose who have been excluded are not simply seeking an equal place in a life determined by those who already have it, but are presenting the challenge of an alternative model of community. They are asking not simply to be included but for the church to change . . . .
>
> —Chris Budden[1]

Woodley's resistance to the dominance of white Christianity is a call for renewal. He calls for white Christians to repent. The implications to be considered in this chapter will, therefore, focus on a response to such a call. Resistance as renewal includes white Christian repentance. Resistance as renewal means, in light of Scripture's testimony to the Creator-God, a fresh understanding of holiness. It means, in the light of the Harmony Way, a renewed recommitment to the communion of the saints. It means, in light of the witness of Jesus Christ, a stress on the agency of God's Spirit in God's mission.

1. Budden, *Following Jesus in Invaded Space*, 90.

## FINDING THE HATE

1. Was the story of the United States of America important in your upbringing? If not, why not? If so, how was it told? Was there another
   national or cultural story more important in your upbringing?

2. What would it mean for you and your circle of friends and family to
   tell the American story as "crisis?"

3. To what extent have you and your church considered the theology
   and practice of corporate or ecclesial repentance? Why/why not?

The dominant culture and the dominant church that Woodley has in view is
a settler culture and settler church. He reminds contemporary readers that
most of the land that America's homes, churches [seminaries], and busi-
nesses are built upon is stolen.[2] A retelling and reteaching of history from
the perspective of marginalized peoples should evoke penitence among
white believers. For Woodley this means deep, practical, and ongoing
"identificational repentance."[3] White Christians can, and should, identify
with the sins of their settler mothers and fathers. We continue to benefit
from their sin, and we harbor in our hearts racism resourced by historical
and contemporary cultural, legal, and institutional injustices. God, argues
Woodley, "still looks for people to stand in the gap in order to heal the land
and the people."[4] He draws from the example of Nehemiah (Neh 1:5–7),
who confessed his own sins, the sins of Israel, and the sins of his ancestors,
despite living in exile. "He had no human reason to confess those sins . . . ."[5]
The church as the body of the self-emptying Christ remains present in the
world in kenotic mode. At the very least, this means a beating ecclesial
heart of repentance for its own sin and for the sin of the world.[6]

---

2. Woodley, *Shalom and the Community*, 131.

3. Woodley, *Living in Color*, 168.

4. Woodley, *Living in Color*, 168. See Douglas, *Stand Your Ground*.

5. Woodley, *Living in Color*, 170, 168.

6. McBride, *Church for the World*. The particular focus of this chapter is ecclesial
repentance in response to Native American suffering. Nonetheless, it should be noted
that there is theological and ethical danger in the more expansive notion of a kenotic
mode of existence for the church. Bergen, quoting Richard Neuhaus, captures the danger
well when he writes that, even in repentance, the church can fall into hegemony claiming too much, as if it was "the world's singular institution of moral credibility" (Bergen,
"Whether, and How, a Church," 139).

Jeremy Bergen's study, *Ecclesial Repentance,* lends support to Woodley's call for corporate repentance. Bergen takes as his point of departure particular examples of the church repenting of past sins (including ecclesiastical disunity, anti-Semitism, slavery, racism, child abuse, sexism, homophobia, colonialism, war, and ecological degradation) as a practice that emerges distinctly in the twentieth century.[7] He begins his study with the 1993 National Native Convocation of the Anglican Church of Canada. During the Convocation, many First Nations peoples witnessed to their experiences in Anglican-governed residential schools. For a week, the Primate of the Church, Michael Peers, listened. Then he offered an apology:

> I have felt shame and humiliation as I have heard of suffering inflicted by my people, and as I think of the part our church played in that suffering. . . . I accept and I confess before God and you, our failures in the residential schools. We failed you. We failed ourselves. We failed God. I am sorry, more than I can say, that we were part of a system which took you and your children from home and family. I am sorry, more than I can say, that we tried to remake you in our image, taking from you your language and the signs of your identity. . . . On behalf of the Anglican Church of Canada, I present our apology. . . . I know how often you have heard words which have been empty because they have not been accompanied by actions. I pledge to you my best efforts, and the efforts of our church at the national level, to walk with you along the path of God's healing.[8]

For Bergen, ecclesial repentance is a church and/or denominational body officially and publicly requesting forgiveness or making a statement of apology or confession for something that was once official practice or policy.[9] Such repentance has significance from at least four perspectives that reflect major themes in post-colonial theology. It puts repentance on the public record (emerging from *particularity*). It contributes to redressing imbalances of power where the penitent is dependent on the response and

7. Bergen, *Ecclesial Repentance.*

8. Anglican Church of Canada, *Apology to Native People,* 1–2.

9. Bergen, *Ecclesial Repentance,* 3, 70–71. There is some controversy around the distinction between "apology" and "repentance." In my judgment, Bergen's distinction that puts both terms in continuity is more satisfactory, and attentive to actual church statements and reparative programs, than contrasting them. In summary, a church apology is repentance that has in view human relationships and the repair of relationships. A statement of church repentance is concerned particularly with restoring relationship with God. For a contrary view see Novak, "Jews and Catholics," 20–25.

priorities of marginalized peoples (actualization of marginalized *agency*). It rewrites, renews, or remembers historical narratives by reforming the testimony of the church in light of marginalized experiences (*hybridizing* testimony). It can anticipate, articulate, and instantiate actions that prevent or seek to prevent the sin of the past from being repeated (grounding *resistance*).[10] While these acts do not constitute in themselves what Christian theologians mean by reconciliation, nor may they be even necessary to a church's commitment to the ongoing elusive work of reconciliation, they can be a contribution to what Bergen calls social reconciliation.[11] They create a language that emerges both from theological convictions (2 Cor 5:18–21) and particular sin, holding before a divided community the ongoing presence of the past and a glimpse of how God's future might be possible. Yet, such contested and controversial public ecclesial repentance may not always be appropriate. Without deep discernment, ecclesial repentance may be done in ways that cause further alienation and harm.[12] This raises an important question at the outset. What are the redemptive outcomes imaged and actualized in ecclesial repentance? To begin to answer that question, the ritual and reparational significance of ecclesial repentance needs to be considered.

Ritual and symbolism are important in ecclesial repentance. Both the words and the actions are to represent an ecclesial body, be expressed in ways that such a body can enter into repentance, and be a witness to wider society. These are complex issues and churches have not always got it right. For example, it was reported that in 2008, when the Episcopal Church (USA) sought to repent for its complicity in slavery at the African Episcopal Church of St. Thomas, Philadelphia, it was not entirely well received. The "Litany of Offense and Apology" was delivered in the context of a church service and all were invited to take part. R. P. M Bowden objected to a liturgy that was penned by a white person who "had no empathy for the pain that we went through."[13] Another leader, Canon Edward Rodman, reflected that such a ritual gave the impression that "repentance has become the office of the victim. What was needed . . . was an apology by

---

10. Bergen, *Ecclesial Repentance*, 279–83.

11. Bergen, *Ecclesial Repentance*, 71, 279.

12. Bergen, "Whether, and How, a Church," 130. As was seen in chapter 5, similar issues are at stake in contested understandings of reconciliation.

13. Kawamoto, "Repentance for Slavery," para. 17. See Bergen, *Ecclesial Repentance*, 77.

one group to another group that has been separate and unequal."[14] Bergen notes, however, that this approach also raises problems. For example, such an approach may imply, once more, that the white-speaking part of the church *is* the church.[15] Symbolically, ritually, and liturgically, both words and actions need to speak to the brokenness of the church. The gathered body is wounded. In the congregation and in the broader church, the voice, testimony, and prophetic judgment of some have been marginalized. At the very least, public repentance needs the embodiment of both countertestimony and testimony, needs the versicle that lays bare injustice and the response that beckons the church to justice. That is to say, corporate repentance must problematize the "we" at work in liturgy.[16]

Bergen suggests that a means to avoid penitential malpractice is to consider the internal fourfold structure (contrition, confession, penance, absolution) of the liturgized sacrament or ministry of reconciliation as it calls the church to the reconciliation it needs and seeks to embody.[17] The first three movements in this ritualized reconciliation will be considered here and absolution considered in the final section of the chapter. *Contrition* is heartfelt sorrow for particular sin and the heartfelt intent of not sinning in such a way again. It is, in Coakley's terms, a desire to align one's will with the divine life-giving will. Corporately, then, ecclesial repentance is not about optics, is not about broadcasting a better message to society, it is not about managing a problem, it is not about progressive politics, it is not even about guilt for a community's sin. It is about being humbled by the convicting work of the Holy Spirit. It is evidence that the judgment of God has been heard and received by a particular community. It is evidence of a community being broken open to deep relationality amidst God's creation across time and space. Evidently, a contrite church *confessing* the specificity of its sins is remarkable.[18] If contrition is indeed a work of the Spirit, then

14. Bergen, "Whether, and How, a Church," 146.

15. Cited in Bergen, "Whether, and How, a Church," 146. See Meridith, "Repenting of Slavery," 105–11. For other reports on the event, see Episcopal News Service, "Episcopalians Gather to Apologize"; Episcopal News Service, "Prayers, Tears and Song." The sermon of the Presiding Bishop can be found here: https://www.episcopalchurch.org/files/attached-files/sermon_by_kjs_10-4.pdf. The Order of Service can be found here: https://www.episcopalarchives.org/sites/default/files/anti-racism/DayOfRepentance_ServiceLeaflet.pdf.

16. Bergen, *Ecclesial Repentance*, 66.

17. Bergen, *Ecclesial Repentance*, 243–83.

18. Beyond the 1993 National Native Convocation of the Anglican Church of

the confession offered will not only demonstrate exposure to the judgment of God, but the expressed confession will ring true to those who have experienced coloniality. If faux contrition is possible, faux confession can be exposed by those who suffer coloniality. They know the depths of their suffering and that suffering becomes a plumb line for any articulated confession. For some, the Episcopal Church's 2008 repentance did not in fact demonstrate a deep enough sense of contrition. In such circumstances, the brokenness and division in the church cannot be veiled liturgically. Rather, just as such suffering and division has been realized in history, it needs to be recognized in ritual. Similarly, Bergen is unsure who the church's confessor can be. In post-colonial theology this is quite clear. Any confession always emerges from and is uttered in intercultural study and intercultural relationship with those who theorize and theologize from the perspective of communities continuing to struggle because of colonialism and coloniality. Bergen recognizes this in part when he writes, "Examination of the church's witness cannot be done apart from the testimony of those who experienced the distortion of that witness and its life-denying effects."[19] In response, life-giving formation is searched after in *penance*. In a very real sense, the characteristics of post-colonialism addressed in this study are done in such a penitential mode. Those in dominant cultures are called to demonstrate a critical awareness of their particularity historically, culturally, theologically, and spiritually (chapters 1 and 2). This will inevitably lead to an openness to the theological voice of those who theologize in response to colonialism and coloniality (chapters 3, 4, and 5). The contextualizing and resisting work of such theologians confronts white theologians with the profound truth that to speak of the God who became incarnate is to speak of the God who became colonized (chapters 6 and 7). The salvation of God then, however wrought, is inextricably linked to a "going beyond" coloniality (chapter 8). That "going beyond" is a call to purgation-into-life. It is the Spirit's call to *penance*. Penance involves acts of reparation. Penance demonstrates that the church has heard, often through the prophetic voice of those who have experienced coloniality, the voice of God's judgment and grace. As Cone rightly recognizes, an apology is not justice.[20] Penance,

---

Canada, other moments of ecclesial repentance, variously received, include an apology from the Anglican Communion (1920); United Church of Canada (1986); the Anglican Church of Australia (1993); the Episcopal Church (1997, 2006, 2008); and the Church of England (2006) (Bergen, *Ecclesial Repentance*, 2–3, 61–77, 205).

19. Bergen, *Ecclesial Repentance*, 254.

20. Cone, *Cross and the Lynching Tree*, 99.

as particular reparative action to particular historical sin, is needed as the fruit of conversion.[21]

The practice of corporate repentance for sin against First Nations peoples, but also others who have experienced coloniality, has not only resulted in steps toward relational repair—however inchoate and inadequate—it has also resulted in shifts in the very understanding of the church. Particularly, ecclesial repentance has had implications for what it means to say that the church is holy. This is where we began this study. The chief issue at stake for the church in the modern and post-colonial era is how Christians can justify the claim that the church is holy. It is to this issue that we turn to next.

## FINDING EACH OTHER

> Apart from Jesus Christ, the church has no basis, no foundation.
> Its identity is something it receives from another. In repentance,
> the church makes clearer what is always the case: the basis of its
> hope is not itself, certainly not its good efforts or best intentions,
> but Jesus Christ.[22]

In ancient biblical and creedal texts the church is declared holy. In the aftermath of the Reformation, Roman Catholic theology stressed that it alone was in apostolic succession and held the true sacraments. Non-Roman Catholic others were "schismatics," "heretics," and "children of Satan."[23] While the church is "something definite and perceptible to the senses" the church, as the mystical body of Christ, is:

> a perfect society, . . . not made up of merely moral and juridical elements and principles. It is far superior to all other human societies; it surpasses them as grace surpasses nature, as things immortal are above all things that perish.[24]

> The Church is holy: the Most Holy God is her author; Christ, her bridegroom, gave himself up to make her holy; the Spirit of

---

21. See Harvey, "Which Way to Justice?" 57–77. She makes a distinction between reconciliation and reparation in a way that Bergen does not. See also Perkinson, *White Theology*, 217–48.

22. Bergen, "Whether, and How, a Church," 140.

23. Bosch, *Transforming Mission*, 461. Bergen, *Ecclesial Repentance*, 172–73; Heb 11:39b–40; Bergen, *Ecclesial Repentance*, 200.

24. Pious XII, *Mystici Corporis Christi* (1943), 14, 63.

holiness gives her life. Since she still includes sinners, she is "the sinless one made up of sinners."[25]

The Creator-God of Woodley's witness who calls God's children into intimate relationship with all of creation will not allow the cry of innocent blood, soaked into the land, to be exculpated by an ecclesiology of the sinless church. The danger of the idea of a sinless church, motivated by a desire for theological coherency, depends upon a logic of abstraction that results in an ironic understanding of holiness unrelated to historical particularism.[26] While this abstraction may be present in Protestant theology, where an emphasis on universal sin can veil particular historical failures, it is particularly prominent in Catholic theology.[27]

Roman Catholic theologians have struggled with a high ecclesiology in the face of complicity in deep historical division, violence, and injustice. The Vatican II document *Unitatis Redintegratio* recognizes that the church "in its members" is "liable to sin."[28] The document *Lumen Gentium* may say more as it depicts a pilgrim church that welcomes sinners and welcomes purification and reform as it journeys to its eschatological God-ordained end. "The Church . . . will attain its full perfection only in the glory of heaven."[29] For some—notably Karl Rahner, Hans Küng, and Joseph Ratzinger—Vatican II opened up the possibility of a church that sins.[30] Bergen's contribution is to examine actual incidents of repentance that, intentionally or unintentionally, shift the church's practice in the direction of Küng and Ratzinger. A variety of statements by popes and bishops in the twentieth century have implied sin on the part of the church.[31] Bergen sees this particularly clearly in the 1997 Drancy statement of repentance by the French bishops for complicity in the anti-Semitic laws of the Vichy government in France during World War II. The bishops confessed to the source of complicity in its very teaching and worship: "for centuries, up until Vatican Council II, an anti-Jewish tradition stamped its mark . . . on Christian doctrine and teaching, in theology, apologetics, preaching and in the liturgy.

---

25. *Catechism of the Catholic Church* (1992), 867.

26. Bergen, *Ecclesial Repentance*, 206.

27. Bergen, *Ecclesial Repentance*, 206. See Moltmann, *Spirit of Life*, 126–28.

28. Vatican II, *Unitatis Redintegratio* (1964), I:3.

29. Vatican II, *Lumen Gentium* (1964), VII:48.

30. Bergen, *Ecclesial Repentance*, 211–12; Rahner, *Theological Investigations*, 288–92. See Catholic Bishops of France, "Declaration of Repentance."

31. Bergen, *Ecclesial Repentance*, 217.

It was on such ground that the venomous plant of hatred for the Jews was able to flourish."[32] For Bergen, such a statement, alongside commitments to deeper relationship with Jews, is nothing less than remarkable. This is not simply the church of today making a judgment about members from its past. Rather, in repentance, the church is "making judgment about an *ecclesial dimension* of its past as church."[33] It is not simply the case that individual sinners in their sinful actions prevent the church from communicating more clearly the grace of God in the world. The church itself has prevented its members from a deeper witness to God's grace.[34] Given this, how now is the holiness of the church to be understood?

A renewed understanding of holiness, that takes into account the growing body of post-colonial theology and acts of ecclesial repentance, will reject any notion that holiness is the achievement of the church's members. It is the gift of God. The church's holiness is not defined or guarded by distinguishing individual sinning members from a sinless body. The holiness of the church is defined by God's presence in the midst of sin and the church as a forgiven fellowship. The historicity and particularity of the church is, therefore, not accidental to its nature. It is of the very essence of its nature. It is holy because it is historical. It is holy because it is dependent upon the grace-filled agency of God.[35] It is holy because it follows on in the wake of Christ's purgation-into-life. Its holiness is its self-emptying and its reception of God's grace. A post-colonial theology, facing the complicities of the church in violent colonialism and coloniality, has a spiritual function. It not only faces the hate, it calls the church to repentance and, thus, to holiness. The question is, how is the gift of God's grace and the call to purgation-into-life discerned? Again, it is important that such a question is understood as particular. The focus here is how a response to the sin identified by Woodley—though the sin identified in engagement with Yeats, Mbiti, and Joh need not be ignored—should be discerned. This particular invitation to discernment, at this juncture, is primarily for white Christians and white-dominated churches. Arising from the call to contrition,

32. Catholic Bishops of France, "Declaration of Repentance."

33. Bergen, *Ecclesial Repentance*, 216. Italics mine.

34. Bergen, *Ecclesial Repentance*, 216–17. See Catholic Bishops of France, "Declaration of Repentance."

35. Bergen, *Ecclesial Repentance*, 225–86.

confession, and penance, a three-dimensional approach to discernment will be considered presently.[36]

First, white Christians need to "sit with it." In more than one occasion, I have found myself involved in consultations and classrooms where emotions run high. White Christians can find counterreadings of history and theological voices that criticize dominant cultures to be threatening. Afraid, we once more exercise our privilege to walk out, check out, or hit out. What I am inviting white Christians to do is not run and not strike, but sit. Sit with the deep criticism that voices like Yeats, Mbiti, Joh, and Woodley provide. Visit with criticism and judgment. Read and reread. Listen and listen again. Learn about the distinct approaches to colonialisms and colonialities and the anti-colonial movements in your own context and across contexts. This is not easy. It is an experience of formation and an expansion of curricula that many of us have never experienced. It is humbling and can sometimes feel humiliating. Yet, this invitation to listen and learn and be formed in intercultural theology is an ongoing process. The pain that Woodley embodies is at least six hundred years old. Taking part in an anti-racism seminar or a march in Washington, DC is not going to redeem this coloniality. Intercultural theology and post-colonial theology are complex and require long-term commitment and local engagement. In the midst of such interculturality, the task is to consider the sin of coloniality that your community, congregation, tradition, or church has been complicit in. During such formation, in the mercy of God, a contrite heart and a humble spirit may be formed as our histories, theologies, and assumptions are decentered. White Christians, with varying degrees of privilege, are accustomed to framing and managing conversations. Contrition means a loss of control. It is a deep recognition that we are dependent on the mercy of God. That realization drives us back to Mary's gospel:

> [T]he Mighty One has done great things for me,
> and holy is his name . . . .
> He has shown great strength with his arm;
> he has scattered the proud in the thoughts of their hearts.
> He has brought down the powerful from their throne
> but has lifted up the humble. (Luke 1:49, 51–52)

---

36. Both Bergen and Woodley suggest a similar approach. See Woodley, *Living in Color*, 162–80, and Bergen, "Whether, and How a Church," 140–48.

To be brought down and to be humbled is what puts white Christians in the position to confess their sins and align themselves with the love, life, and grace of God. We are brought down so that we might receive the Christ.

Second, brought down, we are called to the particularity of confession. Whether this is a public confession, an apology, and/or a request for forgiveness, white Christians must not assume or expect that such responses to coloniality are met with acceptance or absolution. In 1986, the United Church of Canada (UCC) issued an "Apology to First Nations."[37] This came after a direct challenge from a First Nation leader calling the church to apologize. After deliberation, the white leaders of the church penned such an apology. Two years later, Native leaders responded by receiving but not accepting the apology. It was explained that in Native American cultures apologies are lived out:

> On the advice of Elder Art Solomon, a stone cairn was erected on the exact spot where the apology was delivered to symbolize the unfinished and ongoing requirements of the apology. Stones were to be added as signs of healing and progress in the relationship.[38]

Confession is not the means to control the story. It is not putting the pain of the past behind us. It is not closure. It is precisely the opposite. It is, for white Christians, submitting themselves to an agenda which is not their own, one that will only emerge in deeper confession, fellowship, dependence on God's mercy, and in particular, intercultural witness. On the twentieth anniversary of the apology, the statement was reread in the same location. More stones were added to the cairn representing the founding of the All Native Circle Conference,[39] new contextual theological education programs, a Healing Fund for survivors of residential schools, and explorations in traditional spiritualities.[40]

Third, penance means purgation (John 3:30). A complaint that I often hear from white Christians, when invited to read post-colonial theological texts, is "they seem to overlook their own sins or the dysfunction in their own communities" or "at the end of the day, we are all sinners." The latter appeal to the universality of sin has already been addressed in this chapter. The former is rarely, if ever, a justified complaint (remember, post-colonial

37. http://www.united-church.ca/sites/default/files/resources/1986–1998-aboriginal-apologies.pdf.

38. Bergen, *Ecclesial Repentance*, 245.

39. www.allnativecircleconference.com

40. Bergen, *Ecclesial Repentance*, 245.

theologians identify neocolonialism as an ongoing danger) and Woodley is certainly not guilty of this. Indeed, he shares with his readers a public confession that he himself made during a 1997 festival for racial reconciliation. At that festival he made a statement of repentance for the Cherokee involvement in slavery.[41] Even with centuries of suffering and the implications of intergenerational trauma, Woodley recognizes that he begins from a place of weakness. In the case of the UCC's apology, there was evidence that power shifted. The power of white Christians contracted as their confession was challenged to be grounded in healing and reparative action in fellowship with Native believers. Too often we see such contraction as purgation-into-death. We fear that we will lose and others will win. Again, the danger of abandoning the language of sacrifice has unintended consequences. The patriarchal and violent vision of sacrifice dominates our view and forestalls experience of God's grace and the opportunities to build a more humane community. At its 78th General Convention, the Episcopal Church passed a resolution (C019) aimed at responding to systematic injustices. The resolution stated:

> The Episcopal Church confesses that, despite repeated efforts at anti-racism training as well as racial justice and racial reconciliation initiatives, including the passage of more than 30 General Convention resolutions dating back to 1952, the abomination and sin of racism continue to plague our society and our Church at great cost to human life and human dignity; we formally acknowledge our historic and contemporary participation in this evil and repent of it . . . .[42]

> Our Church has enjoyed a unique degree of economic and social privilege in the United States, thanks in part to our origins in the British Empire. . . . The Episcopal Church has a special vocation to examine our history, to say we are sorry, and to participate in the repair and restoration of communities and institutions that struggle to flourish because of systems built to privilege our Church's historic membership.[43]

In light of this resolution, $2 million was set aside for a deeper process of formation and community-based reparation entitled, "Becoming

41. Woodley, *Living in Color*, 169–72.

42. General Convention of the Episcopal Church (USA), "Work for Racial Justice," 310–11.

43. Episcopal Church (USA), *Becoming Beloved Community*, 21.

Beloved Community: The Episcopal Church's Long-term Commitment to Racial Healing, Reconciliation, and Justice."[44] It is too early to say whether such an approach will have significant impact on local communities and the wider church. Nonetheless, this funded initiative has a clear focus (prison reform and financial commitment to two Episcopal, historically Black colleges and universities) and a clear framework. *Becoming the Beloved Community* invites churches into a labyrinthlike process of formation to tell the truth, proclaim God's grace-filled intent, practice the way of love, and repair broken systems and institutions.

4. What do you think it means to say that the church is holy?

5. Given the sins of a settler church and culture highlighted by Woodley, how do you understand contrition, confession, and penance?

## FINDING GOD

The previous section reflected on what it might mean, facing coloniality, to say that the church *is* holy. It also reflected on how the church might discern further ways in which it can live into its call to *become* holy. This section, in light of Woodley's construction of the Harmony Way, considers how this has implications for understanding and teaching the importance of the communion of the saints and the role of God's Spirit in God's mission.

The church claims holiness and it also claims catholicity. In Woodley's demand for ecclesial repentance and practice of ecclesial repentance, there is an assumption that there is continuity between particular times and places. As has been seen, this idea of continuity, through a strong emphasis on interconnectedness or deep relationality, is central to the Harmony Way. Catholicity is not less than this. The ancestral interconnectedness in Christian faith is captured by the idea of the communion of saints. However, this communion is not established simply by an appeal to biological ancestors, nor by historical and cultural antecedents. It is not guaranteed by theological coherence over time. The church as communion is birthed by God's eternal love, by the mission of Christ's love in the face of death, and by the bonding presence of the Holy Spirit.[45] In Christ, ancestors remain bound to the living (Eph 2:16–18; 1 Cor 3:16; Rom 8:38–39). As has already

44. Episcopal Church, *Becoming Beloved Community*.

45. Bergen, *Ecclesial Repentance*, 154–72.

been seen, the work of Christ is a purgation-into-life. Christ gathers up and joins together, in grace, not only the faith of the people, but the frailties of the people. The church as a pilgrim community depends upon the abiding presence of Christ's Spirit opening it to God's grace and God's judgment. Acts of ecclesial repentance may evidence this work of the Spirit, allowing the wholeness of God's future to begin to break in at particular times and in particular places. The abiding Christian community is bound together not only by the merits of its saints, but also by the sins of its saints. The Anglican Church of today is, indeed, the same church that presided over abuse in boarding schools.[46] As with a renewed understanding of holiness, a renewed understanding of communion first and foremost says something about God. The church is holy by virtue of God's abiding presence. The church is catholic by virtue of God's gracious forgiveness.[47]

> Sin . . . belongs to the church not only through Christ's assumption and forgiveness of them, but through the church's own disobedience and transgressions. Yet, because the church is the communion it is because of Christ's forgiveness of sin, this sin of the church does not mean that the church has ceased to be the church. Rather, it is the church in virtue of its connection to Jesus Christ, and its consequent continual reception of his forgiveness.[48]

The mission of God in and toward God's creation is, therefore, ongoing and directed both to those outside the church and those inside the church. The *missio Dei* cannot be straightforwardly associated with the witness of the church. The church can fall into idolatry and present to the world not a testimony of the gospel, but a countertestimony (Rev 2:1–7, 12–17, 18–28; 3:1–6):[49]

> The "bad news" of Jesus Christ requires people to forsake their own ethnic identity for the identity of the dominant culture. . . . The "bad news" of Jesus Christ requires indigenous peoples to accept their status as those meant to be colonized and to cooperate with their own demise. The "bad news" of Jesus Christ asks us to

---

46. This might be seen as a summary of Bergen's much more nuanced and complex argument in *Ecclesial Repentance*.

47. Bergen, *Ecclesial Repentance*, 174–76.

48. Bergen, *Ecclesial Repentance*, 176.

49. See Bergen, "Whether, and How, a Church," 133.

draw our theology, values, and meaning as people from a culture
that wishes to make us self-haters.[50]

Despite this, Woodley does not want to abandon the category of mission entirely.[51] The possibility of a post-colonial understanding of mission comes into view.[52] For him, any new missional understanding and practice must emerge shaped by marginalized voices and take deliberate account of injustice. "The church embodies reconciliation as it hears the cries of the marginalized people, overturns power imbalances and addresses ways to heal individuals and communities, while developing structures to ensure voices are in the future heard and the wrong is not repeated."[53]

Crucial, therefore, to the mission of the church is its ongoing discernment of its failings, which must include discernment about its past ministry as well as its present and future ministry. The mission of the church is, therefore, not simply its "sending." Mission is not simply the self-sending of God in Christ in history. Mission is, crucially, the Spirit of Christ sent *to the church* through the witness of others beyond itself. It is *in*reach as well as *out*reach.

If "mission" is to be a term of ongoing use, then a critical turn will need to be taken before any constructive turn can be considered. As has been seen, an emphasis on particularity in post-colonial theology means historical and contemporary sin is an important point of departure. Injustice in Ireland, Kenya, Korea, and the United States of America becomes spiritually and theologically significant. Many times in the midst of conflict and in sites of conflict, when hateful memories and bloody histories are faced and embodied, I have found myself able only to pray the *kyrie*. Indeed, in my own research and in intercultural partnerships and publications that unveil coloniality and white complicity, I find that I can pray little

---

50. Woodley, *Shalom and the Community*, 150.

51. See Cuéllar and Woodley, "North American Mission and Motive," 74. For a recent argument to abandon the category, see Stroope, *Transcending Mission*. Even as a Professor of Christian Mission, I have mixed feelings about the term. It can have a thoroughgoing theological meaning grounded in particular commitments to the nature of God and God's turning outwards in creative and re-creative acts. However, given the history of missions, I have reservations about the term, not least because of the misunderstandings it creates and the associations it holds, especially in interreligious conversations. Increasingly, my own preference is to name my work not "missiology" but "intercultural theology."

52. For one attempt at this, see Grau, *Rethinking Mission in the Postcolony*.

53. Bergen, *Ecclesial Repentance*, 286.

else but, "Lord have mercy, Christ have mercy, Lord have mercy." Particular practices of ecclesial repentance that are ongoing responses to historical sin have ecclesiological significance particularly in the way that holiness, catholicity, and communion are understood. If it is possible to conceive of post-colonial mission, then this same particularity along with a stress on divine agency will remain central to resistant renewal. The church is not the cause of its own mission. It is the subject and fruit of God's mission.[54] Theological motivations and theological implications of the call to repentance and the practice of repentance have been reflected on in this chapter. The theological nature of coloniality and the need for a theological response to such sin must always be kept in view. This is not the work of a progressive few or the work of some sort of radical wing. To face coloniality and seek a post-coloniality of the heart, framed and nourished by the ritual and liturgy of the church, is to contend for the very soul of the church. It is to take seriously what it means to be the broken body of Christ in a particular place at a particular time. It is to confess, pray, and act together in hope that God's desire for God's people would break in even amidst the hate.

Beyond contrition, confession, and penance in the church's pattern of purgation is the hope of absolution. How is this now understood given the historical and theological implications of the church's complicity in coloniality? Absolution comes ultimately from God. It is, however, embodied in pastoral and sacramental action when a priest absolves the penitent and calls her or him deeper into communion. Absolution, in this sense, is both declared by God and by God's church. This dual reality raises problems in a post-colonial theology. For the same church that sins in coloniality cannot, surely, absolve itself of coloniality. The missiological may, once more, aid our thinking here. If the *missio Dei* cannot simply correspond with the *missio Ecclesiae* (mission of the church) then immediately we have a clue toward a renewed understanding of absolution. The *missio Dei* points to the reality that the Spirit of Christ is at work beyond the church. In circumstances where the church discerns that it must repent of particular sins, those sinned against, or those representing those sinned against, potentially embody the confessor of God amidst coloniality. The Native American leaders who received the UCC apology in 1986 embodied the "not yet" of God's eschatological absolution. They invited the church to do better and enact what it means to be the body of Christ receiving the grace of God toward life. In brokenness, they were called to become witnesses of grace.

54. See Bergen, *Ecclesial Repentance*, 236.

It is not that repentant sinners earn the forgiveness of God or the church. Rather, contrition, confession, and penance are embraced by God in God's larger work of reconciliation. God's work of reconciliation can break into human history and, in the current context, that means grace is received not just at the hands of Christians, but at the hands of others the church has sinned against.[55]

6. To what extent is the communion of saints taught in your context? How does this chapter introduce new impetus or new ideas for inviting others to consider its importance?

7. What are your feelings about the term "mission" and its derivatives? Do you still use the term? Why/why not?

8. What questions are you left with? How might you resource these questions?

---

55. See Bergen, *Ecclesial Repentance*, 260–63.

# 10

# Twenty Centuries of Stony Sleep
## Post-Colonial Theology Today

## REVIEW

Few people on this earth can avoid conflict and the ill effects of conflict. It is a privileged few that can cloister their bodies and minds from the deep seam of hatred that runs through history. Imperialism depends on dehumanizing large numbers of people in order to justify colonization and colonialism. The rhetoric of hate and the reality of violence feed one another. As much as Christians in dominant cultures would want to sequester such hate, rhetoric, and violence away from Christian theology, this is just not possible. Racism, authoritarianism, militarism, land grabbing, ethnocide, and genocide have been theologized implicitly and explicitly. Abstract hate, embodied hate, instrumentalized hate, theologized hate, and memorialized hate are part of the human story. The impossibility of a universally favored, rationally sophisticated, psychologically nuanced, historically subtle, or sociologically observable definition of hate cannot veil the enmity. Look to five centuries of hostility in Ireland. Look to tens of thousands, and possibly hundreds of thousands, dead due to torture and execution in colonial Kenya.[1] Look to 2.5 million causalities of the Korean war.[2] Look to 1900 when

1. Anderson, *Histories of the Hanged*. Elkins, *Britain's Gulag*.
2. Cumings, *Korean War*.

300,000 Native Americans survived as descendants of five million ancestors. Look to the nineteenth and twentieth centuries and five thousand
lynched black men, women, and children. Look to the present-day USA
and the ongoing daylight murder of African-Americans.[3] Hate and death
are in our midst. Any privileged position that can suppress or deny this
serves only to welcome and institutionalize hate. This can happen. This
does happen. The ramifications, especially for black and brown bodies, is
always severe. To deny or dilute the presence of hate in the name of God is
theological malpractice. This must be resisted.

There is resistance in each chapter of this book. Each chapter evidences a bid for some form of contextualization and decolonization. Yeats
resists English hegemony. Mbiti resists the supposed superiority of foreign
theologizing. Coloniality serves to resist any cheap absolution of the present through an appeal to some notion of progress. Joh resists patriarchal
interpretations of the cross that divinize subjugation. Woodley resists white
dominance in the telling of America's story and in the narrating of U.S.
American Christianity. A post-colonial Christian resistance is not simply
a critical stance, it is a constructive move. Post-colonial theology cannot
be reduced to a reactionary movement that has no resources of its own,
or reduced to a movement that simply and always is defined over against
others. A methodological and theological stress on particularity provides a
more transparent point of departure that situates a theologian in relation
to colonialism and/or coloniality. Adopting Yeats heuristically begins to
name and problematize my own particularity and formation in relation to
post-colonialism. Mbiti, beginning from the British colony of Kenya, draws
on Akamba understandings of temporality in reading Christian eschatology. Coloniality is a means to deeper analysis beyond historical colonies.
Subjugation predates and postdates formal colonies. In the midst of *han*,
Joh contends for *jeong* in Christology and on the cross of Christ. Woodley
resists the ethnocide of Native peoples in pointing to the Harmony Way
as gospel. In facing the hate, post-colonial theology deconstructs and
(re)constructs. Post-colonial theology is about criticism, but it is also about
fresh paths in analysis and practice. It is about judgment, but it is also about
grace and life. It is, in short, about a renewed post-colonial imaginary.

The term "post-colonial imaginary" may, in the end, be a way forward
for a clearer understanding of the broader field of post-colonialism and
post-colonial theology. Indeed, it may open up a fresh way of relating one

3. Douglas, *Stand Your Ground*, 173–203.

to the other. As will be seen below, because testimony is central to Christian Scripture, theology, and history, the characterization of theology-as-theory is problematic. Charles Taylor, in defining "social imaginary," writes:

> I speak of "imaginary" (i) because I'm talking about the way ordinary people "imagine" their social surroundings, and this is often not expressed in theoretical terms, it is carried in images, stories, legends, etc. But it is also the case that (ii) theory is often the possession of a small minority, whereas what is interesting in the social imaginary is that it is shared by large groups of people, ... (iii) the social imaginary is that common understanding which makes possible common practices, and a widely shared sense of legitimacy.[4]

What is in view in a *post-colonial* imaginary is an international fellowship for decolonization. It is an international and intercultural fellowship that shares the characteristics of post-colonial theology described in this study. The community exists even though it is not convened or could only ever be partially convened. It is formative for those responding to coloniality in terms of analysis, identity, and practice. It exists transnationally and across a range of experiences and expertise. It is, so to speak, a "communion" of witness from and against coloniality.[5] The post-colonial imaginary has a poetic sensibility or is engaged in a poetic mode. It values the ordinary. It evokes or broadcasts testimony. In the light of such witness, it contends for the relationship between testimony and theory. The post-colonial imaginary is both community and agenda.

In *The Moral Imagination,* veteran peacebuilder John Paul Lederach rightly complains that in any peace process the artists are called upon too late. They are called upon to celebrate the hard-won peace. He wonders how things in our world would be different if the artists were called upon first, and if negotiations were done in a more *poetic mode.* This book has called upon the artists first. Yeats's artistry knew that the transcendental, the religious, and even the theological were at the heart of the most intractable and practical of human problems. His poetic vision opens us to the depths of hate and the imagined ascent of love. Mbiti collects stories and parables and writes poetry. For him, stories are an "actual participation in the art of living."[6] Central to Joh's reading of the cross of Christ is an

4. Taylor, *Secular Age,* 171–72.

5. See Anderson, *Imagined Communities,* 6.

6. Mbiti, *Akamba Stories,* 35.

artistic expression of boundary-crossing, and she makes appeal to a range of cultural products, including film and music. She enters into the complexity of Christology with artistic sensitivity and expression. She opens up the heart in theological and spiritual invitation for those on the margins to write in the center of the page. Woodley too is a curator of wisdom in poetry, sayings, and stories. He too is an author of poetry. Story, he submits, is important to Native Americans because telling the past is a way to the future.[7] Given this, the textuality and literature that these theologian-writers have produced has been taken seriously in intercultural reading. This book takes as its point of departure the particularity of hate through a poetic lens (Yeats), draws upon theologian-artists, and makes numerous references to other artists. It is inevitable that in the conclusion to this study I find myself claiming that one of the threads holding this text together is an artistic or poetic impulse in the face of hate. Pointing beyond the bounds of this work means an invitation to a post-colonial imaginary.

Ngũgĩ wa Thiong'o explicitly makes the connection between artistry and resistance:

> [T]he search for new directions in language, theatre, poetry, fiction and scholarly studies in Africa is part and parcel of the overall struggles of African people against imperialism in its neo-colonial stage. It is part of that struggle for that world in which my health is not dependent on another's leprosy; my cleanliness not on another's maggot-ridden body; and my humanity not on the buried humanity of others.[8]

Writing of the best of contemporary poems, Mary Oliver describes them as brimming from "the particular, the regional, the personal."[9] This is the first attribute of a post-colonial theology. It is concerned with the particularity of place and people in relation to power, empire, and colony (chapters 1 and 2). Famously, wa Thiong'o abandoned writing in English, choosing instead to write in Gikuyu, thus connecting more directly with *ordinary* readers. He committed to a decolonizing dialogue and vision that connected with local communities and nonspecialist audiences. A post-colonial imaginary means scholars close to local communities and local communities close to scholars, resulting in a porosity and subversion of such categories. In poetry, particularity is given voice when "you get your

7. Woodley, *Shalom and the Community*, 118.

8. wa Thiong'o, *Decolonising the Mind*, 106.

9. Oliver, *Poetry Handbook*, 80.

own feeling into your own words."[10] But this is no solitary and individual effort. It is always social. The individual poetic voice emerges from an ageless community of artistry. It emerges from the study of broader traditions, histories, politics, and experiences, drawing from them, illuminating them, critiquing them, and celebrating them.[11] Likewise, a post-colonial theology gives voice or takes heed of the voices that have been suppressed by colonialism and coloniality (chapters 3, 4, and 5). The "ordinary" is, then, defined and valued in a second sense as the theologizing of those "ordered out" of a dominant understanding of theology. Thus the intent and practice of a post-colonial theology is always this admixture of ordinary insight, specialist insight, and marginalized insight. It is a hybridized venture. To say that a poetic voice is hybrid can be to say very little. Poets borrow and they experiment with form, not least because of their exposure to other cultural expressions. Yet, hybridization as seen in the work of Joh (chapter 6) can break open new vision and even new life (chapter 7). Here, again, the theological and the poetical—even in the midst and in a return to grounded particularity—seek some form of transcendence or renewal of life (chapters 8 and 9). I do not want to overdo my estimation of art or the purported artistry of post-colonialism. Suffice it to say, as a practical theology, a post-colonial theology departs from experience, interrogates experience, and must return transformatively to experience. This dogged determination to return or keep connected to the point of departure is also evidence of the poetic mode. As with the poet, the post-colonial theologian testifies to the connectedness between his or her "speaking voice" and his or her "poetic voice," between his or her "original accent and . . . discovered style."[12]

In the introduction to this study I claimed that theology is *testimony*. By now the reader will have a better sense of what I mean by theology-as-testimony. It is (contested) theological articulation emerging from the sociality of experience. It is speech together that gives life. It gives life to Akamba, Korean, Native American Christians, and myriad others that live under restrictive political and theological governance. Rebecca Chopp describes such testimony poignantly as "discourses of survival for hope and of hope for survival."[13] Theology-as-testimony is not universally accepted. Indeed, there is a strong strand in modern Western theology

10. Heaney, "Feeling into Words," 3.

11. Hogan, *Empire and Poetic Voice*, 251.

12. Heaney, "Feeling into Words," 3.

13. Chopp, "Theology and the Poetics," 62.

that distinguishes testimony from theology or, more accurately, contrasts theology-as-theory from theology-as-testimony. On this view, testimony smacks of subjectivity and sectarianism. Theology-as-theory, in contrast, passes judgment, decides credibility, and includes or excludes. "Theory . . . is the clear-headed judge who decides the truth by ordering coherent narratives of history."[14] Chopp sees such distinction and epistemological hierarchy having its roots in European philosophy—she points to Locke, Lessing, Hume, Kant, and Troeltsch—that made any notion of revelation subordinate to particular empirical standards of modernist reason:

> In this trial by reason, testimonies become powerless, emptied of spirit, not convincing for proof. If testimonies cannot give immediate power and truth, what use shall be made of testimony . . . .
>
> Witnesses and testimonies are the stuff to be judged, and the modern theorist is the judge, prosecutor, and jury. If the testimony matches the consciousness of human experience, it is ruled to be credible and appropriate. If not, it is excluded: ruled out as irrational or pagan or simply silenced.[15]

This book does not follow this logic or law. A post-colonial theology is part of an imaginary arising from the "poetics of testimony." This is work that gives life or holds up the lively histories, pain, and visions of God that have been discounted or disallowed. We have already seen this in the authoritarianism of foreign missionaries, and Chopp cites academic conventions that render testimony a particular kind of speaking or writing outside the bounds of "proper" theology. Testimony then must become a particularly inventive mode of theologizing, "for it must create language, forms, images to speak of what, in some way, has been ruled unspeakable or at least not valid or credible to modern reason. Compared to rhetoric, poetics seeks not so much to argue as to refigure, to reimagine and refashion the world."[16]

This refiguring, reimaging, and refashioning in a post-colonial imaginary is already evidenced in the theological writings considered in this study. For each chapter is Christian testimony emerging in colonialism or coloniality toward a clearer Christian testimony in a world where subjugation and suffering continue. A post-colonial theology holds as sacred

14. Chopp, "Theology and the Poetics," 60–61. Chopp particularly has in view here Ogden's *Doing Theology Today*.

15. Chopp, "Theology and the Poetics," 59–60.

16. Chopp, "Theology and the Poetics," 61.

such testimony and seeks to be "responsive to the moral summons of testimony."[17] This does not mean a rejection of theory—where would post-colonial theology be without post-colonial theorists?—but it does mean a distinct view of theory. Theology-as-testimony no longer stands under theology-as-theory but rather in *dialogic relationship* to it.

## RETURN

In Yeats's apocalyptic "Second Coming," "twenty centuries of stony sleep" have created circumstances for a bestial return to Jerusalem. This is not a christological return. It is a nightmarish nativity borne of the failure to testify against hate and against bestial regimes:

> Surely the Second Coming is at hand . . .
> A shape with lion body and the head of a man,
> A gaze blank and pitiless as the sun,
> Is moving its slow thighs, while all about it
> Reel shadows of the indignant desert birds.
> The darkness drops again; but now I know
> That twenty centuries of stony sleep
> Were vexed to nightmare by a rocking cradle,
> And what rough beast, its hour come round at last,
> Slouches toward Bethlehem to be born?[18]

In reading "The Second Coming," one need not subscribe to Yeats's *A Vision* nor his understanding of the twenty-eight phases of the moon as key to understanding human personality. One need not subscribe to his cyclical theory of history divided into dispensations of two thousand years inaugurated each time by the figure of an Initiate or Messiah.[19] Independent of his idiosyncratic philosophy, the poem maintains a kind of prophetic verve. It is tempting to read a range of biblical allusions into Yeats's "Second Coming." The locus of the desert along with the sphinxlike beast could conjure up allusions to an Egyptian superpower. Under the rule of Egypt the people of God were subjugated and eventually released into desert barrenness (Exod 13–14) where they would submit to a beast (Exod 32). Later, under

17. Chopp, "Theology and the Poetics," 65.
18. Yeats, "Second Coming."
19. Yeats, *Vision*, 262–302.

Roman rule, Jesus would reenact and recapitulate their desert temptation (Matt 4). The beast of Yeats's apocalypse will come *from* the desert—reversing or recapitulating the journey of liberation *to* a promised land—and so the empire returns. Such bestial imagery has poetic and ancient precedent. In radical Christianity such imagery is significant, not least in the work of that figure Yeats confessed filled his mind since childhood—Blake.[20] Resourcing the imagination of Blake was, of course, the biblical text including its apocalyptic literature.[21] Whatever virtue there is in discerning biblical allusions in "The Second Coming," and there may be very little virtue in it, the biblical text directly depicts empire and a resistant testimony. Let us briefly return then to Scripture, and particularly, the beasts of John's apocalypse in Revelation 13:

> I saw a beast rising out of the sea. . . . And the dragon gave it his power and his throne and great authority. . . . In amazement the whole earth followed the beast, . . . "Who is like the beast, and who can fight against it?"
>
> The beast was given a mouth uttering haughty and blasphemous words, and it was allowed to exercise authority, . . . it was allowed to make war on the saints and to conquer them. It was given authority over every tribe and people and language and nation, and all the inhabitants of the earth will worship it . . . .
>
> Let anyone who has an ear listen:
> If you are to be taken captive,
> into captivity you go;
> if you kill with the sword,
> with the sword you must be killed.
> Here is a call for the endurance and faith of the saints. (Rev 13:1–10)

The community of Jesus in the province of Asia lived in a world where the preeminence of the Roman empire dominated. Beyond military conquest, the architecture, iconography, public art, rituals, and festivals in the great cities incarnated the emperor's claim to divinity. In the face of such a superpower, the "highly contextual" theology of Revelation stood as anti-imperialist testimony. Christ, not Caesar, is Lord.[22] The empire's military and political hegemony is depicted as bestial (Rev 13; 17). Its eco-

---

20. Yeats, *Vision*, 72. For other influences on the poem see Foster, *W. B. Yeats: A Life I*, 150–51.

21. For a thorough study of this, see Rowland, *Blake and the Bible*.

22. Bauckham, *Theology of the Book of Revelation*, 17, 35.

nomic hegemony is depicted in the image of a harlot or, more accurately, a "rich courtesan" (Rev 17–18). Imperial ideology, however, promises peace (through legionnaire boots on the ground) and prosperity (through screwing ordinary people). Imperial prosperity came at great ecological cost. A widespread network of imports brought to Rome priceless raw materials, luxury goods, and human slaves from locations that included Gaul, Spain, India, the Persian Gulf, Arabia, China, Galatia, Morocco, Egypt, Syria, Greece, Ceylon, Indonesia, and Yemen (Rev 18).[23] The riches that such imported wealth made and the promise and partial fulfillment of the *pax Romana* was intoxicating to many. Lest we forget, Revelation is a *prophecy*. It is an attempt to unveil a theological, spiritual, and ethical reality that is not necessarily apparent.[24] Modern readers benefiting from the satanic nature of systems and structures that serve hegemony are in no more an enlightened state than the original readers of John's Apocalypse. We all need the intervention of the prophetic spirit of God.

The empire is satanic (13:2) and humans are complicit in its rise (13:5, 7, 14). In contrast to an empire centered on the eternal city of Rome, the theology of Revelation provides a scathing critique and a pluralist future vision:

> The maintenance of civilization, of family, nation and property in the name of Christ is blasphemy. It cannot be squared with the way of the Lamb. That is because it too quickly *excludes* the deprived. It puts nations and privilege above human community and the right to possess above the privilege of serving. In Revelation the nation is subordinated to the international "multitude which no one can number" (7.9). That multitude comes from *every* nation.[25]

An argument for a theology that is inherently intercultural and anti-imperialist has ancient and biblical precedent. In current times, debates rage about whether or not superpowers of more recent eras can be fairly compared to the depiction of Rome in the New Testament. If this were so, then such superpowers could be compared to Rome with the obvious hermeneutical corollary that the anti-imperialist censure of Revelation would descend on them also. Further, a call to deeper discernment against the beguiling attractiveness of imperial complicity would be in order. A

---

23. Bauckham, *Climax of Prophecy*, 350–83.

24. Bauckham, *Theology of the Book of Revelation*, 35–47. Bauckham, *Climax of Prophecy*, 343–83.

25. Rowland, *Revelation*, 114.

post-colonial theology invites those of us from the dominant culture to read those theologies marginalized from the center of power as key resources in discerning the presence of God in the life of the world. Even in this short study, particularly in the writing of Mbiti, Joh, and Woodley, it is clear that white Christians do indeed run the risk of aligning the *status quo* with the gospel, and following not the anti-imperial Christ, but the imperialized anti-Christ. "*We* are the ones who allow the process whereby institutions emerge which enable idols like Caesar and Mammon to take the place of God."[26]

The ever-present lure of such idolatry and the dehumanizing rhetoric of colonization unchained a sectarian behemoth in Ulster. While this behemoth has unleashed cousins in other zones of conflict, not least in Kenya, Korea, and the United States of America, the point of departure in this study was Ireland and the settler culture that I was born into. Settler theology seeks to domesticate or baptize the beast in the hope that it will guard contested boundaries and grant peace of mind. It will grant neither safety nor peace. A post-colonial theology is always a call away from the bestial to the humane. It is always a call to recognize that the colonization that oppresses some, dehumanizes all.

"Under Ben Bulben" concludes with famous words that now adorn the headstone in the Church of Ireland parish where Yeats was laid to rest. As a whole, the poem evidences themes—not least, oligarchy and classism—that, as was seen in chapter 1, make Yeats as much a foil as a friend to post-colonialism. A lesson in itself, there are few who now remember the earlier stanzas:[27]

> Under bare Ben Bulben's head
> In Drumcliff churchyard Yeats is laid.
> An ancestor was rector there
> Long years ago, a church stands near,
> By the road an ancient cross.

---

26. Rowland, *Revelation*, 113.

27. Yeats writes: "Irish poets, learn your trade,/ Sing whatever is well made,/ Scorn the sort now growing up/ All out of shape from toe to top,/ Their unremembering hearts and heads/ Base-born products of base beds./ Sing the peasantry, and then/ Hard-riding country gentlemen,/ The holiness of monks, and after/ Porter-drinkers' randy laughter;/ Sing the lords and ladies gay/ That were beaten into the clay/ Through seven heroic centuries;/ Cast your mind on other days/ That we in coming days may be/ Still the indomitable Irishry."

No marble, no conventional phrase;
On limestone quarried near the spot
By his command these words are cut:

*Cast a cold eye*
*On life, on death.*
*Horseman, pass by!*[28]

Despite these famous stanzas, despite the Anglican lineage, and despite the headstone, Yeats may not actually be buried in Drumcliff. After his death in 1939, on the French Riviera, the war intervened and because of dubious actions and records at the graveyard in Roquebrune, the question remains whether the exhumed body was indeed that of the purported problematic progenitor of post-colonialism. The iconoclastic Yeats is in need of icon-elastic language. It seems fitting that the "return" of this most unorthodox of all Irish Protestants, steeped in Victorian occultism and given, even in death, a lukewarm welcome by Anglicanism, would be a "spiritual return."[29] In the last month of his life, and these words have been partially quoted in the introduction to this study, he would write:

> It seems to me that I have found what I wanted. When I try to put all into a phrase I say, "Man can embody truth but he cannot know it." I must embody it in the completion of my life. The abstract is not life and everywhere draws out its contradictions. You can refute Hegel but not the Saint or the song of sixpence.[30]

It is all but fantasy to assume that the poet's return was a return to the faith of Christian Ireland. His chief biographer exegetes these words and Yeats's self-inscribed elegy as a definite narrowing of the gyre, a return to the inspirations of his youth, and a return to the potency of hate in Ireland.[31] Yeats may well be part of a critical post-colonial corpus of literature worthy of being brought into dialogue with theological concerns. He may point toward an answer but he does not possess the answer. The particular

---

28. Yeats, *Collected Poems*, 301.

29. Foster, *W. B. Yeats: A Life: II*, 657. On the nineteenth-century fascination among Irish Protestants with the occult, see Foster, *W. B Yeats: A Life: I*, 45–52. On the doubts around Yeats's burial place and the probability of his return being "spiritual," see Foster, *W. B. Yeats: A Life: I*, 656–59.

30. Foster, *W. B. Yeats: A Life: II*, 650.

31. Foster, *W. B. Yeats: A Life: II*, 632–50.

pathologies of hate and dominance in Ireland cannot simply be healed at Irish wells. I must pass by. Overshadowed by the cross I remain on the way through ancestral crossroads. The spiritual return of Yeats to a Sligo graveyard becomes a waymarker for a deeper truth. A return to humane and humanizing intent and practice, against the dehumanizing brutality of coloniality, is a spiritual return. The intent and practice of a post-colonial theology is a decolonization toward rehumanization. It is, in other words, a matter of salvation.

## CONCLUSION

The seminary I teach at is on high ground. We are fond of calling it "the holy hill." Given the colonialities that the voices in this book resisted, is it possible to speak of holy hills and a holy church? The voices heard in this study disallow any abstract notion of holiness. The church has sinned. Therefore, whatever holiness means, it will have to mean something in the light of the heretical hubris of imperialisms and the church's particular complicity in patriarchy, racism, ethnocide, war, and genocide. Each voice in each chapter resisted particular forms of oppression and called the church to repentance. Herein lies the holiness of hill and church. It is repentance and repair that is the path to God's future *shalom*. It is the gift and presence of the healing spirit of Christ. And just as this penitence has not always been evident in the past, it is not always evident in the present nor, God have mercy, will it be evident in the future. Consequently, a post-colonial theology does not end with unveiling the particularities of imperialist sin and deconstructing the specificities of colonial dominance. It is a continued work of unveiling and a continued call for repentance. It is an abiding suspicion of the rhetoric of progress and an abiding faith in the presence of the Holy One.

Hate is alive and well in the world. So it has been and so it will be. But, God is love. God is eternal love and grace turned outwards in creation and in re-creation. In the worst of circumstances, people have wagered their lives on divine love. In the worst of circumstances, believers have subverted and resisted and imagined that the poetics of grace they have glimpsed—in a lover's touch, a family's solidarity, a community's determination, a song of revolution, or in a vision of the divine—might just be met by the life-giving, over-spilling, just desire of God. The desire to build walls and close doors separating us one from another is exactly what is not needed in theological education and in religious formation. It is exactly what is not needed in the sociality of the church and in the society at large. Anything that blocks thresholds or puts undue pressure on lintels needs to be exorcised. In the final analysis, resistant testimony in colonialism and coloniality is not marginal. It has the power to be liminal. Such witness is the threshold to a renewed vision of God and of each other. It is post-colonial theology in poetic mode. It is, for me, post-colonial theology in penitential mode.

# Bibliography

Achebe, Chinua. *Home and Exile*. New York: Anchor, 2000.

———. *Things Fall Apart*. 1958. Reprint. London: Penguin, 2006.

All Native Circle Conference. www.allnativecircleconference.com.

Allison, Jonathan. "Yeats and Politics." In *The Cambridge Companion to W. B. Yeats*, edited by Marjorie Howes and John Kelly, 185–205. Cambridge: Cambridge University Press, 2006.

Anderson, Benedict. *Imagined Communities: Reflections on the Origin and Spread of Nationalism*. Rev. ed. London: Verso, 2016.

Anderson, David. *Histories of the Hanged: Britain's Dirty War in Kenya and the End of Empire*. 2005. Reprint. London: Phoenix, 2006.

Anglican Church of Canada. "Apology to Native People: A Message from the Primate, Archbishop Michael Peers, to the National Native Convocation Minaki, Ontario, Friday, August 6, 1993." Toronto: Anglican Church of Canada, 1993. http://www.anglican.ca/wp-content/uploads/2011/06/Apology-English.pdf.

Association of Theological Schools. "2017–2018 Annual Data Tables." https://www.ats.edu/uploads/resources/institutional-data/annual-data-tables/2017–2018-annual-data-tables.pdf.

Ateek, Naim Stifan. *Justice, and Only Justice: A Palestinian Theology of Liberation*. Maryknoll, NY: Orbis, 1989.

———. *A Palestinian Theology of Liberation: The Bible, Justice, and the Palestine-Israel Conflict*. Maryknoll, NY: Orbis, 2017.

Athanasius the Great of Alexandria. *On the Incarnation*. Translated by John Behr. New York: St. Vladimir's Seminary Press, 2011.

Bardon, Jonathan. *The Plantation of Ulster: The British Colonisation of the North of Ireland in the Seventeenth Century*. 2011. Reprint. Dublin: Gill, 2012.

Bauckham, Richard. *The Climax of Prophecy: Studies on the Book of Revelation*. Edinburgh: T. & T. Clark, 1993.

———. *The Theology of the Book of Revelation*. Cambridge: Cambridge University Press, 1993.

Bergen, Jeremy M. *Ecclesial Repentance: The Churches Confront their Sinful Pasts*. London: T. & T. Clark, 2011.

———. "Whether, and How, a Church Ought to Repent for a Historical Wrong." *Theology Today* 73.2 (2016) 129–48.

Bew, Paul. *Ireland: The Politics of Enmity, 1789–2006*. Oxford: Oxford University Press, 2006.

Bhabha, Homi K. *The Location of Culture*. London: Routledge, 1994.

———. "Of Mimicry and Man: The Ambivalence of Colonial Discourse." *October* 28 (Spring, 1984) 25–133.

Boff, Leonardo. *Church: Charism and Power*. New York: Crossroads, 1986.

Bosch, David J. *Transforming Mission: Paradigm Shifts in Theology of Mission*. Maryknoll, NY: Orbis, 1991.

Brave Heart, Maria Yellow Horse. "The American Indian Holocaust: Healing Historical Unresolved Grief." *American Indian and Alaska Native Mental Health Research* 8.2 (1998) 60–82.

Brock, Rita Nakashima. *Journeys by Heart: A Christology of Erotic Power*. New York: Crossroads, 1988.

Brooks, Xan. "Joint Security Area" (Review). *The Guardian*, May 3, 2001. https://www.theguardian.com/culture/2001/may/03/artsfeatures4.

Brueggemann, Walter. *Peace: Living toward a Vision*. St. Louis: Chalice, 2001.

Brunner, Larry. *Tragic Victory: The Doctrine of Subjective Salvation in the Poetry of W. B. Yeats*. Troy, NY: Whitston, 1987.

Budden, Chris. *Following Jesus in Invaded Space: Doing Theology on Aboriginal Land*. Eugene, OR: Pickwick, 2009.

Catechism of the Catholic Church (1992). http://www.vatican.va/archive/ENG0015/__P29.HTM

Catholic Bishops of France. "Declaration of Repentance" (Drancy Statement). September 30, 1997. http://www.ccjr.us/dialogika-resources/documents-and-statements/roman-catholic/other-conferences-of-catholic-bishops/484-cefr1997.

Carpenter, Roger M. *"Times are Altered with Us:" American Indians from First Contact to the New Republic*. Chichester, UK: Wiley Blackwell, 2015.

Carter, Warren. *The Roman Empire and the New Testament: An Essential Guide*. Nashville: Abingdon, 2006.

Cavanaugh, William T. *The Myth of Religious Violence: Secular Ideology and the Roots of Modern Conflict*. Oxford: Oxford University Press, 2009.

Chávez, Franz. "Bolivia's Mother Earth Law Hard to Implement." Inter Press Service News Agency, May 19, 2014. http://www.ipsnews.net/2014/05/bolivias-mother-earth-law-hard-implement.

Chopp, Rebecca S. "Theology and the Poetics of Testimony." In *Converging on Culture: Theologians in Dialogue with Cultural Analysis and Criticism*, edited by Delwin Brown et al., 56–70. Oxford: Oxford University Press, 2001.

Cleary, Joe. "Postcolonial Ireland." In *Ireland and the British Empire*, edited by Kevin Kenny, 251–288. Oxford: Oxford University Press, 2004.

Coakley, Sarah. *The Cross and the Transformation of Desire: Meditations for Holy Week on the Drama of Love and Betrayal*. Cambridge: Grove, 2014.

———. "In Defense of Sacrifice: Gender, Selfhood, and the Binding of Isaac." In *Feminism, Sexuality, and the Return of Religion*, edited by Linda Martín Alcoff and John D. Caputo, 17–38. Bloomington, IN: Indiana University Press, 2011.

———. "Pleasure Principles: Towards a Contemporary Theology of Desire." *Harvard Divinity Bulletin* 33.2 (2005) 20–33.

———. *Powers and Submissions*. Oxford: Blackwell, 2002.

———. *Sacrifice Regained: Reconsidering the Rationality of Religious Belief. An Inaugural Lecture by the Norris-Hulse Professor of Divinity Given in the University of Cambridge, 13 October 2009.* Cambridge: Cambridge University Press, 2012.

Coakley, Sarah, and M. A. Nowak, eds. *Evolution, Games, and God: The Principle of Cooperation.* Cambridge: Harvard University Press, 2013.

Cone, James. *A Black Theology of Liberation: Fortieth Anniversary Edition.* 1986. Reprint. Maryknoll, NY: Orbis, 2010.

———. *The Cross and the Lynching Tree.* Maryknoll, NY: Orbis, 2011.

———. *God of the Oppressed.* Rev. ed. Maryknoll, NY: Orbis, 1997.

Cronin, Michael. *A History of Ireland.* Basingstoke, UK: Palgrave, 2001.

Cronin, Mike. "Catholicising Fascism, Fascistising Catholicism? The Blueshirts and the Jesuits in 1930s Ireland." *Totalitarian Movements and Political Religions* 8.2 (2007) 401–11.

Cuéllar, Gregory Lee, and Randy S. Woodley. "North American Mission and Motive: Following the Markers." In *Evangelical Postcolonial Conversations: Global Awakenings in Theology and Praxis,* edited by Kay Higuera Smith et al., 61–74. Downers Grove, IL: IVP Academic, 2014.

Cumings, Bruce. *The Korean War: A History.* New York: Modern Library, 2010.

Daniels, Patsy J. *The Voice of the Oppressed in the Language of the Oppressor: A Discussion of Selected Postcolonial Literature from Ireland, Africa, and America.* New York: Routledge, 2001.

Darden, Lynne St. Claire. *Scripturalizing Revelation: An African American Postcolonial Reading of Empire.* Atlanta: SBL, 2015.

Darwin, Charles. *The Descent of Man, and Selection in Relation to Sex.* 1879. Reprint. London: Penguin, 2004.

Dionysius the Areopagite. *The Mystical Theology and the Divine Names.* Translated by C. E. Rolt. Mineola, NY: Dover, 2004.

Douglas, Kelly Brown. *Stand Your Ground: Black Bodies and the Justice of God.* Maryknoll, NY: Orbis, 2015.

Dube, Musa W. *Postcolonial Feminist Interpretation.* St. Louis: Chalice, 2000.

Dunbar-Ortiz, Roxanne. *An Indigenous Peoples' History of the United States.* Boston: Beacon, 2014.

Duncan, Dawn. "A Flexible Foundation: Constructing a Postcolonial Dialogue." In *Relocating Postcolonialism,* edited by David Theo Goldberg and Ato Quayson, 320–33. Oxford: Blackwell, 2002.

Elkins, Caroline. *Britain's Gulag: The Brutal End of Empire.* London: Pimlico, 2005.

Episcopal Church (USA). *Becoming Beloved Community: The Episcopal Church's Long-Term Commitment to Racial Healing, Reconciliation and Justice.* No loc: n.d.

Episcopal News Service (ENS). "Episcopalians Gather to Apologize for Slavery." October 3, 2008. https://www.episcopalchurch.org/library/article/episcopalians-gather-apologize-slavery.

———. "Prayers, Tears and Song Mark Episcopal Repentance for Slavery." October 3, 2008. https://www.episcopalchurch.org/library/article/prayers-tears-and-song-mark-episcopal-repentance-slavery.

Evershed, Jonathan. "Ghosts of the Somme: The State of Ulster Loyalism, Memory Work and the 'Other' 1916." In *Remembering 1916: The Easter Rising, the Somme and the Politics of Memory in Ireland,* edited by Richard S. Grayson and Fearghal McGarry, 241–57. Cambridge: Cambridge University Press, 2016.

Faden, Gerhard. "No Self, Dōgen, the Senika Doctrine and Western Views of Soul." *Buddhist-Christian Studies* 31 (2011) 41–54.

Fanon, Frantz. *A Dying Colonialism.* 1959. Reprint. New York: Grove, 1965.

———. *The Wretched of the Earth.* 1963. Reprint. London: Penguin, 2001.

Farwell, James. "On Whether Christians Should Participate in Buddhist Practice: A Critical Autobiographical Reflection." *Interreligious Studies and Intercultural Theology* 1.2 (2017) 242–56.

Fitzpatrick, David. "Instant History: 1912, 1916, 1918." In *Remembering 1916: The Easter Rising, The Somme and the Politics of Memory in Ireland,* edited by Richard S. Grayson and Fearghal McGarry, 65–85. Cambridge: Cambridge University Press, 2016.

Foster, R. F. *W. B. Yeats: A Life I: The Apprentice Mage: 1865–1914.* Oxford: Oxford University Press, 1998.

———. *W. B. Yeats: A Life II: The Arch-Poet: 1915–1939.* Oxford: Oxford University Press, 2003.

General Convention of the Episcopal Church (USA). "Work for Racial Justice and Reconciliation." *Journal of General Convention of 2015, The Episcopal Church, Salt Lake City, 2015* (New York: General Convention, 2015), 310–11. https://www.episcopalarchives.org/cgi-bin/acts/acts_resolution-complete. pl?resolution=2015-C019.

Girard, René. *Violence and the Sacred.* Translated by Patrick Gregory. 1972. Reprint. Baltimore: Johns Hopkins University Press, 1977.

Global Alliance for the Rights of Nature. "Bolivia's Leadership." http://therightsofnature. org/bolivia-experience/.

Gonzales, Angela, et al. "Eugenics as Indian Removal: Sociohistorical Processes and the De(con)struction of American Indians in the Southeast." *The Public Historian* 29.3 (2007) 53–67.

Grau, Marion. *Rethinking Mission in the Postcolony: Salvation, Society and Subversion.* London: T. & T. Clark, 2011.

Grayson, Richard S., and Fearghal McGarry, eds. *Remembering 1916: The Easter Rising, the Somme and the Politics of Memory in Ireland.* Cambridge: Cambridge University Press, 2016.

Green, Garrett. "Imagining the Future." In *The Future as God's Gift,* edited by David Fergusson and Marcel Sarot, 73–87. Edinburgh: T. & T. Clark, 2000.

Gugelberger, Georg M., and Diana Brydon. "Postcolonial Cultural Studies." In *The John Hopkins Guide to Literary Theory and Criticism,* edited by Michael Groden et al., 756–68. 2nd ed. Baltimore: Johns Hopkins University Press, 2005.

Hagan, William T. *American Indians.* 4th ed. Chicago: University of Chicago Press, 2013.

Harlow, Barbara. *Resistance Literature.* London: Methuen, 1987.

Harvey, Jennifer. "Which Way to Justice? Reconciliation, Reparations, and the Problem of Whiteness in US Protestantism." *Journal of the Society of Christian Ethics* 31.1 (2011) 57–77.

Hastings, Adrian. *African Christianity.* London: Chapman, 1976.

Hawk, L. Daniel, and Richard L. Twiss. "From Good: 'The Only Good Indian Is a Dead Indian,' to Better: 'Kill the Indian and Save the Man,' to Best: 'Old Things Pass Away and All Things Become White!'" In *Evangelical Postcolonial Conversations: Global Awakenings in Theology and Praxis,* edited by Kay Higuera Smith et al., 47–60. Downers Grove, IL: IVP Academic, 2014.

Heaney, Robert S. "Coloniality and Theological Method in Africa." *Journal of Anglican Studies* 7.1 (2009) 55–65.

———. "Conversion to Coloniality: Avoiding the Colonization of Method." *International Review of Mission* 97.384/385 (2008) 65–77.

———. *From Historical to Critical Post-Colonial Theology: The Contribution of John S. Mbiti and Jesse N. K. Mugambi.* Eugene, OR: Pickwick, 2015.

Heaney, Robert S., John Kafwanka, and Hilda Kabia, eds. *God's Church to God's World.* New York: Church Publishing, forthcoming.

Heaney, Robert S., Zeyneb Sayilgan, and Claire Haymes, eds. *Faithful Neighbors: Christian-Muslim Vision and Practice.* New York: Morehouse, 2016.

Heaney, Seamus. "Feeling into Words." Lecture given at the Royal Society of Literature, October, 1974. https://boginsdotcom.files.wordpress.com/2012/09/feeling-into-words.pdf.

Hempton, David. *Religion and Political Culture in Britain and Ireland: From the Glorious Revolution to the Decline of Empire.* Cambridge: Cambridge University Press, 1996.

Hill, David. "Is Bolivia Going to Frack 'Mother Earth.'" *The Guardian*, February 23, 2015. https://www.theguardian.com/environment/andes-to-the-amazon/2015/feb/23/bolivia-frack-mother-earth/.

Hogan, Patrick Colm. *Empire and Poetic Voice: Cognitive and Cultural Studies of Literary Tradition and Colonialism.* Albany, NY: State University of New York Press, 2004.

Holdeman, David. *The Cambridge Introduction to W. B. Yeats.* Cambridge: Cambridge University Press, 2006.

Horsley, Richard A. *Jesus and Empire: The Kingdom of God and the New World Disorder.* Minneapolis: Fortress, 2003.

———. "Jesus and Empire." In *In the Shadow of Empire: Reclaiming the Bible as a History of Faithful Resistance*, edited by Richard A. Horsley, 75–96. Louisville: Westminster John Knox, 2008.

Howe, Stephen. "Historiography." In *Ireland and the British Empire*, edited by Kevin Kenny, 220–50. Oxford: Oxford University Press, 2004.

Howes, Marjorie. "Yeats and the Postcolonial." In *The Cambridge Companion to W. B. Yeats*, edited by Marjorie Howes, 206–25. Cambridge: Cambridge University Press, 2006.

Innes, Lyn. "Chinua Achebe" (Obituary). *The Guardian*, March 22, 2013. https://www.theguardian.com/books/2013/mar/22/chinua-achebe.

Itumeleng, Mosala. *Biblical Hermeneutics and Black Theology in South Africa.* Grand Rapids: Eerdmans, 1989.

Jay, Nancy. *Throughout Your Generations Forever: Sacrifice, Religion, and Paternity.* Chicago: University of Chicago Press, 1992.

Jefferts Schori, Katherine. "Service of Repentance. St Thomas, Philadelphia. 4 October 2008, 10:30am." https://www.episcopalchurch.org/files/attached-files/sermon_by_kjs_10-4.pdf.

Joh, Wonhee Anne. *Heart of the Cross: A Postcolonial Christology.* Louisville: Westminster John Knox, 2006.

———. "The Transgressive Power of Jeong: A Postcolonial Hybridization of Christology." In *Postcolonial Theologies: Divinity and Empire*, edited by Catherine Keller et al., 149–63. St. Louis: Chalice, 2004.

Johnson, Todd M., and Gina A. Zurlo. "The Changing Demographics of Global Anglicanism, 1970–2010." In *Growth and Decline in the Anglican Communion: 1980 to the Present*, edited by David Goodhew, 37–53. London: Routledge, 2017.

Jones, Christopher R., and Chris Loersch. "Towards a Psychological Construct of Enmity." In *The Psychology of Hate*, edited by Carol T. Lockhardt, 35–57. New York: Nova Science, 2010.

Kane, Ross. "Ritual Formation of Peaceful Politics: Sacrifice and Syncretism in South Sudan (1991–2005)." *Journal of Religion in Africa* 44 (2014) 386–410.

Kawamoto, Janet. "Repentance for Slavery has a Long Way to Go, Say Advocates." *Episcopal News Service*, July 11, 2009. https://www.episcopalchurch.org/library/article/repentance-slavery-has-long-way-go-say-advocates.

Keenan, John P. *The Emptied Christ of Philippians: Mahāyāna Meditations*. Eugene, OR: Wipf and Stock, 2015.

———. *The Gospel of Mark: A Mahāyāna Reading*. Maryknoll, NY: Orbis, 1995.

Keller, Catherine. "The Love of Postcolonialism: Theology in the Interstices of Empire." In *Postcolonial Theologies: Divinity and Empire*, edited by Catherine Keller et al., 221–42. St. Louis: Chalice, 2004.

Kiberd, Declan. *Inventing Ireland: The Literature of the Modern Nation*. London: Vantage, 1996.

Kidwell, Clara Sue, et al. *A Native American Theology*. Maryknoll, NY: Orbis, 2001.

Kim, Chang-Nack. "Korean Minjung Theology: An Overview." *Chicago Theological Seminary Register* 85.2 (1995) 1–13.

Kim, Dong-kun. "Korean Minjung Theology in History and Mission." *Studies in World Christianity* 2.2 (1996) 167–82.

Kinthinji, Julius. "Impunity and Exousia in Mark 1:21–28." In *The Postcolonial Church: Bible, Theology and Mission*, edited by R. S Wafula et al., 43–56. Alameda, CA: Borderless, 2016.

Klawans, Jonathan. *Purity, Sacrifice, and the Temple: Symbolism and Supersessionism in the Study of Ancient Judaism*. New York: Oxford University Press, 2006.

Kristeva, Julia. *Powers of Horror: An Essay on Abjection*. Translated by Leon S. Roudiez. New York: Columbia University Press, 1982.

Kwok, Pui-lan. *Postcolonial Imagination and Feminist Theology*. Louisville: Westminster John Knox, 2005.

Lactantius. *De Mortibus Persecutorum*. http://people.ucalgary.ca/~vandersp/Courses/texts/lactant/lactpers.html.

Lederach, John Paul. *The Moral Imagination: The Art and Soul of Building Peace*. New York: Oxford University Press, 2005.

Lee, Jae Hoon. *The Exploration of the Inner Wounds—Han*. Atlanta: Scholars, 1994.

Lee, J. J. *Ireland: 1912–1985: Politics and Society*. Cambridge: Cambridge University Press, 1989.

Leonard, Gary S.D., ed. *The Kairos Documents*. Durban: University of KwaZulu-Natal: Ujamaa Center for Biblical and Theological Community Development and Research, 2010.

Leopold, Anita, and Jeppe S. Jenson, eds. *Syncretism in Religion: A Reader*. London: Routledge, 2005.

Li, Diyi, and Cory Koedel. "Representative and Salary Gaps by Race-Ethnicity and Gender at Selective Public Universities." *Educational Researcher* (August 16, 2017) 343–54.

Lloyd, David. "Ireland after History." In *A Companion to Postcolonial Studies*, edited by Henry Schwarz and Sangeeta Ray, 377–95. Oxford: Blackwell, 2005.

Locke, John. "Letter Concerning Toleration" (1689). In *John Locke on Toleration*, edited by Richard Vernon, 3–46. Cambridge: Cambridge University Press, 2010.

Mackenzie, Matthew. "Enacting the Self: Buddhist and Enactivist Approaches to the Emergence of the Self." In *Self, No Self? Perspectives from Analytical, Phenomenological, and Indian Traditions*, edited by Mark Siderits et al., 239–73. Oxford: Oxford University Press, 2011.

Mahaffrey, Vicki. *States of Desire: Wilde, Yeats, Joyce, and the Irish Experiment*. New York: Oxford University Press, 1998.

Malina, Bruce J. *The Social World of Jesus and the Gospels*. London: Routledge, 1996.

Mazrui, Alamin M. "Cultural (Re)Construction and Nation Building in Kenya: 1963–1970." In *Kenya: The Making of a Nation*, edited by Bethwell A. Ogot and W. R. Ochieng', 118–31. Maseno, Kenya: IRPS, 2000.

Mbiti, John S. *African Religions and Philosophy*. 1969. Reprint. Garden City, NY: Anchor, 1970.

———. *Akamba Stories*. Oxford: Clarendon, 1966.

———. *Bible and Theology in African Christianity*. Nairobi: Oxford University Press, 1986.

———. "Christianity and African Culture." *Journal of Theology for Southern Africa* 20 (1977) 26–40.

———. "Christianity and Traditional Religions in Africa." *International Review of Mission* 59 (1970) 430–40.

———. "Confessing Christ in a Multi-Faith Context, with Two Examples from Africa." *Metanoia* 4.3–4 (1994) 138–45.

———. "The Future of Christianity in Africa." *Cross Currents* 28.4 (1978–79) 387–94.

———. *New Testament Eschatology in an African Background*. Oxford: Oxford University Press, 1971.

———. "When the Right Hand Washes the Left Hand and the Left Hand Washes the Right Hand, the Two Will be Clean: Some Thoughts on Justice and Christian Mission in Africa." In *Festschrift für Horst Bürkle zum 75. Geburtstag*, edited by Klaus Krämer and Ansgar Paus, 433–64. Herausgeber: Die Weitte des Mysteriums. Christliche Identität im Dialog. Freiburg: Herder, 2000.

McAfee, Noelle. *Julia Kristeva*. London: Routledge, 2004.

McBride, Jennifer M. *The Church for the World: A Theology of Public Witness*. New York: Oxford University Press, 2011.

McClymond, Kathryn. *Beyond Sacred Violence: A Comparative Study of Sacrifice*. Baltimore: Johns Hopkins University Press, 2008.

McDonough, Sean M. *Christ as Creator: Origins of a New Testament Doctrine*. Oxford: Oxford University Press, 2005.

McKay, Stan. "An Aboriginal Christian Perspective on the Integrity of Creation." In *Native and Christian: Indigenous Voices on Religious Identity in the United States and Canada*, edited by James Treat, 51–55. London: Routledge, 1996.

Meeks, Wayne A. *The First Urban Christians: The Social World of the Apostle Paul*. New Haven: Yale University Press, 1983.

———. *The Moral World of the First Christians*. Philadelphia: Westminster, 1986.

Memmi, Albert. *The Colonizer and the Colonized*. 1957. Reprint. Boston: Beacon, 1991.

Meridith, Karen M. "Repenting of Slavery: The African Episcopal Church of St. Thomas, Philadelphia, Pennsylvania. 4 October 2008." *Anglican and Episcopal History* 78 (2009) 105–11.

Middleton, John. *The Kikuyu and Kamba of Kenya.* London: International African Institute, 1953.

Minh-ha, Trinh. *When the Moon Waxes Red: Representation, Gender and Cultural Politics.* London: Routledge, 1991.

Moltmann, Jürgen. *The Crucified God: The Cross of Christ as the Foundation and Criticism of Christian Theology.* Translated by R. A. Wilson. 1973. Reprint. New York: Harper & Row, 1974.

———. *The Spirit of Life.* Translated by Margaret Kohl. Minneapolis: Fortress, 1992.

———. *Theology of Hope.* Translated by J. Leitch. London: SCM, 1967.

———. *The Way of Jesus Christ: Christology in Messianic Dimensions.* Translated by Margaret Kohl. Minneapolis: Fortress, 1993.

Mombo, Esther. "Theological Education in Africa." In *Voices from Africa*, edited by Andrew Wheeler, 127–33. London: Church House, 2002.

Morse, Jedidiah. *A Report to the Secretary of War of the United States, on Indian Affairs.* Washington, DC: Davis & Force, 1822.

Mugambi, J. N. K. *The Biblical Basis of Evangelization: Theological Reflections Based on an African Experience.* Nairobi: Oxford University Press, 1989.

———. *From Liberation to Reconstruction: African Christian Theology after the Cold War.* Nairobi: East African, 1995.

———. "Introduction." In *The Primal Vision: Christian Presence Amid African Religion*, edited by John V. Taylor, xi–xxxv. 1963. Reprint. Oxford: SCM, 2001.

Nandy, Ashis. *The Intimate Enemy: Loss and Recovery of Self under Colonialism.* 1983. Reprint. Delhi: Oxford University Press, 1988.

National Native American Boarding School Healing Coalition. www.boardingschoolhealing.org.

Neill, Peter. "Law of Mother Earth: A Vision from Bolivia." *Huffington Post.* November 18, 2014. http://www.huffingtonpost.com/peter-neill/law-of-mother-earth-a-vis_b_6180446.html.

Novak, David. "Jews and Catholics: Beyond Apologetics." *First Things* 89 (January 1999) 20–25.

Nowak, Martin A. *Evolutionary Dynamics: Exploring the Equations of Life.* Cambridge: The Belknap Press of Harvard University, 2006.

———. "Five Rules for the Evolution of Cooperation." *Science* 314.5805 (8 December 2006) 1560–63.

Nwatu, Felix. "'Colonial' Christianity in Post-Colonial Africa?" *Ecumenical Review* 46.3 (1994) 352–60.

Office of the First Minister and Deputy First Minister (Northern Ireland). *A Shared Future: Policy and Strategic Framework for Good Relations in Northern Ireland.* 2005. https://www.niacro.co.uk/sites/default/files/publications/A%20Shared%20Future-%20OFMDFM-Mar%202005.pdf.

Ogden, Schubert. *Doing Theology Today.* Valley Forge, PA: Trinity, 1996.

Oliver, Mary. *A Poetry Handbook.* Boston: Mariner, 1994.

Oliver, Roland. *The Missionary Factor in East Africa.* London: Longmans, Green, and Co., 1952.

Oppenheimer, Martin. *The Hate Handbook: Oppressors, Victims, and Fighters.* Oxford: Lexington, 2005.

Park, Andrew Sung. *The Wounded Heart of God: The Asian Concept of Han and the Doctrine of Sin.* Nashville: Abingdon, 1993.

Park, Joon-Sik. "Korean Protestant Christianity: A Missiological Reflection." *International Bulletin of Missionary Research* 36.2 (2012) 59–64.

p'Bitek, Okot. *African Religions in Western Scholarship.* Nairobi: East African Literature Bureau, 1970.

PBS. *God in America.* http://www.pbs.org/godinamerica/.

Peel, J. D. Y. *Religious Encounter and the Making of the Yoruba.* Bloomington, IN: Indiana University Press, 2000.

Perdue, Leo G., et al. *Israel and Empire: A Postcolonial History of Israel and Early Judaism.* London: Bloomsbury, 2015.

Perkinson, James W. *White Theology: Outing Supremacy in Modernity.* New York: Palgrave Macmillan, 2014.

Peters, Richard, ed. *Public Statutes at Large of the United States of America, from the Organization of the Government in 1789, to March 3, 1845, Volume 2.* Boston: Little and Brown, 1846.

Pious XII, Pope. *Mystici Corporis Christi* (1943). http://w2.vatican.va/content/pius-xii/en/encyclicals/documents/hf_p-xii_enc_29061943_mystici-corporis-christi.html.

Raheb, Mitri. *Faith in the Face of Empire: The Bible through Palestinian Eyes.* Maryknoll, NY: Orbis, 2014.

Rahner, Karl. *Theological Investigations: Volume VI: Concerning Vatican Council II.* Translated by Karl-H and Boniface Kruger. Baltimore: Helicon, 1969.

Rieger, Joerg. *Christ and Empire: From Paul to Postcolonial Times.* Minneapolis: Fortress, 2007.

Ritchie, Meabh. "'Descent into Terror': Northern Ireland's Worst Year." Channel 4 News. May 7, 2014. https://www.channel4.com/news/1972-troubles-northern-ireland-belfast-ira-video.

Rowland, Christopher. *Blake and the Bible.* New Haven: Yale University Press, 2010.

———. *Radical Prophet: The Mystics, Subversives and Visionaries Who Strove for Heaven on Earth.* London: I. B. Tauris, 2017.

———. *Revelation.* London: Epworth, 1993.

Rowland, Christopher, and Andrew Bradstock, eds. *Radical Christian Writings: A Reader.* Oxford: Blackwell, 2002.

Roy, Judy M. *Love to Hate: America's Obsession with Hatred and Violence.* New York: Columbia University Press, 2002.

Safran, Janina M. *Defining Boundaries in Al-Andalus: Muslims, Christians, and Jews in Islamic Iberia.* Ithaca, NY: Cornell University Press, 2013.

Said, Edward. *Culture and Imperialism.* New York: Vintage, 1993.

Said, Edward W. "Yeats and Decolonization." In *Nationalism, Colonialism, and Literature,* edited by Terry Eagleton et al., 69–95. Minneapolis: University of Minnesota Press, 1990.

Sanneh, Lamin O. *Translating the Message: The Missionary Impact on Culture.* Maryknoll, NY: Orbis, 1989.

Sawyer, Harry. *Creative Evangelism.* London: Lutterworth, 1968.

Schineller, Peter. "Inculturation and Syncretism: What Is the Real Issue?" *International Bulletin of Missionary Research* 16.2 (1992) 50–53.

Scott, A. O. "Dear Enemy: Exchanging Photos and Gunfire" (Review). *The New York Times*, June 15, 2005. http://movies2.nytimes.com/2005/06/15/movies/15join.html.

Smith, Kay Higuera et al., eds. *Evangelical Postcolonial Conversations: Global Awakenings in Theology and Praxis*. Downers Grove, IL: IVP Academic, 2014.

Smith, Maureen. "Forever Changed: Boarding Schools Narratives of American Indian Identity in the U.S. and Canada." *Indigenous Nations Studies Journal* 2.2 (2001) 57–82.

Spivak, Gayatri. *In Other Worlds: Essays in Cultural Politics*. London: Routledge, 1988.

Stanley, Brian. *The Bible and the Flag: Protestants Missions and British Imperialism in the Nineteenth and Twentieth Centuries*. Leicester, UK: Apollos, 1990.

———. *Christianity in the Twentieth Century: A World History*. Princeton: Princeton University Press, 2018.

Starkloff, Carl. *A Theology of the In-Between: The Value of Syncretic Process*. Milwaukee: Marquette University Press, 2002.

Strayer, Robert W. *The Making of Mission Communities in East Africa: Anglicans and Africans in Colonial Kenya, 1875–1935*. London: Heinemann, 1978.

Strong, Rowan. *Anglicanism and the British Empire c. 1700–1850*. Oxford: Oxford University Press, 2007.

Stroope, Michael W. *Transcending Mission: The Eclipse of a Modern Tradition*. Downers Grove, IL: IVP Academic, 2017.

Sugirtharajah, R. S. "Complacencies and Cul-de-sacs." In *Postcolonial Theologies: Divinity and Empire*, edited by Catherine Keller et al., 22–38. St. Louis: Chalice, 2004.

———. *Postcolonial Criticism and Biblical Interpretation*. Oxford: Oxford University Press, 2002.

Sundkler, Bengt, and Christopher Steed. *A History of the Church in Africa*. Cambridge: Cambridge University Press, 2000.

Symons, Arthur. *The Symbolist Movement in Literature*. 1899. Reprint. Manchester: Carcanet, 2014.

Taylor, Charles. *A Secular Age*. Cambridge: The Belknap Press of Harvard University Press, 2007.

Taylor, Mark Lewis. *The Executed God: The Way of the Cross in Lockdown America* Minneapolis: Fortress, 2001.

Taylor, John V. *The Growth of the Church in Buganda*. London: SCM, 1958.

———. *The Primal Vision: Christian Presence Amid African Religion*. 1963. Reprint. Oxford: SCM, 2001.

———. "The Theological Basis for Interfaith Dialogue." *International Review of Mission* 68.272 (1979) 373–84.

Tinker, George E. *American Indian Liberation: A Theology of Sovereignty*. Maryknoll, NY: Orbis, 2008.

Treat, James, ed. *Native and Christian: Indigenous Voices on Religious Identity in the United States and Canada*. London: Routledge, 1996.

Twiss, Richard. *Rescuing the Gospel from the Cowboys: A Native American Expression of the Jesus Way*. Downers Grove, IL: IVP, 2015.

United Church of Canada (UCC). "An Apology to First Nations." http://www.united-church.ca/sites/default/files/resources/1986–1998-aboriginal-apologies.pdf.

United Kingdom Government. *The Agreement: Agreement Reached in the Multi-Party Negotiations* (1998). https://www.gov.uk/government/publications/the-belfast-agreement.

Vatican II. *Lumen Gentium* (1964). http://www.vatican.va/archive/hist_councils/ii_vatican_council/documents/vat-ii_const_19641121_lumen-gentium_en.html.

———. *Unitatis Redintegratio* (1964). http://www.vatican.va/archive/hist_councils/ii_vatican_council/documents/vat-ii_decree_19641121_unitatis-redintegratio_en.html.

Veracini, Lorenzo. *Settler Colonialism: A Theoretical Overview*. Basingstoke, UK: Palgrave Macmillan, 2010.

Virgil. *The Aeneid*. Translated by Sarah Ruden. New Haven: Yale University Press, 2008.

Volf, Miroslav. *Exclusion and Embrace: A Theological Exploration of Identity, Otherness, and Reconciliation*. Nashville: Abingdon, 1996.

Voltaire. *Philosophical Dictionary*. 1764. Reprint. Translated by Theodore Besterman. Harmondsworth, UK: Penguin, 1971.

Wafula, R. S. *Biblical Representations of Moab*. New York: Lang, 2014.

Wafula, R. S., et al., eds. *The Postcolonial Church: Bible, Theology, and Mission*. Alameda, CA: Borderless, 2016.

Warren, M. A. C. *Caesar the Beloved Enemy: Three Studies in the Relation of Church and State*. London: SCM, 1955.

wa Thiong'o, Ngũgĩ. *Decolonising the Mind: The Politics of Language in African Literature*. London: Currey, 1986.

———. *Devil on the Cross*. 1980. Reprint. New York: Penguin, 2017.

Wheeler, Christopher J. "JSA—Joint Security Area" (Review). *Hancinema: The Korean Movie and Drama Database*. February 26, 2011. http://www.hancinema.net/hancinema-s-film-review-jsa--joint-security-area-28144.html.

Wood, David. "Christian Mission with John V. Taylor." *International Review of Mission* 92.366 (2003) 427–33.

———. *Poet, Priest and Prophet: The Life and Thought of Bishop John V. Taylor*. London: Churches Together in Britain and Ireland, 2002.

Woodley, Randy S. *Living in Color: Embracing God's Passion for Ethnic Diversity*. Downers Grove, IL: IVP, 2001.

———. *Shalom and the Community of Creation: An Indigenous Vision*. Grand Rapids: Eerdmans, 2012.

Yates, Timothy E. "Reading John V. Taylor." *International Bulletin of Missionary Research* 30.3 (2006) 153–56.

Yeats, W. B. *Autobiographies*. London: Macmillan, 1955.

———. *Collected Poems*. London: Macmillan, 2010.

———. *On the Boiler*. Dublin: Cuala, 1939.

———. "Purgatory." In *Collected Plays of W. B. Yeats New Edition with Five Additional Plays*, edited by W. B. Yeats, 442–49. 1934. Reprint. New York: Macmillan, 1953.

———. *Synge and the Ireland of His Time by William Butler Yeats with a Note Concerning a Walk through Connemara with Him by Jack Butler Yeats*. Dubin: Cuala, 1911.

———. *A Vision*. Rev. ed. 1937. Reprint. New York: Collier, 1966.

———. *Where There Is Nothing: Being Volume One of Plays for an Irish Theatre*. New York: Macmillan, 1903.

Yeats W. B., and Lady Gregory. *The Unicorn from the Stars and Other Plays*. New York: Macmillan, 1908.

Young, Robert J. C. *The Idea of English Ethnicity*. Oxford: Blackwell, 2008.

———. *Postcolonialism: An Historical Introduction*. Malden, MA: Blackwell, 2001.

———. *Postcolonialism: A Very Short Introduction.* Oxford: Oxford University Press, 2003.

———. "Postcolonial Remains." In *Postcolonial Studies: An Anthology*, edited by Pramod K. Nayar, 125–43. Malden, MA: Wiley-Blackwell, 2016.

———. "What Is the Postcolonial?: Anglican Identities and the Postcolonial." Unpublished Paper, Lambeth Conference (July 21, 2008). University of Kent at Canterbury.

Zick, Andreas, et al. "Prejudices and Group-Focused Enmity." In *Handbook of Prejudice*, edited by Anton Pelinka et al., 273–302. Amherst, NY: Cambria, 2009.

# Name/Subject Index

# Scripture Index

## Scripture Index